W9-DGI-072

STUDIES IN HISTORY, ECQNOMICS AND PUBLIC LAW

EDITED BY THE FACULTY OF POLITICAL SCIENCE OF
COLUMBIA UNIVERSITY

Volume LX]   [Number 1
Whole Number 146

CONSTANTINE THE GREAT AND CHRISTIANITY

THREE PHASES: THE HISTORICAL, THE LEGENDARY, AND THE SPURIOUS

BY

CHRISTOPHER BUSH COLEMAN

AMS PRESS
NEW YORK

Originally Published : New York, 1914

Reprinted with permission of
COLUMBIA UNIVERSITY PRESS

AMS PRESS, INC.
NEW YORK, N.Y. 10003
First AMS Edition : 1968

Printed in Great Britain

PREFACE

IF any defense is necessary for discussing to-day not only the Constantine of history but also the historic ghost of Constantine; *i. e.*, the legends and the forgery which later times produced in his name, it can be found in the fact that starting at one time with a study of the religious revolution which centered in Constantine, and at another with the " Donation of Constantine," forged in the eighth century, I found myself in both instances without any logical stopping-place short of a consideration of the whole field. If in the present work parts of this field are somewhat imperfectly covered, it is my hope that these imperfections may not too seriously impeach the soundness of this procedure. Even the brief summary herein given of the modern critical study of Constantine and Constantinian legends furnishes, in contrast with the early medieval accounts of the emperor, an interesting illustration of the revolution wrought by the modern, scientific-historical spirit. It gains peculiar interest when one considers that Constantine was perhaps the greatest promoter of that other revolution, in which the Christian church gained the mastery of the Roman and Medieval mind, and that the Constantinian legends were among the notable products of the type of piety long promoted by that church. Two of the greatest revolutions in European history thus confront each other, as it were, upon common ground.

I have tried to indicate in the following pages the various items of my indebtedness in the preparation of this work. In some cases, however, mere references are not enough. The writings of Professor O. Seeck have not only given me much information which I would otherwise have missed, but have proved stimulating and fruitful in suggestions. The "Prolegomena" and notes which Professor A. C. McGiffert and Dr. E. C. Richardson contributed some twenty-five years ago to the volume devoted to *Eusebius* in the *Nicene and Post-Nicene Fathers* were among the first guides to introduce me to the field of work in which I have since found much rather unexpected interest. To Lorenzo Valla's *Libellus de falso credita et ementita Constantini donatione*, with its keen wit and able, though defective, historical criticism, I owe my first interest in subjects dealt with in the latter part of my work.

I had originally intended to add an English translation of Valla's Treatise as an appendix to this work. It has seemed best, however, to publish the translation, together with a critical edition of the text, in separate form. This, I hope, may appear within a short time. Among the greatest obligations I owe for help in the present publication is that to Professor Deane P. Lockwood, of Columbia University, for his reading and frequent revision of this translation. Though the publication of this is deferred, many of his suggestions have been of value in other connections.

To Professor J. T. Shotwell, of Columbia University, I am indebted for countless manifestations of efficient leadership in a field of study in which he is master, for suggestions both as to the general plan and as to details, which have always been helpful. For the time and trouble which he has freely given no acknowledgment can be too great. I wish also to express my sense of obligation to Professor W. W. Rockwell, of Union

Theological Seminary, for reading my manuscript and
strengthening the discussion of a number of ½ points by
his comments. Among others who have contributed,
either by direct suggestions or by making it possible for
me to obtain books otherwise inaccessible, are Professors
J. H. Robinson and Munro Smith, of Columbia University, Professor George L. Burr, of Cornell University,
and my colleagues, H. M. Gelston and E. H. Hollands,
now of the University of Kansas. To the editors of the
Series in which this work appears my thanks are due for
courteous and effective co-operation and for help which
has made the burden of publication comparatively easy.

CHRISTOPHER B. COLEMAN.

Butler College, Indianapolis, April, 1914.

TABLE OF CONTENTS

PART TWO

THE LEGENDARY CONSTANTINE AND CHRISTIANITY

CHAPTER I

THE LEGEND MAKERS

CHAPTER II

LEGENDS OF CONSTANTINE'S ORIGIN AND RISE TO IMPERIAL POSITION ; LEGENDS ABOUT HELENA

CHAPTER III

THE HOSTILE, PAGAN LEGEND OF CONSTANTINE

CHAPTER IV

EARLY LEGENDS OF DIVINE AID, CONVERSION, SAINTLINESS

CHAPTER V

LATER LEGENDS OF CONSTANTINE'S CONVERSION AND BAPTISM

PART THREE

THE SPURIOUS CONSTANTINE: THE CONSTITUTUM CONSTANTINI

CHAPTER I

HISTORY OF THE CONSTITUTUM CONSTANTINI

CHAPTER II

EXPOSURE OF THE FORGERY

CHAPTER III

THE "DONATION" IN THE PROTESTANT REVOLUTION. MODERN SCIENTIFIC CRITICISM OF THE "DONATION"

INTRODUCTION

FEW generations have occupied a position of such decisive importance in European history as did that of Constantine the Great. It was the crisis in the rise of Christianity to dominance in European civilization. The part which the Emperor himself took in this momentous revolution makes him one of the most commanding figures of antiquity. It is with this aspect alone of his reign that the following pages deal. Though his military, financial and political arrangements were of considerable significance for subsequent times, I have referred to them only incidentally, and so far as is necessary for my specific purpose. I have, however, attempted to make a fairly full and critical study of Constantine in his relation to Christianity.

This study early divided itself into three sections. First, it was necessary to get at the historical facts, so far as ascertainable, of Constantine's attitude toward Christianity and the Church. Second, the legendary process had to be taken into account by which Constantine's actual position in religious matters was distorted, and in this distorted form influenced subsequent generations. In the third place, consideration had to be given to the extension of this legendary process in a great forgery, the so-called Donation of Constantine. The first Christian emperor may thus be said to have had in European history three distinct spheres of influence, occupied respectively by the real, the legendary, and the spurious Constantine. The latter two have their

own intrinsic importance as well as the first.[1]   They are
of interest also as illustrating the history of the intellectual development of Europe.   No tests of this development are more illuminating than the function played
in various generations by legendary processes and the
reaction of different groups of men toward mistaken
traditional conceptions.

The "historical" rather than the "real" Constantine,
however, must be our point of departure.   Even in fields
where vast funds of original sources of information are
at hand and where an enormous amount of critical work
has been done, it is presumptuous to claim knowledge
of men and of facts as they would appear to the eyes of
omniscience.   The best that we can do under the most
favorable circumstances is to approximate toward the
real men and the real facts; between us and them there
always remains a margin of ignorance, if not of error,
which we may well call the "historical equation."   This
does not mean that we are left with merely "lies agreed
upon," for modern scientific methods are rigorous guides
toward the truth, and though lies remain, even the most
superficial reader knows how far historians are from
agreeing upon them.   In discussing men of the fourth
century, however, it must be admitted that anything like
complete truth seems unattainable.   Information on most
important points often fails us entirely, and, as will be
seen, much information that we possess is open to grave
suspicion.   Yet with reference to Constantine, it can be
said that we possess a mass of evidence which has been
made available in critical editions of sources, and which

[1] *Cf*. Dunning: "Truth in History." *American Historical Review*,
xxix (1914), pp. 217-229.   The point is that primary importance often
attaches not so much to what happened, as to what later ages believed
to have happened.

is being augmented and sifted to such an extent that a
reliable historical discussion of his religious position is
possible. This I attempt to give in Part One.

Legends about Constantine have for the most part
been approached from a mistaken point of view. They
have been used by some as reliable sources and by others
have been scornfully rejected as not worth consideration.
Both attitudes are wrong.

The time has passed for the kind of history that is
made up of unsupported traditions or that fills in its
vacant spaces and obscure origins with untested stories.
Legend usually throws little light upon the actual course
of events, and what light it does throw is generally mis-
leading, so that in reconstructing the past the investigator often does well to ignore it entirely unless he has
some test by which to sort out its genuine basis from its
fable.   Instead of trying to sift out truth from error by
making allowances for probable distortions, he usually
does better if he looks for other sources of information
in documents, in monuments and in traces of earlier
conditions surviving in later institutions.   Scientific research has not only destroyed mistaken legends, but has
been able to displace so many of these by more reliable
facts that the validity of this method can no longer be
doubted.

But though legendary history is doomed, the history
of the legend remains. The story it contains may not
throw much light upon the subject about which it has
grown up, but it reveals the working of the minds of the
people who consciously or unconsciously created it.   A
legend may often be the most direct approach to the
spirit of the time in which it gained currency, and the
clearest illustration of its ideals and its modes of thought.
Its deviation from historical fact is here the most important thing about it.

After the legend becomes crystallized its history is significant. The most obvious value is the influence which it exercises where it is accepted. For an accepted legend has just as much influence as an accepted historical truth. The mistaken belief of American statesmen about the boundaries of Louisiana determined their attitude toward the limitation of Florida and of Mexico precisely as if this belief were correct. Unfounded pagan stories about the early Christians, and unfounded Christian stories about the Jews, had all the potency of verified facts.

A less obvious, but an important value of the history of a crystallized legend attaches to the attitude taken toward it by those whom their generation esteems its scholars. Their acceptance or rejection of it, the tests they apply to it, and the way in which they fit it into their general fund of knowledge shows vividly the intellectual level of their age. A wide study of legends would be one of the most illuminating chapters in the history of history. Part Two, dealing with legends about Constantine, is an attempt to contribute to this end.

The Donation of Constantine takes us into the study of a different field of intellectual activity. Legends are the spontaneous creation of man's fancy. They are often the echo of his own deepest convictions and highest ideals projected into the past and coming back to him as the voices of the dead. But not all the men of the Middle Ages were satisfied to let their imagination play about the tomb of the first Christian emperor. They brought him at length out of his grave and put into his mouth a legal grant of vast powers to the Roman Church and the Roman bishop. Perhaps in the mind of the forger this was not an essentially different act from the earlier legendary processes. Scheffer-Boichorst argues that his chief motive was the glorification of Constantine and Pope Sylvester, to whom the grant was assumed to be made.[1] The late Doctor Hodgkin even suggested, hesitatingly, that the Donation might have been originally composed as an exercise in romancing.[2] But in form at least it was plainly a forgery, and even in the eighth and ninth centuries such forgeries were punishable with death.[3] It was taken seriously and generally accepted as a legal document for nearly six hundred years. It filled so large a place in the thought of Europe that we can justly call it the most famous forgery in history. Dr. Hodgkin even goes so far as to say, "The story of the Donation of Constantine fully told would almost be the history of the Middle Ages."[4]

On the other hand, the unravelling of this skein of forgery is one of the most interesting phases of the development of the modern scientific spirit. The proof advanced by Lorenzo Valla that the document was spurious constitutes in the Renaissance an event emphasized by many writers. In more recent times discussion of various problems connected with the forgery has engaged the energy of many of the foremost historians of Italy, France, England, and especially of Germany, and has produced an extensive and important historical literature. A careful and systematic study of this whole development, such as is attempted in the following pages in Part Three, will throw considerable light upon the workings of both the medieval and the modern mind.

[1] *Cf. infra,* p. 211 *et seq.*

[2] *Italy and Her Invaders,* vol. vii., (1899) p. 135 *et seq.*

[3] *Cf.* Brunner: Das Constitutum Constantini, in *Festgabe für Rudolf von Gneist,* pp. 34-35.

[4] *Op. cit.,* vii., p. 135.

CONSTANTINE AND CHRISTIANITY

PART ONE

THE HISTORICAL FACTS

CHAPTER I

THE PROBLEM

WHAT was the precise part of Constantine in the revolution by which Christianity became the dominant religion of European civilization? The question and its answer have many ramifications. Of little importance for us is the much-discussed matter of the sincerity of his motives. Plausible motives are easily manufactured to fit any point of view and aid immensely in the construction of an interesting, consistent narrative; but the purposes actually controlling a man's conduct are often obscure to himself and, save by means of self-revelation, not often ascertainable by others. Only novelists may postulate a set of motives and develop conduct accordingly; the historian may infer them, but he is not at liberty to reconstruct the course of events upon such inferences. The important questions are really those of conduct and of public influence, and these are matters of record and of fact. If the public policy of Constantine and the course of his religious life, so far as it was in the open, can be ascertained, we shall know all that is here essential. And this knowledge will take us to the very heart of the reciprocal process by which the Roman Empire assumed Christianity, and the Church assumed, so far as in it lay, the control of the future of Europe.

Both phases of this process seem at first sight utterly revolutionary. Under Constantine's immediate predecessors the Roman government bent itself to the task of exterminating Christianity as an alien and hostile power. Under him and his immediate successors the resources of the state were often put at the disposal of the church. The empire, in addition to its already crushing burdens, took up the support of the church and made itself the vehicle upon which the once persecuted religion rode in triumph to its task of establishing the "City of God" upon the earth. The church presents an equally startling contrast in its progress. Not long before this the disciples of Jesus had been a powerless minority, under the control of a political and social system which outraged their religion. Most of them, in the first days in Palestine, and afterwards for several generations, saw no outcome for the hopeless conflict of the new life with the old order except in some great cataclysm in which the existing world-order itself should be utterly destroyed and Christ should reign with his saints in a new heaven and a new earth. In the third century they still thought of their hope and their true citizenship as in heaven, for this world seemed hopelessly hostile and evil. Within a single generation, however, this was, for the leading churchmen, all changed. "A new and fresh era of existence had begun to appear and a light hitherto unknown suddenly to dawn from the midst of darkness on the human race."[1] When that apparent impossibility, a Christian emperor, came upon the scene, and invited into his council-chamber bishops who bore upon their bodies the marks of jail and torture, at least one of those present thought "that a picture of Christ's kingdom was thus shadowed forth."[2] While the future heaven has never passed out of the

[1] Eusebius, *Life of Constantine*, iii, 1.
[2] *Ibid.*, iii, 15.

thought of the church, this shadowing forth of it upon
earth speedily absorbed the energy of a large proportion
of churchmen.   The world was no longer hopelessly
hostile; the church was at home in it, and contemplation
of the speedy and hoped-for destruction of the earth
gave place to an age-long struggle to control and gov-
ern it in the name of him whom it had once crucified.

This double transformation, one of the greatest in the
history of the world, was, however, wrought by forces
which can be, to a large extent, historically analyzed and
estimated.   Many of them had long been working slowly
and almost imperceptibly.   They converged in Constantine, and it is this that gives importance to the question of the part he had in them.   His career is an illustration of the process, and his reign marks its crisis.
It is of great importance, therefore, to find out, so far as
the emperor was concerned, how the government accepted Christianity and how Christians accepted the
governance of the world.

The answer to these questions is not ready at hand.
There is, to be sure, much material, and most of it has
been critically examined from one point of view or
another.   Literature upon Constantine has been almost
steadily produced ever since the beginning of his reign,
and has been recently stimulated by various official celebrations of the sixteenth centennial (1913) of the Edict,
or Rescript, of Milan.   The main facts of his career seem
fairly well established, but historical complacency is
always subject to jolts such as that received from Otto
Seeck's attempt in 1891 to prove that there had never
been any Edict of Milan.   The prevailing views of Constantine's religious position, developed out of many
variant opinions and considerable controversy, must still
be held subject to review and revision.

Until modern times historians generally accepted as an established fact that he openly and sincerely professed Christianity from the time of his victory over Maxentius (312). Gibbon, in " *The Decline and Fall of the Roman Empire*," looked upon him as a supporter of the church, and thought that his conversion may perhaps have been genuine.[1] Niebuhr, however, saw in Constantine a "repulsive phenomenon" of mingled paganism and Christianity, a superstitious man pursuing his own selfish ends.[2] Burckhardt in "*Die Zeit Constantins der Grossen*," an epoch-making work and for years the standard life of Constantine, started with the bold (and unhistorical) proposition that "in the case of a man of genius, to whom ambition and desire for mastery give no rest, there can be no question of Christianity or paganism ; such a man is essentially unreligious."[3] He even characterized Constantine as a "murdering egoist," and ascribes to him as his only religion, a belief in his own conquering genius. His laws accordingly were held to indicate not even a desire to advance the interests of Christianity, but only his use of that religion as part of the political machinery of the empire.

After Burckhardt, the tendency ran strongly toward acceptance of the view that Constantine professed to adopt Christianity for political motives and used it for political purposes, but did not commit either himself or the empire to it. Theodor Keim[4] while contending that Constantine was affected somewhat by Christianity and

---

[1] Chap. xx.

[2] *Lectures on the History of Rome.* Third ed., Eng. trans., 1853, iii, p. 318.

[3] P. 369 (this work appeared first in 1853).

[4] *Der Uebertritt Constantins des Grossen zum Christenthum*, 1862.

came out openly as a Christian at the end[1] interpreted his official actions as hedging between paganism and Christianity. Theodor Zahn[2] pictured him as champion of a vague monotheism, not specifically Christian, till his contest with Licinius, thereafter he was definitely Christian. Marquardt[3] affirmed that Constantine erected heathen temples in Constantinople and that he never broke with Roman religious traditions; it was uncertain whether he ever was a Christian. Brieger[4] inferred from Constantine's coinage and other records that he had a sort of Christian superstition which yet did not supplant his original heathen ideas. Victor Duruy[5] found Constantine's emblems and religious deliverances ambiguous, and the emperor's actions the result of calculation, not of religious conviction or even preference. Herman Schiller[6] endeavored to prove a gradual favoring of Christianity at least to the extent of putting it on a legal level with the old paganism, and concluded that Constantine's policy was to form an official religion balancing the better elements of pagan monotheism with Chris-

[1] Keim rendered the phrase with which Constantine prefaced the announcement of his decision to be baptized, as given by Eusebius in his *Life of Constantine* (iv, 62), "let all duplicity be banished," thus implying that the emperor had previously been two-faced. The Greek term used, ἀμφιβολία, means merely doubt, or uncertainty, and Eusebius, of all men, would not have implied any hypocrisy on the emperor's part.

[2] *Constantin der Grosse und die Kirche*, 1876.

[3] *Römische Staatsverwaltung* (1878), iii, 113.

[4] Constantin der Grosse als Religionspolitiker, *Zeitschrift für Kirchengeschichte* iv (1880), ii, 163.

[5] *Histoire des Romains*, 1870 and later, vol. vii, p. 127 ff.; "Les Premières années du regne de Constantin" in *Compte rendu de l'Académie des Sciences morales et politiques*, xvi, 737-765 (1881), and "La politique religieuse de Constantin," *ibid.*, xvii, 185-227 (1882), and *Revue archaeologique*, xliii, 96-110, 155-175 (1882).

[6] *Geschichte der römischen Kaiserzeit*, 1883-7.

tianity. Victor Schultze,[1] Grisar,[2] and G. Boissier[3] defended his essential Christianity.

The remarkable work of O. Seeck,[4] which has almost superseded earlier writings on the subject, has at length reshaped historical opinion about Constantine. Seeck's conclusion, from a most exhaustive study of all the sources, is that Constantine was favorably inclined to Christianity from the first, that he was definitely converted to adherence to the God of the Christians as his patron and luckbringer during the campaign against Maxentius[5] and that thereafter he supported the Christian church even to the point of subserviency, and introduced Christianity as the state religion so far as conditions permitted. In many of his contentions Seeck has been vigorously attacked by F. Görres[6] and others, yet he and Schultze have exercised dominant influence and have been very generally followed.[7] Duchesne[8] looks upon Constantine as a gen-

[1] *Geschichte des Untergangs des griechischen römischen Heidentums*, 1887–03.

[2] "Die vorgeblichen Beweise gegen die Christlichkeit Constantins des Grossen", in *Zeitschrift für katholische Theologie* vi (1882) 585–607.

[3] "Essais d'histoire religieuse" in *Revue des deux Mondes* July 1886 pp. 51–72, "La Fin du Paganisme" (1891).

[4] *Geschichte des Untergangs der antiken Welt* 1895 *et seq.*, second edition 1897 *et seq.*, third edition 1910 *et seq.*, and numerous articles in historical reviews, especially in *Zeitsch. f. K. G.*   [5] 312 A. D.

[6] *Zeitschrift für wissenschaftliche Theologie* (1892), p. 282 *et seq.*

[7] Eg., J. B. Bury in his edition of Gibbon : *Decline and Fall of the Roman Empire* (1896), vol. ii, append. 19, pp. 566–568; W. K. Boyd : *The Ecclesiastical Edicts of the Theodosian Code, Columbia University Studies in History, Economics and Public Law* vol. xxiv (1905), pp. 16–21. An interesting illustration of this transformation of historical opinion is seen in the revision of current text-books for ancient history in line with Seecks' contentions. *Cf.* G. W. Botsford : *Ancient History for Beginners* (1902), pp. 422–43, and his *History of the Ancient World* (1913), pp. 514–515.

[8] *Histoire ancienne de l'Eglise*, vol. ii, English trans. (1912), pp. 45–71. The first edition was dated 1905.

uine convert and patron of the church.   Ludwig Wrzol[1]
emphasizes Constantine's ascription of victory-giving
power to the Christian God and looks upon most of the
emperor's actions after the battle at the Milvian bridge as
an expression of his desire to be on the right side of this
power.   Ed. Schwartz[2] finds in him sincere attachment
to Christianity in its organized form, but far from admitting his subserviency to the Christian bishops which Seeck
describes, he pictures Constantine as the ambitious seeker
of supreme power and dominating master of the church.
In the first proposition he is thus in agreement with
Seeck, but in the latter with Burckhardt.   One recent
writer[3] turns against the present tendency, to substantial
agreement with Burckhardt's view of the emperor's character and describes him as utterly irreligious and taking
up with Christianity for merely political purposes.   But
in this Geffcken stands almost alone.   On the other
hand, the contributors to the most pretentious of the
books called out by the centennial of the Edict of Milan,
Konstantin der Grosse und seine Zeit,[4] reproduce in
large part that view of the relations of Constantine and
the church most favorable to both. [5]

While, as has been said, the main facts of Constantine's
career now seem clear, the very bulk of this literature,
as well as the differences and contradictions it expresses,

[1] *Konstantins des Grossen persönliche Stellung zum Christentum.
Weidenauer Studien*, I (1906), pp. 227-269.

[2] *Kaiser Constantin und die christliche Kirche* (1913).

[3] Johs. Geffcken, *Aus der Werdezeit des Christentums* (1904), p. 97
et seq.

[4] Edited by F. J. Dölger, 1913.

[5] For other recent discussions see Gwatkin in *Cambridge Medieval
History*, vol. i (1911) p. 10 *et seq.*, and J. B. Carter: *The Religious
Life of Ancient Rome* (1911), p. 117 *et seq.*

calls for a general restatement of his attitude in religious matters, and for a revaluation of its significance. Such restatement must take into account the knowledge which recent years have brought of the general religious condition of Constantine's times. It is possible only on the basis of an examination of all the original evidence. And in this the emphasis must be put upon legal and monumental sources, such as are contained in the Theodosian Code and in coins and inscriptions; for, as will be shown later, the writers of the fourth century had little comprehension of pure historical truth and less devotion to it. Partisanship, eulogy, and defamation were all too common, and these were then, as now, more apt to create legends than to produce adequate appreciation of men and events.

CHAPTER II

THE IMPRINT OF CHRISTIANITY UPON CONSTANTINE'S
LAWS, INSCRIPTIONS AND WRITINGS

1. *Legislation*[1]

CONSTANTINE was a voluminous law-maker; fragments of nearly 300 of his laws are in existence, and we have information about others issued and now lost.[2] He was not a systematic nor a careful legislator; many of his laws are not clear, many are trivial, and many are badly ex-

---

[1] For various phases of this subject *cf.* Seeck's discussion of Constantine's laws in *Zeitschrift der Savigny Stiftung für Rechtsgeschichte, Romanische Abteilung*, x, p. 1 *et seq.*, p. 177 *et seq.* Also Boyd, *op. cit.*

Many of Constantine's laws, but by no means all that are extant, are printed in Migne: J. P., *Patrologiae Cursus Completus Series Latina* viii, cols. 93-400. Most of the extant ones have been preserved in the Theodosian Code and the Constitution of Sirmondi printed with it. Many not found elsewhere, as well as some duplications, are given in Eusebius' *Church History* and in his *Life of Constantine*. Many of these latter, however, are questioned, *cf. infra*, pp. 38, 109. Some laws are found in Augustine's writings against the Donatists, and others are referred to by Jerome and other ecclesiastical writers.

Under the title of Legislation I have included rescripts (rescripta) as well as edicts (edicta, decreta). Strictly speaking, rescripts were answers to inquiries. They were cited as decisions, rather than as legislation. Constantine seems to have begun the custom of issuing laws in rescript form, *i. e.*, in letters to praefects. Seeck dates the custom from December 1, 318. *Cf. op. cit.*, x, pp. 199, 221.

A number of Constantine's laws bearing on Christianity are translated in Ayer, J. C., Jr., *A Source Book for Ancient Church History* (New York, 1913), pp. 263-265, 277-296.

[2] *Cf.* Seeck, *Untergang der antiken Welt*, i, 54.

pressed.   Decadence of legal style had already set in by
his time.

The laws of Constantine show a progressively favorable attitude toward the Christians.   None of his legislation while he was in control of Gaul and Britain alone
has come down to us except references to his religious
toleration.   While he ruled the entire West, but not the
East (that is, from his victory over Maxentius in 312 till
his victory over Licinius in 323) his legislation involved
complete toleration towards Christians, and, in general,
establishment of equality between Christianity and
paganism.   After he became sole emperor, that is from
324 to his death in 337, his legislation became more
definitely Christian and anti-pagan.¹   Seeck, who maintains Constantine's complete adherence to Christianity
after 312, recognizes this distinction.²   A somewhat
detailed analysis of the two periods, 312–323 and 323–
336, is necessary to a full knowledge of the facts.

Before the final victory over Licinius (323) we have
no direct legislation against essential pagan institutions.³
Legislation friendly to the Christians, however, is in
evidence from the time of the victory over Maxentius
(312).   Very soon after that event Constantine and
Licinius, doubtless at the initiative of the former, reached
an agreement at Milan to establish general and complete
religious toleration, and issued a comprehensive edict or
rescript to that effect, specifically putting Christianity

¹ *Cf*. Bury's summary of Schiller's description of Constantine's laws
in Gibbon, *Decline and Fall of the Roman Empire*, ed. Bury, vol. ii,
p. 567.

² He ascribes the absence of a more positively Christian attitude in
the earlier legislation to motives of policy.

³ For legislation limiting magic and the consulting of haruspices, *cf*.
infra, pp. 35–36.

on a level with other legal religions.[1]   This is the famous
and lately controverted Edict of Milan.   The controversy was begun in 1891 by O. Seeck, who denied that
the document given by Lactantius and by Eusebius was
in any respect the work of Constantine, that it was
issued from Milan, or that it was an imperial edict.[2]   He
maintained that these authors gave merely copies of a
rescript issued by Licinius after his victory over Maximinus (or Maximin) Daza, probably as soon as he
entered Nicomedia, the capital of the first conquered
province, reinstating and enforcing the Edict of Toleration of Galerius (311) which Maximinus had not observed.   There would thus be only one edict of toleration, that putting an end to the Diocletian persecution;
and this reissue of it should be called simply the Rescript
of Nicomedia.   Seeck supported his opinion by arguments drawn from the informality of the so-called edict,
from the chronological difficulty involved in the accepted
account, and from the reference, " all conditions being
entirely left out which were contained in our former
letter," etc. ("quare scire dignationem tuam convenit
* * * placuisse nobis ut amotis omnibus omnino con-
ditionibus * * * contendant).   Seeck's article was answered by F. Görres and by Crivelluci.[3]   The former's

---

[1] Eusebius, *Church History*, ix, 9, 12. Our knowledge of its provisions is obtained from two documents, Lactantius, *De Mortibus persecutorum*, xlviii, and Eusebius, *op. cit.*, x, 5, 2-14. Each of these has
its champions as a copy of the original rescript, and by others both are
denied that rank.

[2] " Das sogennante Edikt von Mailand," in *Zeitschrift für Kirchengeschichte*, xii, p. 381 *et seq*. In his later *Geschichte des Untergangs
der Antiken Welt*, he assumed that he had proved his point and merely
remarked in a note that he had not spoken of the Edict of Milan because
in his opinion such an edict never existed. Vol. i (Anhang), p. 495.
(Berlin, 1897).

[3] The former in *Zeitsch. f. wissenschaftliche Theol.*, xxxv (1892), pp.
282-95; the latter in *Studi storici*, i, p. 239 *et seq*.

answer consists largely of ridicule and invective, inter-
spersed freely with exclamation points, but he rightly
emphasizes the obvious fact that there are essential
differences between the Edict of Galerius and this later
edict or letter, the former being polytheistic in tone and
giving bare toleration to the Christians, whereas the
latter is rather monotheistic and provides for a large
measure of general religious liberty together with restoration of confiscated Christian property to its former
owners. The original edict of Milan he thinks has been
lost, but Eusebius and Lactantius reproduce it in giving
respectively a translation and a copy of rescripts published by Licinius in their provinces. The latter writer
also maintains that there was an edict of Milan.

The ablest discussion of the question is that by Hermann Hülle.[1] He accepts an edict of Milan but limits it
to complete religious toleration and ascribes the policy
of restitution of Christian property to later rescripts,
such as that of Constantine to Anulinus in Africa. In
his opinion Lactantius probably gives a rescript issued
afterwards by Licinius for Bithynia, and Eusebius, a later
Palestinian version of this, both being amplifications and
extensions of the brief Milan edict. Valerian Sesan[2]
argues at great length that Eusebius gives a Greek
translation of the original rescript of Milan, and Lactantius a form of it issued by Licinius from Nikomedia.
He holds, however, the untenable ground that both
allude to a lost edict of Constantine's dating from 312.

---

[1] *Die Toleranzerlasse römischer Kaiser für das Christentum*, (Berlin,
1895), pp. 80-106. The same conclusions are reached by V. Schultze in
the articles on Constantine in the *Real-Enzyklopädie für protestantische
Theologie und Kirche*, x, 757-773 (1901).

[2] *Kirche und Staat im römisch-byzantinischen Reiche seit Konstantin
dem Grossen und bis zum Falle Konstantinopels*, vol. i (1911), pp.
128-237.

Another investigator, Joseph Wittig,[1] arrives independently at the same general conclusions as Sesan, combating, however, the assumption of a lost edict of 312.

The meeting of Constantine and Licinius at Milan in 313 and the promulgation there of an edict or rescript of religious toleration are established by adequate evidence beyond reasonable doubt. Lactantius undoubtedly gives, according to his own statement, not this original edict, but a rescript of Licinius' based upon it and issued at Nicomedia. I cannot see in the arguments of Sesan and Wittig sufficient reason for putting Eusebius' version upon a different basis from that of Lactantius and calling it a translation of the original Milan edict.[2] More probably Eusebius gave the version of the rescript which was published in his part of the Empire. How far this rescript reproduces the edict or rescript of Milan it is impossible to say. Hülle's limitation of the latter to religious toleration seems not altogether warranted. It probably not only ordered the recognition of Christianity on exactly the same standing as to toleration as that of the established religions, and not only involved

---

[1] "Das Toleranzreskript von Mailand 313," in *Konstantin der Grosse und seine Zeit*, ed. Franz J. Dölger (1913), pp. 40–65.

[2] Wittig's comparison of differences between the texts is specious rather than convincing. E. g., where Eusebius is briefer, this proves his form to be the original; where he is lengthier, this proves that Lactantius condensed. Where Lactantius represents Licinius as using phrases less vaguely monotheistic and more specifically Christian than Eusebius gives, this shows that Licinius, not being a Christian (*cf.* Eusebius x, 5,4–5, and Lactantius xlviii,4–5), was eager to proclaim his voluntary recognition of Constantine's god, so as to avoid the reproach of being overborn by Constantine! The omission of an introductory section in Lactantius and of the possessive pronoun where Eusebius' version cites former orders as "our former letters" may be significant but furnishes no argument for Wittig's position (*cf.* Eusebius x, 5, 2–3, omitted in Lactantius; *cf.* Eusebius, § 6 and Lactantius, ₰ 6).

the principle of religious liberty, but also directed
the restoration of church property which had been
confiscated from the Christians.[1] The rescript given
by Lactantius differs in a number of places from
the translation given by Eusebius, but both are monotheistic in tone, the latter rather more vaguely so than
the former. What could be more vague than the phrase
quoted by Eusebius, "that so whatever divine and
heavenly power there is may be propitious to us"
(ὅπως ὁ τί ποτέ ἐστι θειότητος καὶ οὐρανίου πράγματος, ἡμῖν . . . . εὐμενὲς εἶναι
δυνηθῇ, for Lactantius' "quo quidem divinitas in sede
coelesti nobis . . . propitia possit existere")?[2] Both
versions concur in ascribing the previous success of the
rulers to divine aid and in assigning as the motive of
the law desire for continuance of divine favor. "So
shall that divine favor which, in affairs of the mightiest
importance, we have already experienced, continue to
give success to us, and in our successes make the com-
monwealth happy."[3] These may well have characterized
the original edict or rescript and have represented Constantine's religious status in 313, for his influence, rather
than that of Licinius, must in this have been dominant.

The policies of complete religious toleration and of the
restoration to Christians of their property formerly confiscated were in any case adopted by Constantine soon
after he became sole emperor in the west. Eusebius
places immediately after the rescript discussed above, a
rescript to Anulinus in Africa, ordering the immediate
restoration to the Catholic church of all property which
had been confiscated from it.[4] This rescript makes no

---

[1] Cf. Eusebius, *Life of Constantine*, i, 14.
[2] Eusebius, *Church History* x, 5, 4. Lactantius, *op. cit.*, xlviii, 4.
[3] Eusebius, *op. cit.*, x, 5, 13. Cf. Lactantius, *op. cit.*, xlviii, 13.
[4] Eusebius, *op. cit.*, x, 5, 15-17.

provision for the compensation of the purchasers and
holders of this property, whereas both the Eusebian and
the Lactantian version of the rescript of Licinius pro-
vide for the compensation from the public treasury of legal
holders of confiscated Christian property.   The rescript
to Anulinus is generally supposed to have been issued
after the edict of Milan, but Wittig argues plausibly that
it antedated the latter and represents a less matured plan
of dealing with the problem.[1] If so, whether at Milan
or elsewhere, Constantine soon provided for reimburs-
ing the losers, for he was always very free with public
moneys.

Among the laws which Constantine issued between 313
and 323 in favor of the church, beyond complete toleration, the following may be noted.

The clergy were exempted from all state contributions.[2]
How substantial this concession was may be seen from
the rush which ensued toward the clerical status.   It
was so great that by 320 another edict was issued limiting
entrance to the clergy to those classes whose exemption
would not make much difference either to the state or to
themselves.   This was not retroactive and did not dis-
turb those who were already clerics.[3]   Great as was the
concession however, it was not an exaltation of Christianity above other religions, for such exemptions were
commonly made to priests of acknowledged religions.

---

[1] *Op. cit.*, pp. 51, 52.

[2] *Codex Theodosianus*, xvi,2,2(319). " Qui divino cultui ministeria religionis impendunt, id est hi, qui clerici appelantur, ab omnibus omnino
muneribus excusentur, ne sacrilego livore quorundam a divinis obsequiis
avocentur. " *Cf.* earlier letter of Constantine's instructing Anulinus to
exempt the clergy of the Catholic church, over which Cæcilian presided, from public duties. Eusebius, *Church History*, x, 7.

[3] *Cod. Theod.*, xvi, 2, 3. (326)

Constantine himself extended substantially the same exemptions to the patriarchs and elders of the Jews, to whom in general he was not friendly. [1]

A law published soon after the victory over Maxentius shows Constantine to be interested in protecting the machinery and the routine of church life from annoyance at the hands of heretics, but more than a friendly interest of this sort can hardly be inferred from it. [2]

In 313 (or 315) the church was freed from "annona" and "tributum." In 320 the laws from the time of Augustus, disqualifying those not of near kinship who remained unmarried or childless from receiving inheritances, were changed, probably in deference to the celibacy of the clergy, allowing celibates to inherit and releasing them from all penalties.[3] In 321 manumission in churches in the presence of the bishop and clergy was made legal and valid.[4] In 321 wills in favor of the Catholic church were permitted. [5]

Constantine's laws on Sunday are of great interest. In 321 he raised it to the rank of the old pagan holidays (feriae) by suspending the work of the courts and of the

[1] *Cod. Theod.* xvi, 8, 2 (a. 330, Nov. 29) and 4 (Dec. 1, 331).

[2] *Cod. Theod.* xvi, 2, 1 (313 (?) Oct. 31). "Haereticorum factione conperimus ecclesiae catholicae clericos ita vexari, ut nominationibus seu susceptionibus aliquibus, quas publicus mos exposcit, contra indulta sibi privilegia praegraventur. Ideoque placet, si quem tua gravitas invenerit ita vexatum, eidem alium subrogare et deinceps a supra dictae religionis hominibus hujusmodi injurias prohiberi."

[3] *Cod. Theod.* xi, 1, 1 (June 17, 315): viii, 16, 1 (Jan. 31, 320) ; Eusebius, *Life of Constantine*, iv, 26.

[4] *Cod. Theod.* iv, 7, 1, cf. *Codex Justinianus*, i, 13, 2.

[5] *Cod. Theod.* xvi, 2, 4 (321). "habeat unusquisque licentiam sanctissimo catholicae [ecclesiae] venerabilique concilio, decedens bonorum quod optavit relinquere," etc. This recognizes the corporate character of the church.

city population on that day, agricultural work, as was usual, being expressly excepted.[1]

In June, of the same year, Constantine published an amendment to the law, keeping the way open for the manumission of slaves on Sunday.[2]

These laws are not positively Christian or pagan, nor are they necessarily ambiguous as to the emperor's religious position. The worship of the sun, "*sol invictus*," and the observance of Sunday were integral parts of Mithraism and the religion of the Great Mother generally. The laws, therefore, might have been issued by a worshipper of the sun. The designation of the day as the venerable day of the sun, "*venerabili die Solis*" and "*diem solis veneratione sui celebrem*," has sometimes been cited as proof of Constantine's seeking at the time to do honor to Mithras, or the sun. Such phrases, however, were common to Christians as well as to pagans. The oriental, probably at first Babylonian, system of a week of seven days, each named from a heavenly body, had very generally supplemented and even supplanted in popular

[1] *Cod. Just.* iii, 12, 3.   "Omnes judices, urbanaeque plebes, et cunctarum artium officia venerabili die Solis quiescant. Ruri tamen positi agrorum culturae libere licenterque inserviant : quoniam frequenter evenit, ut non aptius alio die frumenta sulcis, aut vineae scrobibus mandentur, ne occasione momenti pereat commoditas coelesti provisione concessa." It is surprising that this law is not embodied in the *Cod. Theod.*, as it is presupposed by the law of Constantine in *Cod. Theod.* ii, 8, 1. It may have been included and have been lost in the copies handed down to us. The supposition that it originally included non-Christian terms and was an expression of sun-worship and was therefore omitted from the *Cod. Theod.* occurs to one, but is without any support whatever.

[2] *Cod. Theod.* ii, 8, 1. " Sicut indignissimum videbatur diem solis veneratione sui celebrem altercantibus jurgiis et noxiis partium contentionibus occupari, ita gratum ac jucudum est eo die quae sunt maxime votiva compleri. Atque ideo emancipandi et manumittendi die festo cuncti licentiam habeant et super his rebus acta non prohibeantur."

use the cumbersome Roman numbering of days by kal-
ends, nones and ides, long before this time.[1] Justin
Martyr at Rome, in the second century, used the phrase,
" day of the sun " in describing the worship of the Christians on the first day of the week.[2] Tertullian in North
Africa used it (*dies solis*) in such a way as to show that
it was commonly employed at the end of the second century.[3] No doubt the correct, specifically Christian usage
was to refer to the first day of the week as the Lord's
Day (*dies Domini* or *dies dominicus*), a usage still prevalent in religious speech ; but the name of the sun was
used very generally by the Christians for the first day of
the week even though this heavenly body was a universal
object of adoration among the heathen.   Assuming that
Constantine was a thoroughgoing Christian in 321, he
would probably have proclaimed the day under the name
of " *dies solis.*"

The words "*venerabili*" and "*veneratione sui celebrem*" might be construed as savoring of sun-worship,
but they may refer as well to the worship which from a
very early time characterized the Christian observance
of the first day of the week. The second law with its
emphatic approval of, and provision for manumission of
slaves, certainly gives the whole piece of legislation
the atmosphere of Christianity rather than of Mithraism.

---

[1] *Cf.* Zahn : *Geschichte des Sonntags*, pp. 25, 26, 60, 61 ; Mommsen,
Ueber den Chronographer von 354, pp. 566, 568 ; *Dio Cassius* 37, 19.
In various European languages the days of the week still perpetuate
this oriental influence upon the West through Rome, though German
gods and Christian sentiment have wrought some changes. The names
of the days originally commemorated were, in order: Sun, Moon, Mars,
Mercury, Jupiter, Venus, and Saturn.

[2] *Apology* i, 67. The phrase is used twice here.

[3] *Apology*, xvi ; *ad Nationes*, i, 13.

Eusebius, in his *Life of Constantine*,[1] gives a long list of provisions enacted by Constantine for the most pious observance of Sunday, which are there given as specifically Christian, though the prayer which he says was enforced on that day in the army was merely monotheistic. Allowing for the edifying and eulogistic tone of this source, it seems more probable that Eusebius at most exaggerated the piety of the emperor than that he entirely distorted the object of that piety, and while much of the passage refers to the latter part of Constantine's reign, it unquestionably includes a summary of his first law on Sunday. Taken in connection with this and other evidence these laws seem to have been issued with especial regard for the Christians.

Constantine's laws on the subject of magic and divination, mostly in this period of his legislation (312–323), give no decisive indication of his relation to Christianity. They show indeed his belief in the efficacy of these practices.[2] It was only the private consulting of haruspices and the practice of magic arts against chastity or life, or for other harmful purposes that were forbidden.[3]   Rites

[1] iv, 18–20.

[2] *Cf. Cod. Theod.* ix, 16, 3 (May 23, 321–324). The law of Dec. 17, 320–321, *Cod. Theod.* xvi, 10, 1, permits and even in some circumstances encourages the public consultation of haruspices. " Si quid de palatio nostro aut ceteris operibus publicis degustatum fulgore esse constiterit, retento more veteris observantiae quid portendat, ab haruspicibus requiratur et diligentissime scriptura collecta ad nostram scientiam referatur ; ceteris etiam usurpandae hujus consuetudinis licentia tribuenda, dummodo sacrificiis domesticis abstineant, quae specialiter prohibita sunt. Eam autem denuntiationem adque interpretationem, quae de tactu amphitheatri scribta est, de qua ad Heraclianum tribunum et magistrum officiorum scribseras,ad nos. scias esse perlatam. " *Cod. Theod.* ix, 16, 3, shows belief that charms could affect the weather for the public benefit.

[3] *Cod. Theod.* ix, 16, 1, 2 and 3 ; xvi, 10, 1.

whose object was to prevent disease and drought were not prohibited.[1]

But permission and even encouragement of superstitious rites for certain extraordinary occurrences do not show devotion to pagan religions and absence of any connection with Christianity as some writers on Constantine have inferred. If they did, a large portion of the church

[1] Boyd : *op. cit.*, p. 19 misses the mark when he says "As his panegyrist declares that Constantine fought Maxentius against the counsel of men, against the advice of the haruspices, this legislation [referring especially to commands to collect and transmit to court the replies of the haruspices] does not signify a belief in the divinatory arts, rather an effort to forestall any attempt to make use of divination in any political conspiracy against the fortunes of the Flavian family." The *Anonymous panegyric* (313) referred to (Migne : P .L., viii col. 655, c. ii), in its "contra haruspicum monita" implies rather that Constantine consulted the augurs, but was not discouraged by an unfavorable answer, and the direction of the law in cases of public buildings struck by lightning, "retento more veteris observantiæ, quis portendat, ab haruspicibus requiretur " etc., refer to the observance of accepted practises. Belief in the power of such practises was common among the Christians themselves: they merely asserted the superior magical power of Christian observances. Cf. Lactantius, *de Mort. Pers.* chap. x.

It is barely possible that there may be a connection between the burning of Diocletian's palace, at the beginning of the Diocletian persecution, and Constantine's law in 321 (*Cod. Theod.* xvi, 10, 1). Lactantius it will be remembered (*de Mort. Pers.* cxiv) says that Galerius hired emissaries to set the palace on fire and then laid the blame on the Christians as public enemies. In the Easter "*Oration of Constantine to the Assembly of the Saints*" reproduced by Eusebius, Constantine is reported as saying (chap. 25) that he was an eye-witness of the occurrence, that the palace was consumed by lightning, and that Diocletian lived in constant fear of lightning. For an interesting note upon the beginning of the Diocletian persecution, which still remains obscure, see McGiffert in the *Nicene and Post-Nicene Fathers*, Series ii, Volume i *Eusebius*, pp. 397-400. If, as Professor McGiffert suggests, there was a Christian conspiracy against Galerius, this might establish a connection in Constantine's mind between lightning, haruspices, and plots such as Dr. Boyd assumes. Otherwise, Constantine may have thought that as the Christian God sent lightning against Diocletian the pagan deities or demons might send lightning against him.

would, in many different ages, have to be counted out of Christendom.

Judging from Constantine's legislation in the west discussed thus far, the inference would naturally be that he was friendly disposed toward Christianity, and sought to put it upon a full equality with former official religions of the empire. There was no effort to suppress paganism, or even to make Christianity the one legal religion of the empire.[1]

But with his final conflict with Licinius and his victory in 323,[2] Constantine's legislation seems to become more specifically and completely Christian. A law of 323 expressly forbade any attempt to force Christians to take part in pagan celebrations and gave redress for abuses of this sort.[3]

Several general statements of the greatest importance, chiefly covering the period 323–336, have come down to us from approximately Constantine's time, which if they could be accepted in full would leave no question but that Constantine accomplished a legal revolution, entirely substituting Christianity for paganism in Roman life. One, a law of Emperor Constans in 341,[4] in pro-

---

[1] For a general summary of Constantine's laws in force in the west before the victory over Licinius and put in operation in the east at that time, from the pen of a Christian panegyrist, see Eusebius, *Life of Constantine*, ii, 20 and 21.

[2] Or 324, according to Seeck.

[3] " Quoniam comperimus quosdam ecclesiasticos et ceteros catholicae sectae servientes a diversarum religionum hominibus ad lustrorum sacrificia celebranda compelli, hac sanctione sancimus, si quis ad ritum alienae superstitionis cogendos esse crediderit eos, qui sanctissimae legi serviunt, si conditio patiatur, publice fustibus verberetur, si vero honoris ratio talem ab eo repellat injuriam, condemnationem sustineat damni gravissimi, quod rebus publicis vindicabitur." *Cod. Theod.*, xvi, 2, 5 (May 25, 323[?]).

[4] *Cod. Theod.*, xvi, 10, 2. " Cesset superstitio, sacrificiorum abo-

hibiting sacrifices to the gods implies that Constantine
had earlier made the same sweeping prohibition.   If
such an edict was issued, however, it has been lost.
Jerome [1] tells of a law for the general destruction of
pagan temples. This, too, if issued, has been entirely
lost. Eusebius refers to many laws, which, if his statements are correct and his quotations genuine, would
have put a legal end to many essential features of paganism.[2] Victor Schultze[3] has ably defended these particular summaries of Constantine's laws, but they cannot be
taken as conclusive, in view of Eusebius' probable exaggerations about laws which have been preserved[4] as well
as in view of the general character of his *Life of Constantine*. Even the combined testimony of Constans'
law, Jerome, and Eusebius cannot be accepted as final.
It is contradicted by Libanius,[5] who goes so far as to
say that Constantine did not at all change the legal religion ; by Zosimus,[6] who says that Constantine tolerated
heathen worship ; by later exhortations of Christians
asking for such laws ;[7] and by laws expressly allowing

leatur insania. Nam quicumque contra legem divi principis parentis
nostri et hanc nostrae mansuetudinis jussionem ausus fuerit sacrificia
celebrare, conpetens in eum vindicta et praesens sententia exeratur."

[1] *Chronicle*, under year 335.

[2] *Oration in Praise of Constantine*, 2; 8; 9.   *Life of Constantine*, ii,
44; 45; iii, 55–58; iv, 23; 25.

[3] In *Zeitsch f. K. G.*, vii (1885), p. 369 *et seq.*

[4] Cf. *Life of Constantine*, iv, 18, with Constantine's actual law, *Cod.
Theod.*, ii, 8, 1, and *Cod. Just.*, iii, 12, 3; see above, p. 77. For instances, however, in which Eusebius' statements are confirmed by the
laws which have come down to us, *cf. Cod. Theod.*, viii, 16, 1, with
Life of Constantine, iv, 26; *Cod. Theod.*, iv, 4, 3, and ii, 24, 1, and iv,
4, 1, with *Life of Constantine*, iv, 26, 5.

[5] *Pro Templis*, ed. Reiske (1784).

[6] *Roman History*, ii, 29, 3.

[7] Eg., Firmianus, *de Errore*, p. 39.

divination in the pagan temples.[1] These last may, of
course, have been abrogated by later laws such as
Eusebius and Jerome claim were issued, but there is no
proof of it other than the partisan statements of those
writers.

It seems clear, however, that though Constantine's
later laws may not have gone to the extent assumed by
Eusebius, Constans and Jerome, they show at least an
anti-pagan tendency, in the light of which the statements
of these three authorities must be interpreted as, at
most, exaggerations and not utter misstatements. There
seems to be no doubt that heathen temples suffered
severely from adverse imperial influence;[2] and as early
as 326, in a law looking toward the completion of old
buildings before new ones were begun, it was expressly
provided that temples might be left unfinished.[3]

Several long and rhetorical edicts of Constantine,
notably the " Edict to the Inhabitants of the Province of
Palestine," and the " Edict to the People of the Provinces
concerning the Error of Polytheism" are given in Eusebius' *Life of Constantine,*[4] both purporting to be from

[1] *Cod. Theod.*, xvi, 10, 1 (321); ix, 16, 2 and 3 (319).

[2] *Cf. infra*, pp. 63-64.

[3] *Cod. Theod.*, xv, 1, 3 (326 [362] June 29). " Provinciarum judices
commoneri praecipimus, ut nihil se novi operis ordinare ante debere
cognoscant, quam ea compleverint, quae a decessoribus inchoata sunt,
exceptis dumtaxat templorum aedificationibus."

[4] ii, 24-42, and ii, 48-60, respectively. These with the other documents in this work were labeled forgeries by Crivellucci, Mommsen,
Peter, Burckhardt, Seeck and others: Seeck later accepted them as
genuine, chiefly on the ground that they are documents which would
naturally be in Eusebius' chancery, and with the specific form of address which one would expect in copies sent to Caesarea in Palestine.
Zeitsch. f. K. G., xviii, (1898) p. 321 *et seq.* They are held by Schultze:
Zeitsch. f. K. G., xiv (1894), p. 527 *et seq.*, to be forgeries by a later
hand than Eusebius', largely because (1) the former does not correspond

authentic copies, the former with the emperor's signature and the latter entirely in his own handwriting. If
these are genuine they show that Constantine was at
this time[1] a most zealous Christian, filled with mission-
ary zeal, but determined not to use legal force in the
conversion of pagans.

Many laws were undoubtedly issued after 323 con-
ferring special privileges upon Christian churches and
Christian priests.[2] From all these special privileges
heretics were expressly debarred.[3] Cities which became

with what one would expect it to be from the context, ii, 20–23; (2) the
latter misstates Constantine's age (Constantine says he was a boy, *i. e.*
under 14, at the beginning of the Diocletian persecution in 303, which
in spite of Seeck's contrary opinion seems impossible, *cf.* Eusebius,
op. cit., ii, 51; i, 8, 1; (3) both contain many improbabilities, contra-
dicting other information and other parts of Eusebius' writings; (4)
both are of a nature and style foreign to imperial decrees. It is hard
to see how they can safely be used as authoritative documents.

[1] After his victory over Licinius.

[2] "Neque vulgari consensu neque quibuslibet petentibus sub specie
clericorum a numeribus publicis vacatio deferatur, nec temere et citra
modum populi clericis connectantur, sed cum defunctus fuerit clericus,
ad vicem defuncti alius allegetur, cui nulla ex municipibus prosapia
fuerit neque ea est opulentia facultatum, quae publicas functiones facil-
lime queat tolerare, ita ut, si inter civitatem et clericos super alicujus
nomine dubitetur, si eum aequitas ad publica trahat obsequia, et pro-
genie municeps vel patrimonio idoneus dinoscetur, exemptus clericis
civitati tradatur. Opulentos enim saeculi subire necessitates oportet,
pauperes ecclesiarum divitiis sustentari." *Cod. Theod.*, xvi, 2, 6 (June
1, 326).

"Lectores divinorum apicum et hypodiacone ceterique clerici, qui
per injuriam haereticorum ad curiam devocati sunt, absolvantur et de
cetero ad similitudinem Orientis minime ad curias devocentur, sed im-
munitate plenissima potiantur." *Cod. Theod.*, xvi, 2, 7 (Feb. 5, 330).

[3] "Privilegia, quae contemplatione religionis indulta sunt, catholicae
tantum legis observationibus prodesse oportet. Haereticos autem atque
schismaticos non solum ab his privilegiis alienos esse volumus, sed
etiam diversis muneribus constringi et subjici." *Cod. Theod.*, xvi, 5, 1
(Sept. 1, 326).

exclusively Christian were granted special imperial favors.[1]

A law of 326, or about that year, conferred remarkable civil functions on the church organization, and marks one of the most important of the steps by which, in the Middle Ages, it came to dominate and overshadow the state. Litigants were allowed to bring suits before bishops and even to transfer them thither from the civil judges. The decision of the bishop was to be recognized by government officials as legal and binding. The law thus made the bishop a final court, open apparently to any one, whether Christian or not, who chose to cite his opponent before him. It not only gave legal authority to the judgment which ecclesiastical authorities might pronounce in quarrels between Christians, quarrels which, from the days of St. Paul they had been urged to keep within the church so as to avoid the scandal of suits in pagan courts,[2] but it went far beyond that. It created episcopal courts with far-reaching powers, parallel to, and independent of, the secular courts. It was a recognition of the church, fraught with tremendous consequences for the future.[3]

" Novatianos non adeo comperimus praedamnatos, ut his quae petiverunt crederemus minime largienda. Itaque ecclesiae suae domos et loca sepulcris apta sine inquietudine eos firmiter possidere praecipimus, ea scilicet, quae ex diuturno tempore vel ex empto habuerunt vel qualibet quaesiverunt ratione. Sane providendum erit, ne quid sibi usurpare conentur ex his, quae ante discidium ad ecclesiae perpetuae sanctitatis pertinuisse manifestum est." *Cod. Theod.*, xvi, 5, 2 (Sept. 25, 326).

[1] *Corpus Inscriptionum Latinarum*, iii, 7000. *Cf.* Eusebius, *Life of Constantine*, iv, 37-39.

[2] 1 Cor., vi, 1-7.

[3] "Judex pro sua sollicitudine observare debebit, ut, si ad episcopale judicium provocetur, silentium accomodetur et, si quis ad legem Christianam negotium transferre voluerit et illud judicium observare, audiatur, etiamsi negotium apud judicem sit inchoatum, et pro sanctis

A considerable body of humanitarian legislation shows probably an increasing Christian influence upon Constantine.[1] In his earlier rule in Gaul, though he was extolled by his heathen panegyrist, Eumenius,[2] as one so

habeatur, quidquid ab his fuerit judicatum: ita tamen, ne usurpetur in eo, ut unus ex litigantibus pergat ad supra dictum auditorium et arbitrium suum enuntiet. Judex enim praesentis causae integre habere debet arbitrium, ut omnibus accepto latis pronuntiet." *Cod. Theod.*, i, 27, 1 (June 23, * * *). This law of Constantine's, though the absence of one of the consuls' names leads to the year being omitted in the edition of Mommsen and Meyer, must have been issued about 326, as it is dated at Constantinople, and Crispus was one of the consuls. The building of Constantinople could hardly have been begun much before this, and Crispus was executed that year.

Cf. also Constitutiones Sirmondianae for law of May 5, 333. "* * * Itaque quia a nobis instrui voluisti, olim promulgatae legis ordinem salubri rursus imperio propagamus. Sanximus namque, sicut edicti nostri forma declarat, sententias episcoporum quolibet genere latas sine aliqua aetatis discretione inviolatas semper incorruptasque servari; scilicet ut pro sanctis semper ac venerabilibus habeantur, quidquid episcoporum fuerit sententia terminatum. Sive itaque inter minores sive inter majores ab episcopis fuerit judicatum, apud vos, qui judiciorum summam tenetis, et apud ceteros omnes judices ad exsecutionem volumus pertinere. Quicumque itaque litem habens, sive possessor sive petitor vel inter initia litis vel decursis temporum curriculis, sive cum negotium peroratur, sive cum jam coeperit promi sententia, judicium elegerit sacrosanctae legis antistitis, ilico sine aliqua dubitatione, etiamsi alia pars refragatur, ad episcopum personae litigantium dirigantur. Multa enim, quae in judicio captiosa praescriptionis vincula promi non patiuntur, investigat et publicat sacrosanctae religionis auctoritas. Omnes itaque causae, quae vel praetorio jure vel civili tractantur, episcoporum sententius terminatae perpetuo stabilitatis jure firmentur, nec liceat ulterius retractari negotium, quod episcoporum sententia deciderit. Testimonium etiam ab uno licet episcopo perhibitum omnis judex indubitanter accipiat nec alius audiatur testis, cum testimonium episcopi a qualibet parte fuerit repromissum," etc. *Cod. Theod.*, ed., Mommsen and Meyer, vol. i, part 2, pp. 907-908.

[1] For other contributing factors, *cf.* A. C. McGiffert, " The Influence of Christianity on the Roman Empire," *Harvard Theological Review*, ii, pp. 28–49 (Jan., 1909).

[2] In 310, *Paneg.*, chap. 14, Migne: *Patrologia Latinae*, viii, col. 633 (In *Paneg. Vet.* this is *Paneg.*, no. vii).

formed by nature and rearing that he could not be cruel, he is pictured as ending barbarian wars by the execution of captured kings and the wholesale destruction of prisoners in gladiatorial shows.[1] In his later career, however, he legislated against gladiatorial shows,[2] and in favor of better treatment of prisoners.[3] He also commanded milder treatment of slaves than was customary in earlier laws, and encouraged their manumission.[4] Branding of criminals, for instance, was to be upon the hand, so that the face, made in the image of heavenly beauty, should not be marred. In the laws of the years 319 and 326, dealing with slavery, the distinction made between the death of a slave through cruelty and abuse and his death resulting from punishment of misconduct is the decisive note and an improvement over previous legislation, even though the law expressly exempted the master from penalty in the latter instance.[5] There were edicts issued also in favor of widows and orphans and the poor,[6] edicts encouraging the freeing of slaves, and

[1] *Ibid.*, chaps. 10, 11; *Incerti Paneg.* (Treves, 313), chap. 23; in Migne, *P. L.*, viii, col. 622 *et seq.;* 670-671 resp.

[2] "Cruenta spectacula in otio civili et domestica quiete non placet. Quapropter, qui omnino gladiatores esse prohibemus eos, qui forte delictorum causa hanc condicionem adque sententiam mereri consueverant, metallo magis facies inservire, ut sine sanguine suorum scelerum poenas agnoscant." *Cod. Theod.*, xv, 12, 1 (Oct. 1, 325). *Cf.* Eusebius, *Life of Constantine*, iv, 25.

[3] *Cod. Theod.*, ix, 3, 1 (320); ix, 3, 2 (326); xi, 7, 3 (320).

[4] *Cod. Theod.*, ii, 8, 1 (321); iv, 7, 1 (321); iv, 8, 5 (322), and 6 (323).

[5] *Cod. Theod.*, ix, 12, 1 (May 11, 319); and 2 (April 18, 326). *Cf.* Seeck: *Untergang, etc.*, i, 468, 478.

[6] *Cod. Theod.*, i, 22, 2 (June 17, 334); iii, 30, 1 (Mar. 26, 314); 2 (Feb. 3, 316[323]); 3 (Mar. 15, 326); 4 (Aug. 1, 331); 5 (April 18, 333); ix, 21, 4 (May 4, 329); ix, 42, 1 (Feb. 27, 321). *Cf.* Eusebius, *Life of Constantine*, i, 43, 2; iv, 28. Athanasius *Apologia contra Arium*, 18.

forbidding the exposing of children to get rid of them.[1]

Constantine also issued a number of laws against immorality and immoral religious rites, laws providing for and regulating the punishment of adultery, and a law prohibiting the custom of concubinage,[2] at that time not generally condemned by public sentiment outside the church. These laws may reasonably be inferred to be in sympathy, at least, with the opinion of Christian leaders and advisers of the emperor.

An interesting and apparently specifically Christian turn is found in some laws directed against the Jews. One edict early in Constantine's reign decrees that Jews or their elders or patriarchs who stone a convert to Christianity (ad Dei cultum) or otherwise maltreat him shall be burned, with all their associates in the act.[3]

[1] *Cod. Theod.*, v, 9, 1 (April 17, 331); xi, 27, 1 (May 13, 315), 2 (July 6, 322).

[2] The law of 326 (de concub., *Cod. Just.*, v, 26, 1), forbids a man to have a concubine if his wife is alive. *Cf.* D. S. Schaff, '' Concubinage '' (Christian), in *Encyclopaedia of Religion and Ethics*, iii, 817 (1911). *Cf.* P. Meyer, *Der römische Konkubinat*, (1895).

Cod. Theod., i, 22, 1 (Jan. 11, 316); ii, 17, 1 (April 9, 321 [324]); iii, 16, 1 (331); iv, 6, 2 (April 29, 336) This law, however, was aimed especially at the illegitimate son of Licinius. iv, 6, 3 (July 21, 336); 8, 7 (Feb. 28, 331); 12, 1 [= 11, 1 Haenel] (April 1, 314); 12, 4 [= 11, 5 Haenel] (Oct. 6, 331); ix, 1, 1 (Dec. 4, 316–7); 7, 2 (April 25, 326); 8, 1 (April 4, 326 [?]); 9, 1 (May 29, 326); 24, 1 (April 1, 320); 38, 1 (Oct. 30, 322); xii, 1, 6 (July 1, 319).

[3] '' Judaeis et majoribus eorum et patriarchis volumus intimari, quod, si quis post hanc legem aliquem qui eorum feralem fugerit sectam et ad dei cultum respexerit, saxis aut alio furoris genere, quod nunc fieri cognovimus, ausus fuerit adtemptare, mox flammis dedendus est et cum omnibus suis participibus concremandus. 1. Si quis vero ex populo ad eorum nefariam sectam accesserit et conciliabulis eorum se adplicaverit, cum ipsis poenas meritas sustinebit.'' *Cod. Theod.*, xvi, 8, 1 (Oct. 18, 315).

A later injunction against Jews molesting in any way converts to

Another law forbade a Jew to hold a Christian in servitude.[1]

Any fair summary of Constantine's legislation during the period of his sole emperorship, that is, during the last thirteen years of his life, would show that it was more favorable to Christianity than his earlier legislation, and more alien to paganism. Much of it seems specifically Christian. None of Constantine's later laws justify the theory of Burckhardt, that to the last he remained disposed to balance favors to the Christians with concessions to the pagan element. The law quoted by Burckhardt in favor of certain *sacerdotales* and *flamines perpetui* in Africa, seems merely to guarantee the continuance of their legal and social privileges even after they had ceased to perform any religious functions.[2]

2. *Coinage*

The extant coinage of Constantine is considerable, even after deducting a large number of spurious coins and medals.[3] Many of his coins bear pagan symbols and

Christianity is given in *Cod. Theod.*, xvi, 8, 5 (Oct. 22, 335), " Eum, qui ex Judaeo Christianus factus est, inquietare Judaeos non liceat vel aliqua pulsare injuria, pro qualitate commissi istiusmodi contumelia punienda."

[1] *Cod. Theod.*, xvi, 9, 1 (Oct. 21, 335). Eusebius, *Life of Constantine*, iv, 27. For another law directed toward the Jews, cf. *Cod. Theod.*, xvi, 8, 3 (Dec. 11, 321).

[2] " Sacerdotales et flamines perpetuos atque etiam duumvirales ab annonarum praeposituris inferioribusque muneribus inmunes esse praecipimus. Quod ut perpetua observatione firmetur, legem hanc incisam aeneis tabulis jussimus publicare." *Cod. Theod.*, xii, 5, 2 (May 21, 337). Cf. Aurel. Victor, *Caesars*, 40. Cf. also, Schultze, *Zeitsch. f. K. G.*, vii, p. 369, where it is shown that men of these orders openly declared themselves in inscriptions to be Christians.

[3] For full discussion see Jules Maurice, *Numismatique Constantinienne*, vol. i, 1908, still in progress, and H. Cohen: *Description des Monnaies frappées sous l'Empire romain, communément appelées*

inscriptions such as "Soli Invicti Comiti," though the estimate of these by Burckhardt [1] and others seems to be a gross exaggeration. "Hercules conservator," "Mars conservator," "Victoria," and similar dedications occur more or less frequently.[2] The title "Pontifex Maximus" occasionally occurs, sometimes with a veiled figure representing Constantine as such. But inferences from this must not be carried too far, for succeeding Christian emperors also bore the title.

On the other hand some coins show Constantine looking up as if in prayer.[3] These coins first appear about 325. They correspond in a general way with Eusebius' reference to them as tokens of the emperor's constant practice of prayer [4] and may be understood as an indication of Constantine's professed piety.[5] Coins and medals, one minted at Constantinople, with Constantine's name, and the reverse showing a veiled figure in a four-horse chariot ascending toward a hand outstretched from above need not necessarily be taken as a reflection of

Medailles imperiales edited and continued by Feuardent, 8 vols., second ed., Paris, 1880–1892. For list of older discussions, *cf.* Richardson's bibliography in *Nicene and Post-Nicene Fathers*, second series. vol. i, p. 445 *et seq.* For shorter discussions see Schiller: *Geschichte der römischen Kaiserzeit*, vol. ii, 207, 219; O. Seeck in *Zeitschrift für Numismatik*, xxi (1898), pp. 17–65, and Schultze in *Zeitsch. f. K. G.*, xiv (1894), pp. 504–510.

[1] Zeit Const. d. G., p. 371, "Soli Invicti Comiti" on four out of five.

[2] Grisar, in *Zeitsch. f. Kath. Theol.*, vi, p. 600 *et seq.*, maintains that many of these figures generally assumed to be gods are mere personifications of Constantine's greatness and victories, and cites one of them which has on the reverse an indubitable Christian emblem.

[3] For prints of these see Cohen, *op. cit.*, vii, pp. 240, 256, 311, 400.

[4] *Life of Constantine*, iv, 15.

[5] Schultze, in *Zeitsch. f. K. G.*, xiv (1894), p. 504 *et seq.*

Elijah's translation.[1] They may represent the apotheosis
of the emperor, as similar coins are said to have been
made for his father, Constantius, who was not a Christian.

Schiller's summary of Constantine's coinage is sug-
gestive, and the gradual development which he finds
seems justified, though his insistence upon the ambiguity
of signs generally accepted as Christian betrays a strong
bias in favor of his theory that Constantine tried to
straddle between Christianity and paganism.   He shows
that in Constantine's western mints coins[2] appear with
Mars, genius pop. Rom. and with *Sol invictus*; that
the first two ceased in 315 or earlier, and that the
last disappeared, perhaps by 315, at any rate before 323.
Coins with *Juppiter* stamped on them were not issued
in the west but in the east from the mints of Licinius.
Gradually non-commital legends, such as *Beata tran-
quillitas* took the place of pagan inscriptions.   Finally
coins with the monogram ☧[3] were issued, and toward
the end of Constantine's life series were issued showing
soldiers bearing the labarum with this monogram.

3. *Inscriptions*

Two inscriptions have been the center of controversy
in connection with Constantine's position in religious
matters, one on his triumphal arch at Rome, and the
other at a building in Hispellum.

The middle panels of the attic, on both the north and
the south side of the Arch of Constantine, above the

---

[1] See Schultze.

[2] Roman imperial coinage usually bore a well-defined clue to the mint
that put it out.

[3] In some instances this was a sign of the mint. For this sign, *cf.
infra*, p. 77 *et seq.*

central passageway, bear the following dedicatory inscription:

> IMP . CAES . FL . CONSTANTINO MAXIMO
> P . F . AVGVSTO . S . P . Q . R .
> QVOD INSTINCTV DIVINITATIS MENTIS
> MAGNITVDINECVM EXERCITV SVO
> TAM DE TYRANNO QVAM DE OMNI EIVS
> FACTIONE VNO TEMPORE IVSTIS
> REMPVBLICAM VLTVS EST ARMIS
> ARCVM TRIVMPHIS INSIGNEM DICAVIT

or in full, modern form:

"Imp(eratori) Caes(ari) F(lavio) Constantino Maximo P(io) F(elici) Augusto S(enatus) P(opulus) q(ue) R(omanus) quod instinctu divinitatis mentis magnitudine cum exercitu suo tam de tyranno quam de omni eius factione uno tempore iustis rempublicam ultus est armis arcum triumphis insignem dicavit." This may be translated: "To the Emperor, Caesar Flavius Constantius Maximus, Pius, Felix, Augustus, inasmuch as by his divine inspiration and his great mind, with the help of his army, he has justly avenged the republic at the same time upon the tyrant and upon his entire party, the Senate and the Roman People do dedicate this arch notable for triumphs."

This inscription, commemorating the victory over Maxentius (312), is almost universally assigned to the year 315, the date of Constantine's assumption of the title Maximus. The arch is generally believed to have been erected between 312 and 315, in large part out of materials taken from other monumental works, especially from works of Trajan and other emperors of the second century. The theory that the arch was constructed in Trajan's time and worked over for Constantine's benefit has been advocated at various times. Strong arguments against this theory were advanced by such authorities as

Bunsen [1] and Nibby. [2] De Rossi, also, who made a careful examination in 1863, when Napoleon III had plaster casts made of parts of the arch, reported that the dedicatory inscription quoted above was carved in marble blocks, which were an integral part of the structure itself, and that there was every indication that it was the original and the only inscription ever carved there. [3] Lanciani, after examination of the staircase and rooms in the attic, pronounced the inside of the structure to be built with a great variety of materials taken from monuments belonging to the Fabii and to the Arruntii. He pronounced the bricks, however, contemporary with Constantine. [4]

Recently, A. L. Frothingham, whose *Monuments of Christian Rome* (1908) described the arch as erected in the time of Constantine, has argued that it was originally erected in the time of Domitian, that it was afterwards "undedicated" and mutilated, that it was used in the third century as a sort of imperial "triumphal bulletin-board," and that its "Odyssey" ended with its final dedication to Constantine. [5] He bases his new opinion (1) on the well-know frequency with which Domitian had arches erected; (2) on the bas-relief from the mausoleum of the Haterii showing an unidentified monument where the Arch of Constantine now stands— between the Arch of Titus and the Colosseum, and facing the latter; (3) on the decree of *memoriae damnatio* passed against Domitian after his death; (4) on the fact

---

[1] *Beschreibung der Stadt Rom* (1837), vol. iii, part i.

[2] *Roma nell'anno MDCCCXXXVIII* (1838), part i, p. 443 *et seq.*

[3] *Bullettino di Archeologia cristiana del Cav. G. B. de Rossi* (Rome), I, No. 7 (July, 1863); No. 8 (Aug., 1863), Miscellaneous (1863).

[4] *The Ruins and Excavations of Ancient Rome* (1897), pp. 191–192.

[5] *Century Magazine*, vol. lxxxv, pp. 449–455 (Jan., 1913).

that triumphs were granted and arches built for victories
over foreign foes alone, not for victories in civil wars;
(5) on the phrase in the inscription quoted above,
"arcum triumphis insignem dicavit," which he translates,
"do dedicate herewith . . . this arch, famous for its
triumphs;" (6) on his belief that the set of eight medal-
lions over the smaller passageways representing hunting
scenes are in the style of Domitian and were part of the
original decoration, while the rest of the ornamentation
was inserted later; (7) and on the "series of eight
niches with half-figures of emperors being crowned by
victories" under the two smaller arcades. This argument as a whole seems plausible, but is by no means
convincing. The connection of the first three points
with the Arch of Constantine is purely speculative, the
second one being also weakened by the fact that the unidentified arch on the Haterian bas-relief, which Frothingham identifies as an arch of Domitian later converted
into the Arch of Constantine, plainly represents a structure with openings on all four sides (quadrafrons) afford-
ing passageway not only from north to south, but from
east to west; quite a different structure from the one we
are considering. The fourth point, while well taken, is
not conclusive; there may well have been exception in
the fourth century, and the argument would tell as
effectively against the dedication of an old triumphal
arch as against the erection of a new one. The fifth,
sixth and seventh points involve question of interpretation of literary and archæological evidence, in which the
weight of opinion is against Mr. Frothingham. Moreover, the history of the arch as he reconstructs it would
certainly be unique in the Roman empire, involving more
difficulties than does the generally accepted account.[1]

[1] For the Arch of Constantine, in addition to the works cited above,

Our interest, however, is in the dedicatory inscription. It will be seen that this ascribes Constantine's victory partly to his army, but primarily to the prompting of divinity and his greatness of mind, " Instinctu Divinitatis Mentis Magnitudine." The phrase is colorless and absolutely indecisive as between paganism and Christianity. It does not even necessarily refer to any special manifestation of providence, pagan or Christian. Victories have in all times been ascribed to divine favor irrespective of the religion involved and even of the circumstances of the battle. Constantine's earlier triumphs in Gaul had long before this been ascribed by pagan panegyrists to something like "instinctus divinitatis, mentis magnitudo."[1]   The monotheism of the conqueror may be inferred from the inscription, since if Constantine had been a pagan of the old type there would probably have been specific reference to Jupiter, Apollo or some other pagan deity. One would infer, also, that he was not at this time a zealous Christian, nor thought to be such, otherwise some distinctively Christian phrase would have been used. It is possible, however, that the indefiniteness of the phrase represents the thought of the pagan Senate rather than the emperor's attitude.

The matter has been complicated by the theory that "instinctu divinitatis" was not the original inscription, but a correction carved later over the original phrase.

cf. Jordan, *Topographie der Stadt Rom im Altertum*, ed. Huelsen (Berlin, 1907), vol. i, part 3, pp. 45 *et seq.;* H. Grisar, *Geschichte Roms* (1901), vol. i, p. 172.; E. Petersen, *Vom altem Rom* (Leipsic, 1911), p. 66 *et seq.*

Photographs of the Arch and other reproductions have been frequently published. Detailed descriptions with excellent photographic reproductions are given by J. Leufkens in *Konstantin der Grosse u. seine Zeit*, ed. by Dölger, pp. 161-216, and plates iii, iv, v, vi.

[1] *Cf. infra*, p. 131 *et seq.*

It has even been asserted that the original inscription was "NVTV. I. O. M.," "at the nod of Jupiter Optimus Maximus."[1] This theory, however, seems utterly untenable. The spacing of the inscription would be very peculiar, indeed, if such a phrase had really been a part of it, and close study of the attic of the Arch seems to afford no grounds for assuming that the inscription ever contained other words than are now to be seen in it.[2]

In the ruins of a building in the little Umbrian city of Hispellum an inscription[3] recites that the emperor granted a petition for the erection of a temple in honor of the gens Flavia to which he belonged, for the celebration there of certain festal performances with the stipulation that the temple was not to be polluted with the frauds of tainted superstition, "ne aedis nostro nomini dedicata cuiusquam contagiosae superstitionis fraudibus polluatur." In spite of Burckhardt's opinion to the contrary,[4] this probably meant the prohibition of pagan rites, and the building was intended apparently, not as a place of worship, but as a place for game and other celebrations, including, it must be admitted, gladiatorial shows.[5]

A third inscription[6] shows that privileges were given to localities on account of all their inhabitants being

---

[1] For full assertion of this theory and references, see Burckhardt, *Zeit Constantins d. Grossen*, pp. 343-344, 475-6.

[2] *Cf. supra*, p. 49; also Seeck, *Gesch. d. Untergangs der antiken Welt.*, i, p. 491; Dessau, 694; Keim, *Der Uebertritt Constantins, d. G. zum Christentum.*

[3] Ascribed to 336-337 A. D., Dessau 705 ; Orelli 5580; printed in Muratori *Inscr.* iii p. 1791 as spurious, but now generally accepted as genuine.

[4] *Zeit Constantins d. G.* p. 382.

[5] Cf. Seeck : *Gesch. d. Untergangs d. antiken Welt.* i, 471.

[6] *C. I. L*, iii 7000 "quibus omnibus quasi quidam cumulus accedit quod omnes ibidem sectatores sanctissimae religionis habitare dicantur."

" adherents of (our) most sacred religion." Taken with Eusebius' account [1] of special honor being shown Gaza and a town in Phoenicia on the same ground, this is proof of the emperor's active interest in, and association with Christianity after he became sole emperor.

4. *Writings*

Aside from coins and inscriptions a considerable body of direct evidence on Constantine's religion has been preserved, chiefly by Eusebius, in the form of speeches and letters attributed to him.[2] The longest of these is the Easter sermon, or " Oration of the Emperor Constantine to the Assembly of the Saints," which Eusebius appended to his Life of Constantine as a sample of the discourses which he says Constantine was in the habit of delivering to the court and even to the public.[3] This is held by Schultze,[4] chiefly on the ground of contradictions which it involves to Eusebius' narrative, and some close, even verbal resemblances to Lactantius, to be not a speech of the emperor's, but some Latin document copied by Eusebius. Since Eusebius did not hear the speech and was only at rare intervals at the court,[5] such a mistake was within the realm of possibility. But I am inclined to think that its obvious dependence upon Lactantius and its variations from Eusebius' own statements,[6] do not militate against the speech being Con-

---

[1] *Life of Constantine*, iv, 37, 38.

[2] For lists, with comments, see Richardson's " Prolegomena" in *Nicene and Post-Nicene Fathers*, Second Series, vol. i, *Eusebius*, pp. 436–439. *Cf.* also *infra*, p. 109 *et seq.* For imperfect and uncritical edition of Constantine's *Works*, cf. Migne, *P. L.*, vol. viii, 93–581.

[3] *Life of Constantine*, iv, 29–32.

[4] *Zeitsch. f. K. G.*, viii (1886), p. 541 *et seq.*

[5] *Life of Constantine*, iv, 33; 39; 46.

[6] *Eg.* Lactantius, *Divine Institutes*, i, 4–7, iv, 18–19, and Constantine,

stantine's. Lactantius, as the tutor of the emperor's
sons and a member of his household, probably influenced his religious conceptions as much as any one else,
certainly more than Eusebius. Constantine may well
not only have read his writings, but also have used them
without acknowledgment in his speeches. Indeed, Lactantius may have written the speech for the emperor to
deliver.

Many letters purporting to be Constantine's have been
preserved, some in Eusebius' *Church History*, more in
his *Life of Constantine*, and a few elsewhere. Those
whose genuineness is practically unquestioned, and those
which are in doubt, do not vary greatly in tone. They
are characterized by a loose, difficult style, in many cases
made worse by translation from Latin into Greek.[1] If
we restrict ourselves to those whose genuineness there
is no reason for questioning, we get a picture of one on
terms of official intimacy with the leading bishops, writing as one personally interested in the welfare of the
church, and as a believer in its teachings. From a theological point of view they expound a somewhat vague

---

Oration to the Saints, chaps. xviii–xxi, maintain that the Sibyl and
other heathen sources foretold the Christian revelation and Christ,
while Eusebius, *Oration in Praise of Constantine*, chap. ix, expressly
declared they did not.

[1] Among the most important in Eusebius, not mentioned in the discussion of legislation, are the following: *Church History*, x, 5, 18–21;
21–24; *Life of Constantine*, ii, 46; 64–72; iii, 17–20; 30–32; 42; 52–53;
60; 61; 62; iv, 36. Athanasius gives several bearing on himself and the
Arian controversy; *e. g. Apol. contra Ar.*, lix; lx; lxi; lxii; lxviii; lxx;
lxxxvi. Augustine, also, *Ep.*, lxxxviii. Gelasius of Cyzicus gives several letters, the genuineness of which is open to question, in his *History
of the Council of Nicea* (in Labbe, *Concilia*, 2 (1671), pp. 103–286).
For a list of 44 letters, not including all the above and giving some
from other sources, *cf*. Richardson, Prolegomena, in *Nicene and Post-
Nicene Fathers*, Second Series, vol. i, *Eusebius*, pp. 436–439.

monotheism linked rather clumsily to a revelation in
Christ which is represented in the organized church.
The Christian church, and Christians, are therefore the
representatives and the protégés of God. Immortality
is occasionally emphasized, but there is little attempt
after, or feeling for, those teachings and experiences,
which in all ages have constituted the highest types of
Christianity.

The most characteristic passages, varying phases of the
dominant note, are those in which Constantine speaks of
the favor of God as the source of his own great achievements and success. " I myself, then, was the instrument
whose services he chose, and esteemed suited for the ac-
complishment of his will. Accordingly, beginning at the
remote Brittanic ocean, through the aid of divine power
I banished and utterly removed every form of evil which
prevailed." [1] "But now that liberty is restored, and that
serpent, [Licinius, Constantine's brother-in-law] driven
from the administration of public affairs by the providence of God, and our instrumentality, we must trust
that all can see the efficacy of the Divine power." [2]
" Under thy guidance have I devised and accomplished
measures fraught with blessings : preceded by the sacred
sign I have led thy armies to victory. * * * For thy
name I truly love, while I regard with reverence that
power of which thou has given abundant proofs, to the
confirmation and increase of my faith." [3]

[1] Eusebius : *Life of Constantine*, ii, 28, quoting Constantine.

[2] *Ibid* ii, 46.

[3] *Ibid* ii, 55 *Cf. Oration of Constantine to the Assembly of the Saints*,
(his Easter sermon) appended to the *Life of Constantine*, chap. 22, 1;
chap. 26. Also Eusebius : *Church History* x, 7, 1 and 2.

CHAPTER III

IMPERIAL PATRONAGE OF CHRISTIANITY; ATTITUDE TOWARD PAGANISM

1. *Church Building*

Aside from legislation and other evidence already cited, many phases of imperial patronage of religion are disclosed by writers of Constantine's time. Thus, in the erection of buildings, in the entourage of the court, and in the attitude of contemporary Christian and pagan leaders, one can trace the dominance of one or another religious influence.

Constantine followed the example of many of his predecessors in erecting innumerable buildings. Early in his career, in Gaul, he rebuilt the public structures of Autun.[1] Nazarius extolled his building as well as his restoration of order in Rome immediately after the victory over Maxentius.[2] His friendly attitude toward Christianity was, therefore, naturally shown in the erection of churches. Eusebius abounds in sweeping statements of wholesale erection of Christian memorials, basilicas and churches throughout the empire.[3]

Zosimus, the pagan historian, with characteristic spleen, tells of his wasting public money on many useless buildings,

[1] *Cf.* the panegyric of Eumenius (310) at Treves, chap. 22, and the oration of formal thanks the following year, Migne, *P. L.,* viii, cols. 639, 641.

[2] *Panegyricus* of 321, Migne, *P. L.,* viii, col. 605 *et seq.* (chap. 33).

[3] *Cf. Oration in Praise of Constantine,* chaps. 9 *et seq.; Life of Constantine,* i, 42; ii, 45 and 46; iii, 1, 47 and 50.

56

some of which were so badly constructed that they had to be torn down. The Theodosian Code bears testimony to his zeal for building, at the time of the rearing of many structures in Constantinople, by his instructions for establishing schools of architecture.[1]

Many important church structures were, beyond reasonable doubt, built by him or through his influence, and by members of his family.[2] Most of our information about churches built in the eastern part of the empire comes from Eusebius' *Life of Constantine*. Aside from general statements about the zeal of the emperor and of his mother, Helena, in this cause the biographer refers specifically to the following: the Church of the Sepulchre[3] and its adjacent basilica, in Jerusalem; a church on the Mount of Olives,[4] a basilica in Bethlehem[5] and at Mamre;[6] a church at Heliopolis,[7] at Antioch,[8] at Nicomedia;[9] the Church of the Twelve Apostles at Constantinople,[10] in which Constantine's own sepulchral monument was built. Of most of these Eusebius gives a glowing description, and in the case of the Church of the Sepulchre at Jerusalem and the Church of the Twelve Apostles at Constantinople, he gives a detailed and elaborate account. These two, and the church at

---

[1] xiii, 4, 1.

[2] Ciampini, *De sacris aedificiis a Constantino Magno constructis synopiis historia*, Rome, 1693, is still one of the chief sources of information about these, though his identifications are not always accepted by modern archæologists.

[3] iii, 25-40; *cf.* also *Anonymi itinerarum* (Bordeaux pilgrim), A. D. 333, Migne, *P. L.*, vol. viii, col. 791.

[4] iii, 41-43; *cf.* also Bordeaux pilgrim, *loc. cit.*

[5] *Ibid.* Cf. Bordeaux pilgrim, col. 792.

[6] iii, 51-53; *cf.* also Bordeaux pilgrim, *loc. cit.*

[7] iii, 58.   [8] iii, 50.

[9] *Ibid.*   [10] iv, 58-60.

Antioch must have been magnificent and costly structures.
One of Eusebius' continuators, Socrates, who spent a large
part of his life in Constantinople, tells of another church
in that city named Irene (Peace), which he says Constantine considerably enlarged and adorned.[1] It may originally have antedated Constantine at Byzantium, or may
have been built in the first instance by the emperor, perhaps
shortly after his victory over Licinius and the restoration
of peace to the empire.

Rome is the only city in the West in which the erection
of any particular churches can be assigned, on any considerable historical evidence, to Constantine and his family.
Even here much is left uncertain. He unquestionably gave
the bishop at Rome at least the temporary use of the Lateran
palace, which had come into his possession through his
wife, Fausta. In 313 Bishop Miltiades presided there over
the well-known conference called at Constantine's direction
to settle the incipient Donatist schism in Africa. In connection with this palace, or out of part of it, Constantine
built the basilica (and adjacent baptistery) which, under
the name of the Lateran, was to become for centuries the
" mother and head of all the churches of the city and the
world." In early days it was called the Basilica of Constantine (not to be confused with the great civil basilica
which, begun by Maxentius, was, after his defeat and death,
finished by his conqueror, and became the basilica of Constantine), and in later days became St. John of the Lateran,
in honor of John the Baptist.[2] No vestige of its original
features now remain.

---

[1] *Ecclesiastical History*, ii, 16; i, 16, 2.

[2] On this church, *cf.* Lanciani, *Ruins and Excavations of Ancient
Rome*, pp. 339-343; Frothingham, *Monuments of Christian Rome*, p. 24.
Niebuhr, *Vorträge über alte Länden u. Völkerkunde*, p. 399, accepted
Constantinian origin for the Lateran buildings alone. Gregorovius, *Rome*

In the case of the Lateran, as of other churches which Constantine may have built or enlarged, the ecclesiastical structure must have been overshadowed by the magnificent buildings of ancient Rome with which it was surrounded. The *Notitia* which was edited about 330 and which enumerated the important public buildings of the city, did not mention a single Christian Church.[1] Eusebius, in connection with Rome, mentions only Constantine's benefactions to the churches; he names no churches which he built there, but refers only to his "enlarging and heightening" and "embellishing" the sacred structures.[2] Though Eusebius wrote with only a distant knowledge of Rome, his statement counts for something against the later extravagant traditions of Constantine's church building at Rome. The *Liber Pontificalis,* also, which, though compiled more than two hundred years after Constantine, embodied information from earlier documents, while it is full of descriptions of lavish embellishments and endowments, gives only a very modest list of churches as of Constantinian origin.[3]

Another palace within the city walls, the Sessorian, apparently furnished room for an ecclesiastical structure by the conversion of its main hall into a church. This was the Jerusalem church, and later became the "Holy Cross in Jerusalem" (*Santa Croce in Gerusalemme*), from the

---

in the Middle Ages, i, pp. 88-95, after naming seven churches which tradition ascribes to Constantine, added: "We can ascertain nothing definite of these buildings; and perhaps St. John Lateran alone owes its origin to the Emperor."

[1] *Cf.* Frothingham, *Monuments of Christian Rome,* p. 31.

[2] *Life of Constantine,* i, 42.

[3] *Cf.* the account it gives of Sylvester's pontificate. *Cf.* also Duchesne's discussion in the introduction of his edition of the *Lib. Pont.,* vol. i, p. cxl *et seq.*

preservation in it of the principal relic of the True Cross.[1]
A parish church inside the old city, that of Equitius, afterwards *SS. Silvestro e Martino ai Monti,* is claimed by the
Liber Pontificalis for the episcopate of Sylvester, Constantine's contemporary, and its remains are so assigned by
many archaeologists.[2] If this be correct it was probably one
of the beneficiaries of the emperor's generosity, even
though the bishop of Rome was its builder.

Outside the walls, according to the *Liber Pontificalis,* a
large basilica of St. Peter was erected (on the Vatican
Hill), a smaller basilica of St. Paul (on the Via Ostiensis),
a basilica of St. Lawrence (on the Via Tiburtina), a basilica
of St. Agnes (on the Via Nomentana), and one of SS.
Marcellinus and Peter (on the Via Praenestina). The
mausoleum of Constantina (incorrectly called Constantia)
near the basilica of St. Agnes, was apparently used as the
baptistery of the latter and should therefore be included
in the list.[3] While it is by no means certain that all of these
buildings owed their origin to Constantine, his family, or
pontiffs contemporary with him, such is the very general
opinion of archaeologists and of church historians.[4] It is
probable also that these and other churches received some,
if by no means all, of the ornaments and endowments which
later were described in such detail in the *Liber Pontificalis.*
Though tradition has doubtless exaggerated the extent of
Constantine's building, adorning and endowing of churches,

[1] *Cf.* Frothingham, *op. cit.,* p. 24; Lanciani, *op. cit.,* pp. 397 *et seq.*

[2] Frothingham, *op. cit.,* pp. 22-23.

[3] For a short account of all these buildings, *cf.* Frothingham, *op. cit.,*
pp. 24-31.

[4] For short summaries of Constantine's church building, *cf.* W. R.
Lethaby and C. H. Turner, in *Cambridge Medieval History,* vol. i, pp.
609-611, and 158 respectively. The argument that Constantine was at
Rome only at long intervals and for short stays does not, as is sometimes assumed, prove that he did not order extensive building there.

it is not too much to say that he was in this regard not only
the earliest, but one of the most profuse of imperial patrons
of the church.

2. *Constantine's Actions at Rome*

In the campaign against Maxentius, Constantine made
use of the cross and the monogram among his military insignia, perhaps as a result of a dream.[1] After his entry
into Rome he is said to have erected in the city a statue of
himself holding a cross in his hand, and inscribed with the
following phrases, " By this salutary sign, the true proof
of bravery, I have saved and freed your city from the yoke
of the tyrant," *etc.*[2] These references in Eusebius are our
only evidences and they have been questioned,[3] but their
repetition by him in different circumstances, especially in
the *Church History* and in the oration at Tyre in 314, has
something of cumulative evidence. The probability of such
a statue being erected is great, and is increased by the fact
that Maxentius declared hostilities by overthrowing and
defacing statues of Constantine at Rome.[4] I am therefore
inclined to accept Eusebius' statements.

The honor of apotheosis granted to Diocletian (soon
after 313) probably by the Senate, is sometimes cited as
evidence that Constantine was not a Christian at this time,[5]
but not much weight ought to be attached to it. Rome was

[1] For discussion of stories of Constantine's conversion in this connection, *cf. infra*, pp. 78 *et seq.;* 135 *et seq.*

[2] Eusebius, *Church History,* ix, 9, 10; 11; x, 4, 16; *Oration in Praise
of Constantine,* ix, 9, 18; *Life of Constantine,* i, 40.

[3] *Cf.* Brieger in *Zeitsch. f. K. G.* (1880), p. 45.

[4] Nazarius, *Panegyricus* (321), chap. 12.

[5] *Cf.* Burckhardt, *Zeit Constantins d. G.,* p. 345. This was the last
time this was done in the old pagan sense.

still strongly pagan; the act was very natural, and probably a mere formality.

On the other hand, Constantine, in the latter part of his reign, during his last visit to Rome, seems to have taken a definite stand against public ceremonies which involved recognition of the old gods. He refused on this occasion to lead the military procession of the equestrian order and present himself before the Jupiter of the Capitoline hill.[1] Something of a riot is said to have resulted from his defiance of the public sentiment which supported the ceremony.

3. *Personal Favor Shown Churchmen and the Church*

Of great significance is the unquestioned fact that Constantine employed (317) a Christian rhetorician, the well-known writer Lactantius, as the tutor of his sons, especially Crispus. All of his children were given a distinctively Christian education and the sons who succeeded him in imperial power carried out a decisively Christian policy in the government.[2]

Christian bishops were continually present at Constantine's court after 312. Hosius, bishop of Cordova in Spain, may have been with him in his campaign against Maxentius; he certainly accompanied him on an expedition later, and seems to have been very influential at court.[3] Eusebius of Nicomedia for many years enjoyed the favor of the emperor as well as that of his family. Eusebius of Caesarea delighted to recount expressions of royal appreciation

[1] Zosimus, ii, 29. Though Zosimus is not always a reliable source, there is no reason to reject this story. *Cf. infra,* p. 63, n. 6.

[2] *Cod. Theod.,* xvi, 10, 2 and 4. *Cf.* Boyd, *op. cit.,* pp. 21-23. See also Eusebius, *Life of Constantine,* iv, 52. For Lactantius, *cf.* Jerome, *de Vir. Ill.,* 80.

[3] Eusebius, *Church History,* x, 6, 2; *Life of Constantine,* ii, 63; Socrates, i, 2. 1; Athanasius, *Apol. c. Ar.,* 75.

which he received at his appearance before Constantine and in letters from him.[1] At the Council of Nicea the emperor showered attentions upon the bishops, and especially upon those who had suffered during the persecutions.[2] Making all allowance for exaggerations by Eusebius and other ecclesiastics who were dazzled by the eminence thus given them, the direct patronage bestowed upon the church and upon many leading churchmen must have been exceedingly liberal. Ammianus Marcellinus complained of his disorganizing the post service by giving Christian bishops free use of it in attending councils.[3]

He granted public money to various clergymen and churches,[4] and spent large sums on church buildings.[5] So far as we know he took little or no part during his later life in pagan ceremonies.[6]

4. *Attitude Toward Paganism*

Reports of the destruction of pagan temples by Constantine's orders and of his approval of their destruction by the people come down to us from nearly all sources. Most, if not all of these, refer to the last ten years of his life. Some

[1] *Life of Constantine,* iv, 33-36; 46; iii, 61.

[2] *Ibid.,* iii, 15, 22. *Cf.* also Theodoret, i, ii, 1.

[3] xxi, 16, 18.

[4] Eusebius, *Church History,* x, 6, Constantine's letter to Cecilian, bishop of Carthage, informing him of an appropriation, and authorizing him to draw on the treasury.

[5] *Cf. supra,* p. 56 *et seq.*

[6] For his refusal to take part in the military procession of the equestrian order to offer public vows to Jupiter on the Capitoline Hill, *cf. supra,* p. 62. Zosimus elsewhere affirms that Constantine tolerated heathen rites, and even took part in them (ii, 29, 3), but his statements to that effect in part refer to the earlier years of Constantine, in part are trivial, and are always under the suspicion of extreme partisanship. It can readily be seen that entire removal of pagan elements in all public ceremonies or absolute refusal to participate in such unpurified occasions would in any case be difficult and unnecessary as well as impolitic.

such cases may be traced to a desire to suppress immoral
and licentious rites, a feeling not limited to the Christians.[1]
Some were doubtless due to the necessity of replenishing
Constantine's notoriously disordered treasury, though Eusebius maintains that the removal of gold, silver and brass
ornaments and coverings of statues was effected in order
to expose the bare wood to the derision of the multitude.[2]
But though the motive was avarice, the process shows no
friendship for paganism. Many statues, also, and other
ornaments were removed from heathen temples for the
beautification of the new city of Constantinople.[3] Not
only were repairs stopped on old temples, but many such
buildings must have been demolished and their materials
used for other purposes. There can be no doubt but that
the emperor's attitude greatly encouraged the process of
the destruction of pagan antiquity.[4] Though no general
law for the destruction of pagan temples has come down
to us from this time, a law of Constans presupposes the
gradual destruction of such edifices during the last years of
Constantine's reign.[5]

Constantine's pro-Christian and anti-Pagan policy, however, does not seem to have been so pronounced as to make

[1] *Eg.*, the shrine of the heavenly goddess at Aphaca on Lebanon about
330 (Eusebius, *Life of Constantine*, iii, 55) ; and the temple at Heliopolis, supplanted by a church liberally supplied with almsmoney (*ibid.*,
chap. 58).

[2] Eusebius, *Life of Constantine*, iii, 54 and 57, copied from his *Oration in Praise of Constantine*, ch. 8. It may be noted that in chapter
54 Eusebius says this was done not by military force, but by a few of
the emperor's own friends. This looks like mercenary pillage.

[3] *Cf. infra*, pp. 65-66.

[4] *Cf.* Eusebius, *Life of Constantine*, iii, 54-58 ; *cf.* Lanciani, *The Destruction of Pagan Rome* (1903), pp. 30 *et seq.*

[5] *Cod. Theod.*, ix, 17. *Cf.* also Eunapius, *Vita Aedes*, 37, ed., Boise-
sonade, Amsterdam, 1822.

an open and sharply-defined break. Eusebius himself after summarizing his legislation for the relief of Christians in the west between 312 and 323 adds, " But his munificence bestowed still further and more numerous favors on the heathen peoples and the other nations in his empire. So that the inhabitants of our regions [the East] with one consent proclaimed their own happiness," *etc.*[1] Pagans continued in the court of Constantine up to the very last.[2] Yet a story has been preserved of a heathen philosopher, Kanonaris, executed for persistent denunciation of Constantine's destruction of the old religion.[3] We are told, also, through Eunapius, Zosimus and Suidas, concerning Sopater, a neoplatonist friend of the emperor's or possibly a magician, who was executed at Constantinople after 330. According to one version this was on the accusation of keeping back by magic the Egyptian grain ships. It may have been brought about by a court intrigue of the Christian faction.[4]

There are even some reports of pagan elements in the buildings and dedicatory exercises of Constantinople. Burckhardt[5] has emphasized the following: Glycas[6] tells of an astronomer Valens brought there to cast the horoscope of the new city. Sopater, also, is said to have performed mystic symbols as a magician.[7] There are also re-

---

[1] *Life of Constantine,* ii, 22.

[2] For one of the " self-imagined philosophers "; *cf.* Eusebius, *Life of Constantine,* iv, 55.

[3] Burckhardt, *Zeit Constantins d. G.,* p. 447, on basis of "Anonymus" in Banduri, *Imperium orientale,* p. 98.

[4] *Cf.* Zosimus, ii, 40.

[5] *Zeit Constantins d. G.,* pp. 382, 480 *et seq.*

[6] *Chronicle,* part iv. A poor source, from the twelfth century or later.

[7] This on basis of Joannes Lydus, *De Mensibus,* iv, 2.

E

ports of the erection of heathen temples to the Divine
Mother, to Castor and Pollux, and to Tyche, and of the
performance of an annual ceremony in which the image of
Tyche figured.[1]   On the face of the evidence, however, the
first two seem very uncertain, while the temples seem to
have been monumental structures built to hold statuary,
without any cults connected with them, and the ceremonies
were probably without any religious significance whatever.[2]

The friendliness of Christian writers to Constantine and
the hostility of subsequent pagan writers is of itself almost
conclusive evidence that he took his stand openly with the
former.   That he had some pagan panegyrists, especially
early in his reign, is to be accounted for by the fact that
only later did he assume Christianity, and then only gradually.[3] That there was little or no specifically pagan opposition to him during his life is explained by the fact that
pagan leaders do not seem to have been aware that the issue
between the two religions was being permanently decided
in that generation.   It could not have been seen until the
reign of Julian that the attitude of one emperor could be so
decisive or that a future restoration of paganism was forever out of the question.   Diocletian's persecution had not
only failed to destroy the church, but it had failed to per-
suade earnest supporters of pagan religions that Christianity was dangerous to them.   However, with Julian's unsuc-
cessful attempt to turn the tide back to paganism, there
came a change so noticeable that Bury uses it as one basis

---

[1] On the basis of Zosimus, ii, 31 ; Philostorgius, ii, 17 ; Sozomen, v, 4,
and *Chronicon Paschale*, ad. ann. 330.

[2] *Cf.* Grisar, *Zeitsch. f. Kath. Theol.*, vi (1882), pp. 587 *et seq.*, and
Strzygowski in *Analecta Graeciensia* (Graz., 1893).

[3] *Cf.* Eusebius, *Life of Constantine*, ii, 23, 47.

for determining the date of pagan writings.[1]   Those who
were most in earnest about paganism were thereafter apt
to be bitter toward Constantine, even to the extent of
maligning and slandering him.

5. *Constantine's Activity in Church Affairs, and his Motives*

The friendliness of Christian writers toward Constantine is so evident that it needs no proof nor comment. Eusebius, and his successors, united in extolling Constantine
not only as the first Christian emperor, but as their deliv-
erer and their divinely sent prince.   None ventured upon
serious criticism of him, and, in Christian writings, even
the most harmless suggestion of any imperfection in him
was usually veiled by reference to the evil influence of
others.[2]

We may conclude, then, that imperial patronage as well
as the legislative power of the emperor was exerted in-
creasingly in favor of the Christians, and that the total
effect of his reign was an overwhelming asset to the church.
Acts and tendencies to the contrary were only incidental to
a gradual change in that direction and to the natural survival of earlier conditions.   Such, beyond reasonable doubt
was the retention by him until his death, and indeed by
his immediate successors, of the title Pontifex Maximus,
which designated the emperor as honorary head of the old
official religions.

The spirit or purpose dominant in this use of imperial
power and patronage is not altogether clear, important as
this is for the understanding of the history of the church.
Of two such authoritative historians as Seeck and Ed.
Schwartz, the former exhibits Constantine as dominated

[1] *Cf.* his edition of Gibbon, *Decline and fall of the Roman Empire,*
ii. appendix 1, p. 534, under Praxagoras.

[2] *Cf.* Eusebius, *Life of Constantine,* iv, 29, 31.

by religious or superstitious motives and by those whom he
looked upon as representatives of the divine power,[1] the
latter speaks of " the sovereign high-handedness with which
he ruled the church.[2] Neither extreme is warranted. There
is no evidence that the first Christian emperor sought to use
the church organization for any political ends or to impose
upon it any task alien to its own conception of its ends.
The evidence that he devoted resources of the state to the
support of the church is abundant; there is none that he
used even the moral resources of the church for the support of the crown. Statements to the latter effect are
merely inferences, and for the most part based on *a priori*
reasoning. And yet Constantine was far from putting
himself unreservedly under the control of the church leaders. His attitude toward the whole situation was that of a
statesman, not that of a fanatic. Nor did he, apparently look upon the church organization as an institution
superior to, and independent of, the imperial power. He
took an active part in its management.[3] The chief interest
he displayed on this score was that the ecclesiastical machinery should run smoothly and that the cult of the supreme God, the God who gave victory, should be maintained in full efficiency.

Shortly after he was established in control of the West
he took a hand in the troubles in Africa out of which the

[1] Seeck throughout represents Constantine as unselfish and not at all
ambitious. He even expounds his military career on the basis that he
tried his utmost to uphold Diocletian's system of governing the empire, that he had no desire to increase his own power or territory, and
that all his wars were defensive. *Cf. Untergang d. antiken Welt*, i, p.
112, *et passim*. This preposterous proposition I can explain only as an
extreme reaction against Burckhardt's exposition of Constantine as the
embodiment of unscrupulous ambition, and as an instance of Seeck's
habit of assuming a motive for his characters and then construing
everything in accordance with that motive.

[2] *Kaiser Constantin und die christliche Kirche*, p. 70.

[3] *Eg. cf.* Eusebius, *Life of Constantine*, i, 46.

Donatist schism developed. He gave his support from the first to the regular organization,[1] but submitted matters in dispute to Miltiades, bishop of Rome, and three of his colleagues from Gaul.[2] In this and in some subsequent matters Constantine employed the bishop of Rome in the West as a " kind of secretary of state for Christian affairs,[3] and contributed not a little to the growing power of the Roman see. When the vindication which Caecilian, the regular bishop, received from this Roman tribunal failed to quiet the African disturbance, the emperor convoked the famous Synod of Arles (314) which also condemned the schismatics and took advantage of the occasion to draw up various rules for church discipline.[4] As the schism, instead of subsiding, grew in violence, Constantine tried to settle it himself by summoning leaders of the two factions and hearing them in person. Deciding in favor of Caecilian, he sent commissioners to restore peace in Africa, meanwhile retaining these contestants in Italy. They escaped to Carthage, however, and the struggle continued. For a while Constantine tried forcible expulsion of the Donatists from churches, but later gave this up and contented himself with stating his disapproval of the schismatics and urging the Catholic leaders to have patience.[5]

[1] *Cf.* letters in Eusebius, *Church History*, x, 5, 15-17; x, 6, 1-5; x, 7, 1-2.

[2] *Ibid.*, x, 5, 18-20. Fifteen Italian bishops were later joined to these four.

[3] The phrase is from George Finlay, *History of the Byzantine Empire*, Book I, iii, sec. 3.

[4] *Cf.* letters of Constantine: Eusebius, *op. cit.*, x, 5, 21-24, and Migne, *Patrologia Latina*, vol. viii, p. 487. *Cf.* also the *Sylloge Optatiana*, in the Vienna *Corpus Scriptorum Ecclesiasticorum Latinorum*, vol. xxvi, p. 206. Seeck, dates the council, 316, *Zeitsch. f. K. G.*, x, 509.

[5] For a clear discussion of this procedure with references to sources, *cf.* Duchesne, *Histoire ancienne de l'Eglise*, Eng. trans. *Early History of the Church*, vol. ii, pp. 92-97.

Constantine's participation in the next great ecclesiastical controversy of his reign, the Arian trouble, ran a course somewhat parallel to the preceding. The conflict was in full blast at Alexandria when Constantine gained control of the East. He tried by letters, carried in person by Hosius to Bishop Alexander and to Arius, to induce them to restore peace by mutual toleration of differences of opinion.[1] This failing, and in view, also, of a widespread difference in the time of the observance of Easter, Constantine proceeded to summon a great council at Nicea. The bishop of Rome, so far as we know, did not figure in the preliminaries of the council. There was no one in the East holding a central position corresponding to his, so Constantine assumed immediate direction of the affair. At the first session of the council he made his entrance in state, and replied in a set speech to the oration of thanksgiving with which he was addressed.[2] He followed the debates and occasionally took part in the discussion. The decisions of the council both as to the proper date for observing Easter, to which the emperor himself attached most importance, and as to the doctrinal questions raised by the Arian controversy were confirmed by imperial letters.[3] The further course of the controversy also

---

[1] Eusebius, *Life of Constantine*, ii, 63-73; giving a copy of the long letters.

[2] For the part taken by Constantine in the proceedings of the council, cf. *Realencyklopädie für prot. Theol. und Kirche*, xiv, 12, 30-45.

[3] Such, substantially, is Eusebius' account. *Cf. Life of Constantine*, iii, 6-23; also i, 44. This is the most important contemporary description, but tells little about the debates, about the course by which decisions were reached, or even about the decisions themselves. The literature on the Council of Nicea is extensive, and important points are still obscure. Duchesne's account, *op. cit.*, vol. ii, pp. 98-124, gives clearly the generally accepted version, if indeed there may be said to be such a thing.

substantiates Eusebius' comparison of Constantine to a "general bishop constituted of God." [1] But it is not necessary here to go into the temporary success of the Arian reaction, the recall of Arius from banishment, and the first triumph of Athanasius' enemies, resulting in his exile and imprisonment at Trèves. Constantine, while hopelessly at sea as to the theological aspects of the controversy, controlled the proceedings and gave preponderance to those whom he favored, and exile to those whom he condemned.[2]

Constantine did not succeed in stifling ecclesiastical controversy by government pressure. But he undoubtedly contributed to the realization of the purpose for which he labored, the unity of the church in the support of the cultus of the Supreme God. His dictum, "whatsoever is determined in the holy assemblies of the bishops is to be regarded as indicative of the divine will," [3] involved in his mind the co-operation of state and church in winning and keeping the favor of this Supreme God, the bestower of all success. It however involved also the subsequent development of a state church with intriguing bishops, an iron organization and thought-confining dogma linked to a military absolutism.[4]

---

[1] *Op. cit.*, I, 44.

[2] Our chief, but by no means our only, source of information on these matters is the writings of Athanasius. For a modern account based largely on these writings, and judiciously favorable to their author, *cf.* Duchesne, *op. cit.*, ii, pp. 125-152. For an account almost bitterly hostile to Athanasius, and extremely distrustful of his statements, *cf.* Seeck, *Untergang d. antiken Welt,* vol. iii, pp. 431, *et passim.*

[3] Eusebius, *op. cit.*, iii, 20.

[4] *Cf.* Ed. Schwartz, *Kaiser Constantin u. d. christliche Kirche,* pp. 169-171.

CHAPTER IV

THE "CONVERSION" OF CONSTANTINE, AND THE RELIGIOUS REVOLUTION OF HIS TIME

1. *Various Early Accounts*

CONSTANTINE came into direct contact with the East as emperor only after his final triumph over Licinius. His reign henceforth, as we have seen, was not only favorable to the Christians, but was essentially the reign of a Christian sovereign. It was in this capacity that the historian Eusebius, who lived in Palestine, first came to fully know him. It was very natural, therefore, that Eusebius in his *Church History,* which he wrote during and almost immediately after Constantine's rise to power,[1] should assume that Constantine had been a Christian from the beginning of his career.[2] Throughout the work there is no word of a conversion of Constantine, of any miraculous vision instrumental in the process, or of any need of his being converted at all. On the contrary, it tells how, before the campaign against Maxentius in 312, he " took compassion upon those who were oppressed at Rome [the Christians under Maxentius], and having invoked in prayer the God of heaven, and his Word, and Jesus Christ himself, the Saviour of all, as his aid, advanced with his whole army, proposing to restore to the Romans their ancestral lib-

---

[1] For the dates of the various parts of the Church History, *cf.* the critical apparatus of the edition of Schwartz and Mommsen.

[2] viii, 13, 14; ix, 9, 2; 3; 9-11.

72

erty." [1] Eusebius' later version of the matter, which he gives in his *Life of Constantine,* written some fifteen or twenty years after the passage quoted above, is quite different. It contains a description of the emperor's sudden conversion by a miraculous apparition in the heavens interpreted the following night in a dream. This episode will be discussed later; [2] but the question whether a sudden conversion of some sort or other took place must be considered here. Legends from pagan sources, as well as Eusebius' *Life of Constantine,* incorporate the view that the emperor underwent such an experience. The sources of information examined in our previous chapters do not point to such a conclusion, but we may well look into other evidence.

2. *Constantine's Early Paganism*

Constantine apparently identified himself with paganism during the time he ruled north of the Alps as the successor of his father, Constantius. Eusebius' early opinion to the contrary is discredited not only by his later contradiction of it, but by his remoteness from Gaul. [3] That he, following in his father's footsteps, extended toleration to the Christians is certain; but various pagan emperors had previously done the same. This is no proof that he himself entertained Christian views. That his father was a Christian and conducted his household as such is implied in Eusebius' *Life of Constantine;* [4] but this is, on such a point, questionable authority, and the particular passages con-

[1] *Ibid.,* ix, 9, 2. It will be noted that this marks the inception of the campaign, and that the opening engagements of the war follow it in paragraph three.

[2] *Cf. infra,* p. 135 *et seq.*

[3] The addresses in Lactantius' *Div. Inst.* implying that Constantine was a Christian in 311 or earlier, have been shown to be interpolations. *Cf.* Brandt's ed. in CSEL. xix, 668.

[4] i, 16-18; ii, 49; this latter purporting to quote Constantine.

cerned are unquestionably highly overdrawn.[1] Some slight
evidence in support of Eusebius' eulogy there may be in
the fact that Constantius gave one of his daughters, Constantine's sister, what seems to be a specifically Christian
name, Anastasia (Resurrection), though in any case this
name may have been proposed by a Christian mother.[2]
Eusebius himself, however, in his *Church History,* speaks
of Constantius' being ranked by his subjects among
the gods and receiving after death every honor which
one could pay an emperor.[3] Lack of substantial evidence for Constantius' being a Christian, leads one
to accept the general opinion that, while probably a
devout monotheist and certainly tolerant toward the Christians, he was not himself one of them. As for Constantine in Gaul, the only local and strictly contemporary
evidence we possess is found in the panegyrics of Eumenius
and an anonymous orator, generally identified as Nazarius.
Eulogistic orators are not unimpeachable historical sources,
but these two take at least relatively high rank among those
who spoke in honor of Constantine. Eumenius was one of
the foremost scholars of his time, the head of a considerable literary circle at Autun, in Gaul,, and enjoying the personal and financial support of the emperor.[4] His panegyrics, and the anonymous one referred to above, show detailed familiarity with Constantine's career in Gaul. There
is no reason for questioning their statements about his re-

[1] For discussion of the reliability of Eusebius' *Life of Constantine,*
cf. infra, pp. 107 *et seq.*

[2] *Cf.* on this Seeck, *Untergang d. antik. Welt,* i, pp. 61, 473.

[3] viii, 13, 12. The remoteness of Eusebius from the West would not
invalidate his statements about such official matters to the same extent
as it would his statements about the personal religious convictions of a
Western ruler.

[4] For a modern account of the school at Autun, *cf.* G. Block, in Lavisse's *Histoire de France,* vol. i, part ii (1900).

ligious affiliations, for panegyrists, even though they were otherwise untrustworthy, could be relied upon not to offend the convictions of the subject of their praise. What they have to say about their prince's religion, furthermore, is told incidentally, as patent fact, not as argument or proof, but as basis for obviously acceptable praise. Both orators represent Constantine as a devout pagan of monotheistic belief.

Eumenius, in a panegyric delivered in 310, in the presence of his royal patron, refers to a visit of the latter to the Apollo temple at Autun before a renewed attack upon the Franks, and proceeds to extol the divine qualities of the young ruler, and to recite the favor of Apollo to him. " For thou sawest, I believe, thine Apollo, accompanied by Victory, offering thee the laurel crowns." " Now all temples seem to call thee to themselves, especially our Apollo, in whose seething waters perjuries, which thou must have hated most of all, are punished." " Immortal gods, when will you grant that day on which this god most manifest, universal peace restored, may go about among those groves of Apollo himself, and among the sacred abodes, and the breathing mouths of the springs. . . . Thou wilt assuredly marvel at that abode of thy very divinity." [1]   The orator

---

[1] *Panegyric* 310, chaps. 20, 21, 22; in *Pan. Vet.*, no. vii, and in Migne, *P. L.*, viii, col. 637 *et seq.*

" Ipsa hoc si ordinante fortuna, ut te ibi rerum tuarum felicitas admoneret, diis immortalibus, ferre quae voveras, ubi deflexisses ad templum [of Apollo] toto orbe pulcherrimum, imo ad praesentem, ut veniste, deum. Vidisti enim, credo, Constantine, Appollinem tuum, comitante victoria, coronas tibi laureas offerentem," *etc.* " Jam omnia te vocare ad se templa videantur, praecipueque Apollo noster, cujus ferventibus aquis perjuria puniuntur, quae te maxime oportet odisse."

" Dii immortales, quando illum dabitis diem, quo praesentissimus hic deus omni pace composita, illos quoque Apollinis lucos et sacres sedes et anhela fontium ora circumeat. . . . Miraberis profecto illam quoque numinis tui sedem," *etc.*

closes with a delicately worded, but urgent suggestion that Constantine repair the public buildings and especially the temple of Autun. The formal thanks of that city for its restoration and for the grant of the imperial name, Augustodunum, presented to Constantine by Eumenius in the panegyric of the following year, show that the allusions to Apollo were not ungrateful.

The whole episode is reinforced by a reference in Julian's Orations [1] to a special Helios cult of Constantine's, by Eumenius' emphasis upon his relation to Apollo, and by the frequency of the tokens of the Sun-god [2] on Constantine's coinage.

The anonymous panegyric of 313, usually attributed to Nazarius,[3] informs us that Constantine invaded Italy to fight Maxentius against the advice of men, and the warnings of soothsayers ("contra consilia hominum, contra Haruspicum monita"), showing that he had consulted the omens. This oration was delivered after the return of Constantine to Gaul from his victory over Maxentius, and perhaps the effect of that campaign [4] upon the religious ideas of Constantine are reflected in the questioning monotheism of the orator in his peroration.[5]

---

[1] *Oration*, vii, p. 228 D (ed. Hertlein).

[2] Apollo, Mithras, "Soli Invicti Comiti."

[3] *Incerti Paneg. Constantino Augusto*, 313, in Migne, *P. L.*, viii, especially col. 655, chap. ii. *Cf.* also, *supra*, p. 36; *infra*, p. 132, n. 1.

[4] *Cf. infra.* pp. 77-79.

[5] *Ibid.*, chap. 26, "Quemobrem te [Jove], summe sator, cujus tot nomina sunt, quot gentium linguas esse voluisti, quem enim te ipse dici velis scire non possumus: sive in te quaedam vis mensque divina est, qua toto infusus omnibus mercearis elementis, et sine ullo extrinsecus accedente vigoris impulsu per te ipse movearis: sive aliqua supra omne coelum potestas es, quae hoc opus tuum exaltiore naturae arce despicias: te, inquam, oramus et quaesumus," *etc.*

For light upon this whole subject from another angle, *cf. infra*, pp. 131-132 *et seq.*

3. Campaign against Maxentius, and Adoption of Christian Labarum

In this campaign against Maxentius there took place an episode which an early Christian legend fixed upon as the definite conversion of Constantine to Christianity.[1] Modern historians have occasionally denied the occurrence of the episode, and looked upon it as merely the later invention of the emperor or of his pious biographers. There seems, however, to be no reason for rejecting the simple and straight-forward account of the narrator of the earliest version of it which has come down to us. Lactantius (Lucius Caelius Firmianus) was for some years a member of Constantine's household and the tutor of his son Crispus.[2] In his *De Mortibus Persecutorum* he says that "Constantine [encamped in the neighborhood of Rome, opposite the Milvian bridge] was directed in a dream to cause the heavenly sign to be delineated on the shields of his soldiers,

---

[1] A pagan legend dated the conversion much later. On this, cf. *infra*, pp. 127 *et seq.*

[2] I think we are on safe ground now in accepting Lactantius' authorship of the *De Mortibus Persecutorum*. Cf. R. Pichon, *Lactance* (Paris, 1901), pp. 337-360; Harnack, *Die Chronologie der altchristlichen Litteratur*, vol. ii (Leipsic, 1904), pp. 421 *et seq.*; O. Bardenhewer, *Patrologie* (Freiburg, 1910), p. 181; Monceaux, *Histoire litteraire de l'Africa chretienne depuis les origines jusqu'à l'invasion arabe*, vol. iii (Paris, 1905), pp. 340-342. Brandt, one of the greatest authorities upon Lactantius, attempted to prove what had often been surmised before, that the book is by an imitator of Lactantius, in "Ueber die Entstehungsverhaltnisse der Prosaschriften des Lact. u. des Buches de mortibus persecutorum," in *Sitzungsberichte der Wiener Akad.*, vol. cxxv, Abh. vi (1892), but his case now seems definitely lost. For an excellent, brief summary of the matter, see Bury, in his edition of Gibbon's *Decline and Fall of the Roman Empire* (1896), vol. ii, pp. 531-533. For the life of Lactantius, see Brandt, "Ueber das Leben des Lact.," in *Sitzungsberichte der Wiener Akad.*, vol. cxx (1890).

The *De Mortibus Persecutorum*, in any case, must have been written soon after 313.

and so to proceed to battle. He did as he had been commanded, and he marked on their shields the letter X,
with a perpendicular line drawn through it and turned
round thus at the top, being the cipher of Christ, ☓
Having this sign, his troops stood to arms." [1]

In this account there is nothing said about a miraculous
vision or about Constantine being converted to Christianity.
All that the author tells is that in a dream the promise of
victory was associated with the use of the monogram of
Christ, and that the event turned out as the dream foretold.
The dream itself is, of course, not susceptible of historical
proof, but Constantine's use of the monogram of Christ's
name, for the first time, during this campaign, and his use
of it thereafter, is supported by abundant evidence.[2] Its use
in the first instance may have come as well from a dream
as from anything else. That political or military considerations could scarcely have led him to take this step, and
that they could not have played any large part in Constantine's adoption of Christianity, is clearly proved by Seeck.[3]

---

[1] Chap. 44.

[2] Cf. supra, p. 47, infra, pp. 79-81; and in addition to Eusebius' reiter-
ated statements, Lactantius, de Mort. Persec., chap. 44; Prudentius, In
Symmachum, ii, lines 464-486. Also many coins and medals. For the
monogram on helmets, see Numismatic Chronicle, 1877, pp. 44 et seq.,
plate i (article by Madden, "Christian Emblems," etc.). A labarum
containing the Christian emblems was probably long after deposited in
the palace at Constantinople, Cod. Theod., vi, 25; Theophanes,
Chronogr., p. 11. For some other evidence, see Schultze, Zeitsch. f.
K. G., xiv (1894), pp. 521 et seq.

[3] Deutsche Rundschau, April, 1891, pp. 73-84, and repeatedly in his
Untergang d. antiken Welt. The Christians constituted a very small,
almost negligible part of the army and, so far as we know, had as yet
taken no part in politics. Italy was predominantly pagan, and Rome
especially so. There could have been no inherent military or political
advantage in displaying Christian emblems there. Cf. also Fedele Savio,
La Conversione di Costantino Magno e la Chiesa all' inizio del secolo
iv, in La Civilta Cattolica, 1913, vol. i, pp. 385-397.

That some curious natural phenomena in the heavens may have impressed the contestant for Italy and led to the use of the cross is possible, but hardly meets the requirements of any of our sources. Eusebius' detailed account of a heavenly apparition is followed by a reference to a dream the following night, and this is to some extent a corroboration of Lactantius. Where the former goes beyond the latter, we have merely an instance of legend-making powers at work.[1]

All that the incident involves, then, was the association of victory with the use of the wonderful monogram. It was a superstitious age, and Constantine in fact used the labarum bearing this monogram, and the monogram itself, as a magical charm, a fetich. For him and for the Christians generally, including their bishops, divine power resided in it; its use brought success and good luck. By it Constantine probably felt that he prevailed over his enemies. What he adopted before the battle of the Milvian Bridge, was not Christianity but a luck token.[2] The cross had by this time become generally used by Christians as a magic sign before which demons fled.[3] Constantine used both the monogram of Christ and the cross. It is often difficult in reading the accounts of Eusebius and later writers to tell to which of the two they refer.

The monogram ☧ had not always been an exclusively Christian sign; it was used on oriental banners in pre-Christian times, probably as one of the many symbols of

---

[1] Cf. infra, p. 135 et seq.

[2] Eusebius, Life of Constantine, i, 31; ii, 6-7; ii, 16; Oration in Praise of Constantine, chap. 6, 21; chap. 9; chap. 10. Many of these passages embody fetichism pure and simple.

[3] Lactantius, Divine Institutes, iv, 27; De Mort. Persecut., chap. 10. For earlier accusation that Christians worshiped the cross, see Tertullian, Apology, chap. 16, and Ad Nationes, i, 13.

the sun.[1]   It appears on coins in the late third, in the second, and the first centuries before Christ.[2]   But it is apparent that Constantine's Christian friends regarded it as an emblem of their religion.   We have no evidence that his pagan contemporaries regarded his use of it as indicating adherence to the sun-god.[3]

The cross also was used symbolically by others than the Christians.   It has been, among various peoples, a common object in nature worship.[4]   Early Christian writers speak of its recurrence in nature and of its general symbolism apart from their own religion.[5]   It was in such universal use among the Christians, however, as a religious token and sign of magic power that by the time of Constantine it must have been regarded almost as their property.[6]   It is interesting to note that for Eusebius it was a symbol of immortality rather than a token of Christ's sacrificial or vicarious death.[7]

That a great general would expect divine help through using a symbol, that he would attribute his victory to a

---

[1] *Cf.* Zahn, *Constantine d. Grosse u. die Kirche,* p. 14.

[2] Rapp, "Das Labarum u. der Sonnenkultus," in *Jahrbuch des Vereins von Altertumsfreunden im Rheinlände,* 1866, pp. 166 *et seq.*

[3] Bury is a little over-cautious in his statement: " It is not clear that Constantine used it as an ambiguous symbol, nor yet is there a well-attested instance of its use as a Christian symbol before A. D. 323 (*cf.* Brieger, in *Zeitsch. f. K. G.,* iv (1881), p. 201)."

[4] It was commented, for instance, that it was one of the emblems in the Temple of Serapis at Alexandria at the time that temple was destroyed. Sozomen, vii, 15; Socrates, v, 17.

[5] Justin Martyr, *First Apology,* chaps. lv, lx; Tertullian, *Apology,* xvi; *Ad Nationes,* i, 13.

[6] *Cf.* references, *supra;* also Tertullian, *De Corona,* 3.

[7] Eusebius, *Life of Constantine,* i, 32, and elsewhere when he mentions the cross.

divine monogram, is difficult for us to realize to-day, but as Seeck and others have shown, it was very natural in the fourth century. It was much more natural than free-thinking and absence of superstitious considerations. The clear-minded man who, himself uninfluenced by religious forces or fears of supernatural power, used these for the ends of his own ambition, as Constantine is sometimes assumed to have done, would have been the exception at that time, if not an impossibility.[1] Lactantius apparently believed that Licinius, who was not of that author's religion, was taught in a dream by an angel a magic formula in the shape of a vague monotheistic prayer, which, repeated in the presence of the enemy, insured victory.[2]

4. *Constantine's Christianity*

Having adopted the magical symbol of the Christian God, and finding it successful, Constantine pursued this primitive allegiance to its logical end. He favored the church which represented this God, and allied himself more and more with its officers and its teachings. His conversion was thus a gradual process extending from the war with Maxentius, or earlier, and ending only with his last illness. Certain episodes mark the stages of this development; the victory over Maxentius, the attainment of sole emperorship by the victory over Licinius,[3] and probably also the Council of Nicea. In the first two cases the deciding factor was the success with which the Christian God

[1] Burckhardt, and others, in picturing Constantine as such a man, came near creating a modern legendary Constantine as the product of nineteenth-century free-thought. *Cf. infra*, p. 99.

[2] *De Mort. Pers.*, 46. Seeck, in his *Untergang d. antiken Welt*, accepts Lactantius' account of the battle which followed, in every detail, even to the successful carrying-out of this plan.

[3] *Cf.* Seeck, *Untergang d. antiken Welt*, i, pp. 61, 472-3.

F

crowned his arms.[1] In neither was the change so great
as it has usually been considered. To the end of his days
probably his chief conception of Christianity was that of a
cult whose prayers and whose emblems ensured the help of
the supreme heavenly power in military conflicts and political crises, and whose rites guaranteed eternal blessedness.
Of the inner experiences of Christianity and of the doctrines of that religion, other than the broadest monotheism,
he seems to have had little conception.

The great Arian controversy seemed to him " intrinsi-
cally trifling and of little moment " involving " not any of
the leading doctrines or precepts of the Divine law " but
concerning " small and very insignificant questions." [2]
Upon the proper day for observing Easter, however, vital
issues depended. " A discordant judgment in a case of
such importance and respecting such a religious festival, is
wrong," " discrepancy of opinion on so sacred a question
is unbecoming." [3] At the court Easter was celebrated with
gorgeous ceremonies, and martyr's days and other sacred
occasions were carefully observed.[4]

5. The Transition from Paganism to Christianity in the Roman Empire

In all of this, Constantine did not differ greatly from the
current notions of his day, pagan and Christian. Most
men seem to have been seeking charms to give them success
in this life and happiness hereafter. Belief in one supreme

[1] Cf. the prayer which Eusebius said was enforced in the army, Life
of Constantine, iv, 20.

[2] Eusebius, Life of Constantine, ii, 68-71, reproducing letter to Alexander and Arius.

[3] Op. cit., iii, 18 and 19, reproducing letter of Constantine respecting
the Council of Nicea.

[4] Op. cit., iv, 22 and 23.

heavenly power, in the future life, and in the necessity of expiatory rites, was common to Roman paganism of the fourth century, modified as it had become by prevalent influences, and to Christianity.[1]

Remembering the presence of numerous Orientals in Gaul[2] and Constantine's connection with the cult of the sun,[3] the transformation of Roman religious life as described by Cumont is illustrated and confirmed by the case of Constantine. " The last formula reached by the religion of the pagan Semites and in consequence by that of the Romans, was a divinity unique, almighty, eternal, universal and ineffable, that revealed itself throughout nature, but whose most splendid and most energetic manifestation was the sun. To arrive at the Christian monotheism only one final tie had to be broken, that is to say, this supreme being, resident in a distant heaven, had to be removed beyond the world." [4]

" The principal divergence [between Christianity and the later Roman paganism] was that Christianity, by placing

[1] For the gradual change in the tone of the panegyrists and others from polytheism to monotheism, see Pichon, *Les derniers Écrivains profanes*, Paris, 1906. A beautiful illustration of this is the peroration of the anonymous panegyric delivered before Constantine in Gaul in 313. *Cf. supra*, p. 76. It was certainly not a long step for the orator of this occasion instead of declaring (chap. 2) that Constantine was under the care of the supreme mind, while other mortals were left to the lesser gods, to omit the lesser gods entirely in his peroration. *Cf. infra*, p. 132 *et seq.*, and *supra*, p. 76, n. 5.

[2] *Cf.* Cumont, *Oriental Religions in the Roman Empire*, pp. 107 *et seq.*

[3] Eumenius, *Panegyric. Cf. supra*, pp. 75-76; Julian, *Orat.*, vii, f. 228, and numerous coins inscribed to " Soli Invicti Comiti." See also Preger, *Konstantinos-Helios*, in Hermes, xxxvi, 1901, pp. 457 *et seq.*

[4] *Op. cit.*, p. 134. *Cf.* page xxiv. *Cf.* also p. 288, where Cumont quotes with approval Loeschke's statement calling Constantine's letters " ein merkwürdiges Produkt theologischen Dilletantismus, aufgebaut auf im wesentlichen pantheistischer Grundlage mit Hilfe weniger christlicher Termini und fast noch weniger christlicher Gedanken."

God in an ideal sphere beyond the confines of this world, endeavored to rid itself of every attachment to a frequently abject polytheism. . . . As the religious history of the empire is studied more closely, the triumph of the church will, in our opinion, appear more and more as the culmination of a long evolution of beliefs."

What was true of Constantine was thus in a measure true of the Empire at large. Christianity and paganism in the fourth century did not constitute two fixed, unchanging, irreconcilable enemies. " The upper class were for generations far more united by the old social and literary tradition than they were divided by religious belief. . . . In truth the line between Christian and pagan was long wavering and uncertain. We find adherents of the opposing creeds side by side even in the same family at the end of the fourth century." [1]

The later persecutions seem to have been continued more by governmental policy than by popular desire. There was even a general reaction among the people against this policy. Lactantius was able to give as one of the reasons why God permitted the persecutions the fact that " great numbers are driven from the worship of the false gods by their hatred of cruelty." [2] The triumph of Christianity was comparatively peaceful and left paganism in many instances unembittered. " No advocate appeared; neither god nor demon, prophet nor divines, could lend his aid to the detected author of the imposture [of paganism.] For the souls of men were no longer enveloped in thick darkness, but enlightened by rays of true godliness, they deplored the ignorance," etc.[3]

---

[1] Dill, *Roman Society*, 2d ed, p. 13. *Cf.* also E. F. Humphrey, *Politics and Religion in the Days of Augustine* (New York, 1912), pp. 26-39, *et passim*, for the situation at the end of the fourth and beginning of the fifth century. *Cf.* also, *infra*, p. 96.

[2] *Divine Institutes*, v, 24.

[3] Eusebius, Oration in Praise of Constantine, viii, 8.

The religious revolution under Constantine was not unique in the history of the empire though it proved to be the greatest one. Mithraism and a revival of the cult of Apollo had prevailed in the court of Diocletian. Christianity came to the front under Constantine, and Neoplatonism was fostered by Julian. This oscillation was not due entirely to an even balance of power between bitter enemies, but in part, also, to uncertainty and a wavering border line.

On the pagan side there had long been a movement unconsciously leading in the direction of Christianity. Paganism " after three centuries of Oriental influence . . . was no longer like that of ancient Rome, a mere collection of propitiatory and expiatory rites performed by the citizen for the good of the state: it now pretended to offer to all men a world conception which gave rise to a rule of conduct and placed the end of existence in the future life. It was more unlike the worship which Augustus had attempted to restore than the Christianity that fought it. The two opposed creeds moved in the same intellectual and moral sphere, and one could actually pass from one to the other without shock or interruption. . . . The religious and mystical spirit of the Orient had slowly overcome the whole social organism and had prepared all nations to unite in the bosom of a universal church." [1]

On the Christian side the sense of irreconcilable conflict between the world and the gospel no longer dominated all church life. Belief in the speedy end of the world and apocalyptic descriptions of a miraculous millennium, which had at first offered to many the only hopeful outcome of this conflict, were gradually relegated to the byways of ecclesiastical thought. In the third century, the great Alex-

[1] Cumont, *Oriental Religions, etc.*, pp. 210-11.

andrian theologians had completed the reconciliation of
the new revelation and the old philosophy in an evolution-
ary interpretation of Christianity.[1] Without surrendering
its claim to finality or the necessity of the exclusion of all
other gods and religions from the mind of the believer, the
new faith found many points of contact and support in
the growing monotheism of paganism. Nor were the
Christians, as we have seen, free from the fundamental religious notions of the fourth-century piety generally; belief in magic, in good and evil spirits, in the constant inter-
ference of the supernatural in human affairs, and in success and victory as the ultimate test of the reality and
supremacy of the god whose aid was invoked.[2]

The center of Constantine's Christian life and that of
many of his contemporaries is to be sought, not in any
theological or moral convictions, but in the identification of
his fortunes, his luck one might say, with the Christian
god. Eusebius, perhaps unwittingly, tells us as much when
he closes his " Oration in Praise of Constantine " with the
tribute of divine revelations to the Emperor:[3]

Yourself, it may be, will vouchsafe at a time of leisure to
relate to us the abundant manifestations which your Saviour
has accorded you of his presence, and the oft-repeated visions
of himself which have attended you in the hours of sleep. I
speak not of those secret suggestions which to us are unre-
vealed: but of those principles which he has instilled into your
own mind, and which are fraught with general interest and
benefit to the human race. You will yourself relate in worthy
terms the visible protection which your Divine shield and
guardian has extended in the hour of battle; the ruin of your
open and secret foes; and his ready aid in time of peril. To

[1] *Cf.* the chapters upon the Hellenizing of church theology in Harnack, *Dogmengeschichte.*

[2] *Cf. infra*, pp. 95-96.

[3] Chap. 18.

him you will ascribe relief in the midst of perplexity, defence in solitude, expedients in extremity, foreknowledge of events yet future.

6. Constantine's Baptism

Only one contemporary source, Eusebius' *Life of Constantine,* distinctly affirms and describes Constantine's entrance into membership in the Christian Church.[1] He is, to be sure, spoken of as " pious " and " God-beloved " in the *Church History,* but the same terms are applied to Licinius, whom nobody has ever accused of being a Christian, and whom Eusebius afterwards likened to " some savage beast of prey, or some crooked and wriggling serpent." [2] In spite of the friendly relations between Constantine and the church organization, in spite of the part he took in the church council at Nicea and possibly at Arles, in spite of public proclamations of Christian faith with which he is accredited, there is no evidence nor contemporary report of Constantine's becoming even a catechumen until the last few days of his life. For that and his baptism the only account we have is in his Life by Eusebius.

Here we are told that the emperor, convinced that his end was near,[3] sought purification for the sins of his past

---

[1] iv, 61-64.

[2] *Church History,* 9, i ; *Life of Constantine,* ii, i.

[3] iv, 61-62. The fact that Constantine was not baptized until his last illness does not indicate that he then for the first time accepted Christianity. Fear of the penalties inflicted for mortal sin after baptism was a powerful motive for the postponement of the rite. In many other cases than Constantine's it was deferred till the approach of death, and was sometimes even administered upon the sick-bed (clinical baptism). Constantine's leniency toward the Novatianists (*cf. Cod. Theod.,* xvi, 5, 2), who were very rigorous in their treatment of those who had " lapsed " after baptism, may possibly be an indication of sympathy for their position in this respect. On this whole subject, *cf.* Dölger, *Konstantin d. Grosse u. s. Zeit,* pp. 429-447.

career in " the mystical words and salutary waters of baptism ". He prayed " kneeling on the pavement in the
church itself, in which he also now for the first time received the imposition of hands with prayer " [the process
of becoming a catechumen]. Meeting the bishops whom
he had summoned at the suburbs of Nicomedia, he explained that he had deferred baptism hoping to have it administered in the river Jordan, but since God decreed
otherwise he requested it " without delay ".[1] If he were
destined to recover and associate with the people of God,
and unite with them in prayer as a member of the church, he
would prescribe for himself thenceforth such a course of
life as befitted His service.

" After he had thus spoken, the prelates performed the
sacred ceremonies in the usual manner, and having given
him the necessary instructions, made him a partaker of the
mystic ordinance. Thus was Constantine the first of all
sovereigns who was regenerated and perfected in a church
dedicated to the martyrs of Christ; thus gifted with the
divine seal of baptism, he rejoiced in spirit, was renewed,
and filled with heavenly light."

" At the conclusion of the ceremony he arrayed himself
in shining imperial vestments, brilliant as the light . . .
refusing to clothe himself with the purple any more." This
account in the *Life of Constantine* alone, a source not
above suspicion, a eulogy rather than a biography, can
hardly by itself establish the baptism of Constantine as an
historical certainty. But it is confirmed by the best writers
of the following generations with some additional facts
implying independent sources.[2] There seems therefore no

---

[1] Or " hesitation ".

[2] Jerome (Chron., A. Abr. 2353) adds that Constantine was baptized by
Eusebius of Nicomedia (" Constantinus extremo vitae suae tempore ab
Eusebio Nicomedeni episcopo baptizatus in Arianum dogma declinat ").

reason to doubt the truth of the narrative, and it is accepted by practically all modern historians.[1]

7. Ethical Aspects of Constantine's Life.

A survey of Constantine's Christianity would not be complete unless it took unto account certain ethical aspects of his life and reign which have been occasionally cited as proof that he was never at heart really a Christian.

Criticism of his character from pagan sources was not wanting. His vanity was freely commented on. Eutropius, Constantine's pagan secretary, and later the friend of Julian, criticized his administration after the adoption of Christianity.[2] Ammianus Marcellinus complained of his prodigality towards his friends.[3] Julian criticized him severely in the *Caesars* for extravagance, minimized his achievements, and accused him of luxury and dissoluteness.[4] Zosimus wrote bitterly of his waste of public money,[5] of his favors to undeserving persons, and of the

This may be an inference from the place where the ceremony was performed, but since Eusebius of Nicomedia was not orthodox, one is led to think Jerome would not have given his name without direct evidence calling for it. Inasmuch as Jerome, apparently, did not use the story of Constantine's conversion through a miraculous vision, and other episodes from Eusebius' *Life of Constantine* which would naturally appeal to him, it may be that he did not even know this work. *Cf.* also Mommsen, *Chronica minora*, i, p. 235.

[1] For a complete and scholarly summary of the overwhelming evidence for the baptism of Constantine, *cf.* F. J. Dölger, "Die Taufe Konstantins u. ihre Probleme," in *Konstantin d. Grosse u. s. Zeit* (1913), pp. 381-394.

[2] x, 6 and 7 (ed. Ruehl, Leipsic, 1887): "In primo Imperii tempore optimis principibus, ultimo mediis comparandus," "Interfecit numeros amicos."

[3] xvi, 8: "Proximorum fauces aperuit primus omnium Constantinus."

[4] *Cf. infra.*, pp. 124-127   [5] Book i.

crushing burden of taxation imposed by him. [1] He closes his account of Constantine with a register of his weaknesses, mistakes and crimes. In the *Epitome* under the name of Sextus Aurelius Victor the first ten years of Constantine's reign are praised, in the next twelve he is said to have been a robber, and in the last ten a dotard on account of his enormous squandering. [2]

Some of these criticisms are supported by the evidence of Christian writers, also, especially the indictment of extravagance and favoritism,[3] which seems to have been amply warranted by the facts.[4]

One fixed standard of Christianity, one of its cardinal requirements, chastity, Constantine apparently frequently violated. Heathen panegyrists praised him, indeed, for his chastity and his conduct toward women in his campaigns.[5] Julian, however, in his *Caesars* accused him of living luxuriously and dissolutely in time of peace.[6] If this be set down as malicious gossip, it is reinforced by the rather infrequent and perfunctory praise by Christian writers,[7] where, had there been an opportunity, we would expect extravagant praise and jubilant comparison with

---

[1] Book ii, chap. 38, ed. Bekker (Bonn 1837), p. 104.

[2] Trachala [from the Greek, τραχαλᾶς, one of Constantine's epithets] decem praestantissimus, duodecim sequentibus latro, decem novissimis pupillus ob immodicas profusiones," chap. 41.

[3] Eusebius, *Life of Constantine*, i, 43; iv, 1; 4; 31; 54 and 55.

[4] For one of the fullest recent characterizations of Constantine see Seeck, *Geschichte des Untergangs der antiken Welt.*, i, pp. 45–75.

[5] *Incerti auctoris panegyricus Maximiano et Constantino dictus* (307), chap. iv, in Migne, *P. L.*, viii, col. 612; *Incerti Panegyricus* (313), chap. vii, in Migne, *P. L.*, viii, col. 660, and chap. xvii, col. 667; *Nazarius panegyricus* (321), chap. xxxiv, in Migne, *P. L.*, viii, col. 605.

[6] *Cf. infra*, p. 125.

[7] *Eg.* Eusebius, *Oration in Praise of Constantine*, v, 4.

heathen emperors. The fact seems to be that his oldest
son Crispus was the son of a concubine, Minervina,[1] and
that either Constantius or Constantine II, born within a
few months of each other, was also illegitimate. Seeck
gives some evidence that he was not free from irregular
relations during most of the time of his marriage with
Fausta, 307–326.[2]

In another respect also Constantine deviated from the
standards of primitive Christianity and the standard of
the better Christians of his own day. He was exces-
sively fond of display and his vanity was notorious.
Most of his panegyrists, doubtless with assurance of his
approval, mingled their outrageous flattery with praise
of his personal appearance. He was the first emperor
to be pictured wearing a diadem. He adorned himself
with gems, bracelets, jewelled collars, robes with em-
broidered gold,[3] and even with false hair of different
colors.[4]

The most telling indictment of Constantine, however,
grows out of the execution of certain persons closely
related to him, such as Licinius, his colleague and
brother-in-law, Crispus his son, and Fausta his wife.[5]

[1] Zosimus, ii, 20, 2; Vict. *Epit.*, 41, 4; Zonaras, xiii. Eusebius by ig-
noring Crispus entirely in his *Life of Constantine* (*Cf.* iv, 40 and 49),
though he had written very highly of him in his *Church History* (x, 9,
4), may have been influenced by the fact that Crispus was illegitimate,
as well as by the fact that he had been executed by his father's orders.

[2] *Untergang d. antiken Welt.*, i, 476; iii, 425; iv, 3, 377.

[3] Caricatured by Julian in the *Caesars*, cf. *infra*, p. 126.

[4] *Cf.* Gibbon, *Decline and Fall of the Roman Empire*, ed. Bury, ii,
205; Richardson in *Nicene and Post-Nicene Fathers*, Second series, vol.
i, Eusebius, p. 427. Eusebius speciously covers the real facts of his
gorgeous descriptions by ascribing a superior mental attitude to the
emperor. *Life of Constantine*, iii, 10; *Oration in Praise of Constantine*, 5, 6.

[5] To complete the list of executions in his family there could be

The execution of Licinius in 325, a year or two after he had surrendered upon promise of security, was by pagan writers and hostile historians called a violation of faith. By early Christian writers and by friendly historians it was ascribed to the continual plotting of Licinius which made his death necessary. [1] The execution of Crispus and Fausta has been attributed by some to their adultery, by some to a false accusation against Crispus by Fausta, and the subsequent crime of the latter, and by others to family dissensions and sultanism such as occurred in the case of Herod the Great.[2]

added the earlier death of his father-in-law, Maximianus, of another brother-in-law, Bassianus, and the later execution of his nephew, son of Licinius and Constantia (though this son of Licinius was perhaps illegitimate). Even if all of these executions were justifiable, as some of them certainly were, it is an appalling list.

[1] *Cf. Fasti* of Hydatius in Mommsen: *Chronica minora*, i, p. 232; Eutropius, x, 6, 1: Zosimus, ii, 28, 2 and ii, 29: the last two look at it as a violation of Constantine's oath made when Licinius surrendered; Eusebius, *Life of Constantine*, ii, 18: *Anon. Vales.*, v, 29: Socrates, *Church History*, i, 4: Zonarus, xiii, all four of whom exonerate Constantine of any violation of faith. Seeck, *Untergang der antiken Welt*, vol. i, p. 183, holds that the execution was necessary, and forced on Constantine by his army.

[2] For the execution of Crispus and of Fausta, see Seeck, "Die Verwandtenmorde Constantins des Grossen," *Ztsch. f. wiss. Theol.*, xxxiii (1890), 63 *et seq.*, and his *Untergang der antiken Welt*, in chapters devoted to Constantine. For list of evidences see Seeck, *Untergang der antiken Welt*, iii, 424-5, and add to that list Philostorgius, *Church History*, epitomized by Photius, Book ii, chapter 4; Ammianus Marcellinus, xiv, 6; see also Bury's discussion in his edition of Gibbon: *Decline and Fall of the Roman Empire*, ii, 558. Eusebius ignores the whole matter, but in two lists of the emperor's sons, which he gives after Constantine's death (*Life of Constantine*, iv, 40 and 49), he omits Crispus entirely, thus implying his official execution. Monuments and other memorials (*e. g.*, C. I. L., 10, 517) have been discovered with Crispus' name erased, thus strengthening the theory of his disgrace.

It has been maintained by some, even recently, that Fausta was not executed at all but was living as late as 340, three years after Constan-

It is, however, hard to see how the obscure question of the guilt of those executed and of the motives of the emperor has any bearing on the religious question. If the executions were unjustifiable they would be condemned by a pagan as much as by a Christian conscience; if they were in the mind of Constantine unavoidable there was nothing in either his Christianity or his paganism to prevent them. No one could argue from the execution of Don Carlos, that Philip II of Spain professed paganism rather than Christianity. These family crimes, whether Constantine's or his victims, may show that he was suspicious or cruel, or difficult to get along with,

tine's death. Gibbon hazarded this as a possibility (*Decline and Fall*, *etc.*, ed. Bury, ii, pp. 211–212). Ranke (*Weltgeschichte*, iii, 521 asserts it, as does Victor Schultze, *Zeitsch. f. K. G.*, viii, p. 534, followed by Boyd: *Ecclesiastical Edicts of the Theodosian Code* (Columbia Univ. Studies, *etc.*, vol. xxxiv), p. 17. The evidence upon which this view was based does not compare in amount with the evidence on the other side and is extremely faulty, the principal pieces being the fact that Julian Orat., i (p. 10 ed., Hertlein) eulogizes Fausta as he would not have done had she been executed and guilty of a crime (her guilt is not necessarily involved in the question) and the existence of the *Anonymi Monodia* (ed. Frotscher *Anon. Graeci oratio funebris*, Freiberg, i. S., 1855) formerly supposed to be (and so labeled in one MS.) a funeral oration on Constantine, the eldest son of Constantine the Great killed in 340. This explicitly states that the mother of the dead prince survived him; but it has been clearly proved to be a much later writing and to refer to some Byzantine emperor late in the Middle Ages. (Seeck, *Zeitsch. f. Wiss. Theol.*, 1890, p. 64); Wordsworth: "Constantine the Great and his Sons": "Constantius i," in Smith and Wace: *Dict.*, i, (1877), p. 630; Bury, in *op. cit.*, ii, p. 534. A heretofore neglected bit of evidence lies in a letter in Eusebius' *Life of Constantine*, iii, 52, purporting to be from Constantine, referring to the benefit of information given him by his "truly pious mother-in-law" (Eutropia, mother of Fausta), evidently after the execution of Fausta. This would seem to tend either to disprove the execution or to justify it; in view of the other evidence probably the latter. Seeck: *Die Verwandtenmorde Constantins des Grossen*, pp. 63–77, holds the execution of both Crispus and Fausta to have been caused by their joint misconduct.

and hence they may affect our judgment of his character, and of the kind of Christianity he experienced; but they do not prove that he did or did not profess Christianity.

In view of all the foregoing, it will be seen that it is easy to pronounce harsh judgment on Constantine. One of the foremost of present-day writers upon the period says, "The personal morality of the first emperor, who, though not a Christian, at least died as a baptized Christian, was not much above that of an oriental sultan."[1]   Not to pause over the question whether even an "oriental sultan" may not have a high standard of personal morality, the implied criticism has much justification.   Yet it must be remembered that Constantine compared more than favorably with the other emperors of his century.   Moreover, judging from Christian writings of the time which have been preserved, it may be doubted whether the ethical element of that religion was emphasized then as much as it is usually assumed to have been emphasized.[2]   So far as we can judge, Constantine conceived his own service of the Supreme God to be chiefly by way of promoting his cult and his church, and to this task he was true.

8. *Summary*

If our interpretation of the evidence be correct, the answer to the question of Constantine's religious position would be about as follows: He was at first a pagan inclined toward monotheism, and friendly in his attitude toward the Christians.   In his government he extended more and more favors and privileges to the Christians, and before 323 put Christianity on a level with official

---

[1] Schwartz, *Kaiser Constantin u. d. christliche Kirche*, p. 70.

[2] *Eg. cf.* the course of the whole Arian controversy as told by Socrates and other continuators of Eusebius.   *Cf.* also, *infra*, p. 102.

paganism.   After 323, when he was sole emperor, he
used his imperial influence very extensively for Christianity and against paganism.[1]   Personally, he allied himself to the Church organization, without joining himself
to it, associated intimately with Christian priests, took
part in councils and identified himself in sympathy with
church affairs so far as ceremonies and preservation
of unity were concerned.   He professed belief in that religion as a whole, in the lordship of the Christian God
over the world, in his revelation through Christ, and in
his providence over his people.   He believed that his
own remarkable successes were miraculously furthered
by his use of Christian symbols and by his course toward
the church.   He was by no means above reproach in
either his private or public life.   He probably prepared
for death by a resolution to live a better and more Christian life if he recovered from his illness, and by entering
the church through a momentary catechumenate and
through baptism.

The importance of Constantine's religious development for the light it throws on the history of religion
has generally been obscured by the emphasis put upon
the profitless question, impossible to answer, whether his
real motives were political or sincerely religious.   There
are few men of the fourth century, that critical century in
the history of religion in Europe, about whom we have
so much information, reliable and otherwise.   I believe
that the more this information is studied from the point
of view first mentioned, the more it will tend to con-
firm the theory that Christianity did not come down
into the middle ages through the Roman Empire like
a knife cutting through some foreign substance, but
that it entered into the complex of imperial religious

[1] *Cf.* in addition to references given *supra*, Eusebius, *Life of Constantine*, ii, 23; 27.

life along with other oriental influences and came out,
the dominant religion of Europe, by way of a very general synthesis.[1]   The Christian writers upon whom
church historians have relied as their sources over-
emphasized contrasts and did not realize this synthesis,
unconscious as it largely was.   We recognize that pagan
stories about the early Christians were slanders; it is becoming generally recognized that many of the early
Catholic stories about the heretics were slanders; it is
very probable that many of the Christian stories about
the pagans, emphasizing the contrast between the two
religions, were slanders.   Stories of the conversion, the
piety and sainthood of Constantine have their reverse
side in sensational denunciations of pagans in such books
as Lactantius' *De Mortibus Persecutorum*, and in many
paragraphs in other writings.[2]   The contrast between
religions seems to have been overdrawn as much as was
the contrast between the character and deaths of their
several champions.

[1] There was not a great deal of difference between Constantine consulting the omens at the Temple of Apollo at Autun, and Constantine
seeking miraculous guidance in battle in his tabernacle as described by
Eusebius, *cf. supra*, p. 76; *infra*, pp. 134-135.   Nor did Aquilinus, the
Christian, who sought cure for his sickness by spending the night at a
Christian temple (Sozomen ii, 3) differ greatly from those who slept in
the temple of Esculapius (Eusebius, *Life of Constantine*, iii, 56).   In fact
in some localities the transition from paganism to Christianity seems to
have been facilitated by Christianizing pagan shrines and retaining methods of healing and divination used by the pagan priests and oracles,
adopting, however, the name of some saint or angel recognized by the
Christians.   The church at which Aquilinus was healed had formerly
been a famous miracle-working shrine.   *Cf.* Mary Hamilton, *Incubation, or the Cure of Disease in Pagan Temples and Christian Churches*
(1906), pp. 109-118, 138-140 *et passim*.

[2] *Cf.* for instance, the account of Galerius' death, Lactantius, *op. cit.*,
chap. 33; the death of Maximinus in Eusebius, *Church History*, ix, 10,
14-15; the death of the heretic Arius, in Socrates, *Church History*,
i, 38.   For a discussion of the last mentioned, see Seeck, *Untergang d.
antiken Welt*, iii, p. 426 *et seq.*, p. 438 *et seq.*

PART TWO

THE LEGENDARY CONSTANTINE
AND CHRISTIANITY

CHAPTER I

1. *Significance of Legends about Constantine*

THE part which Constantine actually played in the religious revolution of the fourth century is scarcely more significant than the place taken in that and subsequent times by legends about him. Even in his own generation, it was not only the actual emperor, but the emperor as idealized, that influenced the thoughts of men and the course of events. Few men at the time tried honestly to discriminate between the two. After the lapse of sixteen centuries this discrimination, though the necessity for it is recognized, is exceedingly difficult. Many of those who discard in largest measure material from earlier writers as legendary have unquestionably created from the remainder a Constantine as legendary as that one described by their predecessors. Such has Burckhardt's Constantine been shown to be; a Machiavellian prince who had no conviction but that of his own destiny, a cold, clear-sighted, free-thinking, ambitious statesman, rising to supreme power by playing with the religious faiths of his subjects,—a being who existed only on the pages of over-skeptical historical critics, and yet a powerful influence upon the thought of a whole generation.

Even if we should be fortunate enough accurately to distinguish the real facts from legends, the latter so long dominated the thought of the world that they have become a part of history.[1]   Their origin and acceptance, also, bring into clear relief the intellectual life of the ages through which they have come to us.

2. *Lack of the Historical Spirit in the Time of Constantine*

The early and luxurious growth of legends about Constantine is explained partly by the relative weakness of the investigative and historical spirit of the Romans.   History among them never reached the position of an independent science.   In the educational curriculum it formed a sub-classification under rhetoric.[2]   Rhetorical schools, not formal histories, were the chief means of instructing new-comers to Rome in history.[3]   It was only natural that historical incidents were generally distorted for rhetorical purposes, and that it became the fashion in imperial times to incorporate manufactured documents when authentic ones were not at hand.[4]

There seems to have been something of an historical revival in the time of Diocletian and Constantine.   But this was in no sense scientific, it was not even spontaneous.   The *Scriptores Historiae Augustae,* for instance, while pretending independence and impartiality, were in part imitators

[1] For in illuminating discussion of the part of legends in the history of the world, *cf.* Dunning, " Truth in History," *Am. Hist. Rev.* xxix (1914), pp. 217-229.

[2] *Cf.* Cicero, de leg. 1, 2, 5, and de or. 2, 9, 36.

[3] H. Peter: *Die Geschichtliche Litteratur über die römische Kaiserzeit bis Theodosius I, und ihre Quellen,* i, 10, 61-64.

[4] For illustrations on a wholesale scale, *ibid.,* i, 248. *Cf.* from another point of view, O. Seeck: "Urkundensfalschung des 4n Jahrhunderts," *Zeitschr. f. K. G.,* xxx, (1909, June), p. 181. *Cf.* also, H. Peter, *Wahrheit und Kunst Geschichtschreibung und Plagiat in klassischen Altertum,* Leipzig, 1911; Reitzenstein, *Hellenistische Wundererzäh-lunger,* 1906.

of Suetonius, in part mere rhetoricians, and in part sub-
sidized flatterers of the reigning monarch.

Diocletian, a soldier and statesman of first rank, was a
crude patron of letters and Constantine followed in his footsteps.[1] The most notable expression of revived interest in
literary and historical matters was the rebirth of Roman
rhetoric. Gaul was one of its greatest seats, and the panegyric was its most characteristic utterance.[2] Fifty-three
panegyrics from between 289 and 321 have come down
from Gaul, mostly from Treves.[3] Nazarius and Eumenius,
two of the leading lights among these rhetoricians, eulo-
gized Constantine in more than one rhetorical flight. Eusebius, in the East, went even beyond them in praise of his
royal patron. Peter's criticism of imperial Roman biog-
raphies holds true of much of this panegyrical rhetoric.
" Amid the confusion of petty, insignificant details, errors,
exaggerations, careless and malignant fabrications, all judgment and ability to distinguish between the possible and
the impossible was lost. People believed, without asking
the question whether it was possible or not, whether it was
true or not." [4]

Constantine's imperial influence did not improve historical standards. Not a highly-educated man,[5] he was notor-

---

[1] Peter: *Gesch. Litt.*, i, 95-96.

[2] For school at Autun, and Eumenius, see G. Bloch in Lavisse: *Histoire de France*, vol. i, part ii (1900), pp. 388-398. Translated in part
in Munro & Sellery: *Medieval Civilization.*

[3] Peter: *Gesch. Litt.*, i, 46-49, 95.

[4] i, 150.

[5] Julian, Or. 2, 94 a. p. 102 H.; Aurelius Victor, *Caes*, 40, 13;
Eusebius, *Life of Constantine*, iii, 13 (where the emperor addressed the Council of Nicea, an eastern assembly, in Latin, and used
a Greek interpreter) iv, 32; Exc. Val. 2, 2 ("litteris minus in-
structus"); *Anon. Vales.* p. 471; Cedrenus, p. 473.

iously vain.[1] Judging by the panegyrics to which he listened and which he praised and rewarded, he encouraged the wildest flights of legend-breeding imagination.

Historical writing among the Christians was as unreliable as among the pagans of the empire. Forgeries, present in religious writings of the heathen, were equally numerous in Christian writings. Even the leading bishops were " ready to prove the truth of their faith by lies." [2]

3. Incentives to Legend-Making

Incentives to embellish Constantine's career with touches of imagination were, from the first, very strong. The imperial throne always distorted accounts of the character and career of one who occupied it by intensifying all the lights and shadows. In this particular case there were pagan writers to do injustice to a Christian ruler. But most of all, there were Christians whose imagination was quickened by the emergence of their church from persecution into full religious liberty and even to supremacy in the state. They beheld the change wrought, moreover, not through any struggle and victory of their own, but through the wonderful military achievements of one who, always fighting against odds, never knew defeat; a conqueror who raised the church from the dust and honored her in the imperial court.

Every apprehension of the evils under the pressure of which all had suffered was now removed; men whose heads had drooped in sorrow now regarded each other with smiling countenances, and looks expressive of inward joy. With proces-

---

[1] *Nicene and Post Nicene Fathers, Eusebius,* p. 427; Victor, *Epitome,* 61, 63, (Antwerp edition 1579) p. 51; Eutropius, 10, 7; Eunapius *Vit. aedes,* p. 41, (Amst. 1822).

[2] Seeck, *Untergang d. antiken Welt,* iii, 210-212, 431 *et seq.,* with specific illustrations from Ambrose of Milan and Athanasius.

sions and hymns of praise they first of all, as they were told, ascribed the supreme sovereignty to God, as in truth the King of Kings: and then with continued acclamations rendered honor to the victorious emperor, and the Caesars, his most discreet and pious sons. The former afflictions were forgotten and all past impieties forgiven, while with the enjoyment of present happiness was mingled the expectation of continued blessings in the future.[1]

Thus the final victory of Constantine and Christianity over persecution and Paganism fired the imagination of those who were to make the history and the legends of the future. A state dinner at the council of Nicea gave the church historian an overpowering contrast between the days of tribulation and of triumph: " detachments of the body guard and other troops surrounded the entrance of the palace with drawn swords, and through the midst of these the men of God proceeded without fear [only a few years before, most of them had been criminals in the eyes of the law] into the innermost of the imperial apartments, in which some were the emperor's own companions at table, while others reclined on couches arranged on either side. One might have thought that a picture of Christ's kingdom was thus shadowed forth, and a dream rather than a reality." [2]

European civilization turned on the axis of this man's reign. It is no wonder that he received the tribute of innumerable legends. The desire to know and to tell more than the plain facts about such a great man, the curiosity

[1] Eusebius: *Life of Constantine*, ii, 19.

[2] *Ibid.*, iii, 15. It is perhaps worthy of note that this reflection came to Eusebius at the imperial banquet rather than during the deliberations of the council. He also rather naively remarks that " not one of the bishops was wanting at the imperial banquet."

which in other circles bred a host of legends about Alexander the Great, and Charlemagne, created legends about Constantine. They began in the emperor's lifetime and as the worldly greatness increased to which Constantine opened the door for the church, these legends also developed. Through his triumphal arch at Rome there marched, no longer Roman soldiers but Christian priests whose fervor pictured the victor in strangely distorted perspective.

For them a great religious revolution had been wrought, and the more wonderful they made it, the more it accorded with their inner feelings. This gave a peculiar impetus to the legend-making process. For the emotional stress connected with religious movements seems more fruitful of legends than any other, more even than the emotion of patriotic and family pride. Think, for instance, of the swarm of legends which developed about early Buddhism, Christianity, and Mohammedanism. Almost every religious change, such as the introduction of a new religion, gives rise to a penumbra of this sort. The explanation is undoubtedly to be found not only in the general credulity of the ages in which such changes take place, if indeed this can be proved, but also in the character of the emotional and mental activity attending religious agitation and devotion. Religion, finding its explanation of human life and fortunes in the will of God or gods, encourages the embellishment of events with providential wonders. In this realm the mysterious and the inexplicable becomes accepted as self-evident fact.[1]

Many religions emphasize truth. But this must usually be understood as meaning, not historical or scientific truth, as these terms are used to-day, but as another term for the

[1] *Cf.* H. Delehaye, *The Legends of the Saints*, London, 1907.

content of the teaching of these several religions. In
Christian documents, for instance, the word "truth" is
used not so much in the former as in the latter sense; it is
often synonymous with the revealed content of Christian
teaching, with the "gospel".[1]

At times one is tempted to think that the love of truth,
which is the basis of all genuine historical criticism, and
of all other scientific work as well, is a comparatively modern product. It almost seems as if it were a new faculty
acquired in the slow evolution of the human mind. If this
be too strong a statement, born of impatience at the occasional audacity and success of legend-makers, a study of
the Constantinian legends shows that many former generations, when plain historical facts lay ready at hand, pre-
ferred to create and accept fanciful stories.   ,

It is perhaps invidious to designate individual writers
in this connection, for most legends are the product of
many minds, the work of whole generations rather than of
isolated persons. Those who bore a conspicuous part in
the making of the legends about Constantine will be discussed later in connection with these legends. Two men,
however, are so pre-eminently conspicuous in the process
that they require mention here, namely, Constantine himself, and Eusebius, his first biographer.

4. *Constantine's Part in the Process*

The legend of Constantine's descent from Claudius [2]
and of his hereditary right to the imperial purple was so
obviously to his own advantage that it is only reasonable to

---

[1] *Cf.* articles on ἀλήθεια in Moulton & Geddes, *Concordance to the
Greek New Testament*; Thayer, *Greek-English Lexicon of the New
Testament*; Cremer, *Biblico-Theological Lexicon of New Testament
Greek*.

[2] *Cf. infra*, pp. 112-115.

assume that it was promulgated at his instance. Legends
of miraculous manifestations and of his extraordinary piety
may also, with considerable probability, be laid at his door.
Eusebius repeatedly ascribed extraordinary statements of
that nature to the emperor. Though his assurances to the
reader that he merely repeated imperial utterances are not
altogether convincing, one can not but suspect Constantine of being aware how greatly the good bishop was awed
in his ruler's presence, and how easy and pleasant it would
be to create an exaggerated idea of his own Christian devotion.[1] The most famous instance of this is the story of
the miraculous conversion of Constantine, which Eusebius
assures us the emperor told him and confirmed with an
oath.[2] I am inclined to believe that Eusebius' account of
this conversion was not wholly his own invention, for his
own earlier version of the facts, which he had already
given out in the *Church History,* was quite inconsistent
with the story of the miraculous conversion.

Stories of the miraculous protection of the special guard
who surrounded and defended the divine standard in battle,
with which Eusebius says the emperor regaled him,[3] may
well record the emperor's superstitious attitude toward
this wonderful charm, but they bear the marks, also, of
exaggeration common to the tales which men of war often
tell to men of peace.

For he said that once, during the very heat of an engagement,
a sudden tumult and panic attacked his army, which threw
the soldier who then bore the standard into an agony of fear,
so that he handed it over to another, in order to secure his own
escape from the battle. As soon, however, as his comrade had

---

[1] *Life of Constantine,* iii, 60; 61; 62; iv, 33-36.

[2] *Ibid.,* i, 28-29. *Cf. supra,* pp. 77-79, and *infra,* pp. 136-140.

[3] Eusebius: *Life of Constantine,* ii, 7-9.

received it, and he had withdrawn and resigned all charge of
the standard, he was struck in the belly by a dart, which took
his life. Thus he paid the penalty of his cowardice and un-
faithfulness, and lay dead on the spot; but the other, who had
taken his place as the bearer of the salutary standard, found
it to be the safeguard of his life. For though he was assailed
by a continual shower of darts, the bearer remained unhurt,
the staff of the standard receiving every weapon. It was indeed a truly marvellous circumstance, that the enemies' darts
all fell within and remained in the slender circumference of
this spear, and thus saved the standard-bearer from death; so
that none of those engaged in this service ever received a
wound. This story is none of mine, but for this, too, I am indebted to the emperor's own authority, who related it in my
hearing along with other matters.

That Constantine was not averse to receiving credit for
religious virtues even on contradictory counts is shown, if
we can accept Eusebius' rendering of his conversation and
his speeches, by his advancing in one place a claim to life-
long possession of Christian piety, and in another place
describing his radical and sudden conversion to that religion.[1]

5. *Eusebius of Caesarea*

But making all allowance for the assistance of the emperor, Eusebius himself in his *Oration in Praise of Constantine* and his *Life of Constantine* was the chief creator
of the legend of a saintly emperor. Of the former of
these, the author himself said in the latter,[2] " we have
woven, as it were, garlands of words, wherewith we en-
circled his sacred head in his own palace on his thirtieth

---

[1] Eusebius, *Oration of Constantine to the Assembly of the Saints*
(the Easter Sermon), chap. 26; *Life of Constantine*, ii, 49 and 51;
i, 27. Compare these with *Life of Constantine*, i, 28-32.

[2] Chapter i.

anniversary." The first part [1] is a eulogy of Constantine's devoutness and religious leadership, and of the magical efficacy of the " salutary sign " by which he conquered, mingled with analogies of Christianity in the natural world. The last part, often considered a separate oration, is a general exposition of the true doctrine of God and of the incarnation of the Word. The first part alone concerns us. It is a panegyric which from the point of view of historical trustworthiness is not superior to the low level of the time to which it belongs. Extravagant in its praises almost to the point of blasphemy,[2] its statements are often gross exaggerations,[3] and above all it violently twists all of Constantine's motives into the most unselfish promptings of saintliness.[4] Eusebius shows in Constantine nothing but a superstitious holy-man who turned his own chambers into an oratory, and his household into a church, and who had oft repeated visions of the Saviour.[5]

The viciousness of this one-sided eulogy is modified by the fact that Eusebius himself gives notice in the prologue that he proposes not a narrative of "merely human merits" or " merely human accomplisments " but " those virtues of the emperor which heaven itself approves, and his pious actions." He wants to " close the doors against every profane ear, and unfold, as it were, the secret mysteries of our emperor's character to the initiated alone." He thus frankly

[1] Chapters i-x.

[2] *Eg.* i, 3 and ix, 18, compared with Constantine's domestic tragedies.

[3] *Eg.* i, 3; 8, 9; 9, 10 compared with actual law on Sunday *Cod. Theod.* ii, 8, 1 and *Cod. Just.* iii, 12, 3.

[4] iii, 5 and 6 attribute Constantine's overthrow of Diocletian's system and his attainment of sole rulership to an imitation of God's sole and undivided government of the universe. i, 6; and v, 5-7 attribute his gorgeous apparel to popular demand which he himself despised.

[5] ix. 11 : 18.

avows his intention of painting upon the background of Constantine's career, the traits of an ideal Christian emperor for the edification of a Christian assembly. It may contain historical truth, but that is not its main purpose. It intentionally ushers us into the realm of legend.

The same is true of the *Life of Constantine* written shortly after the emperor's death,[1] and in places built upon material from the Oration.[2] There is more historical material in the later work but its tone is the same as that of the earlier. Eusebius not only extols Constantine as the divinely-appointed emperor to whose elevation no man contributed,[3] but attributes to him repeated, direct, and miraculous revelations of God, who " frequently vouchsafed to him manifestations of himself, the divine presence, according to him manifold intimations of future events." [4] It is a serious question how much reliance to place even in the speeches, laws and letters of Constantine embodied in the *Life,* occasionally with professions that they are copied from documents in Constantine's own handwriting or with his signature.[5] This ostensibly original material was savagely attacked along with the general reliability of the Life, by Crivellucci, in 1888,[6] and by H. Peter in 1897,[7] and the

---

[1] i, 2.

[2] *Cf.* ix, 8; viii; ix, 15; ix, 17 of the *Oration* with Book ii, 16; iii, 54, 55; iii, 50 and iii, 41 of the *Life* respectively. The notes in the English translation in the *Nicene and Post Nicene Fathers, Eusebius,* pp. 591 and 593 make the strange mistake of assuming that the *Oration* uses the *Life,* though the former was written first and is mentioned in the latter.

[3] i, 24　　　　　[4] i, 47.　　　　　[5] ii, 47; ii, 23.

[6] *Storia della relazione tra lo stato e la chiesa,* vol. i, appendix, "Della fede storia di Eusebio nella vita di Costantino." He calls it a historical novel.

[7] *Die geschichtliche Litteratur über die römische Kaiserzeit bis Theodosius I und ihre Quellen.* He calls it " methodical falsification of history," i, 249-250, 405 *et seq.*

worthlessness of these documents was assumed by
Mommsen and by Seeck. Benjamin in Pauly-Wissowa,
Real Encyclopädie der classischen Altertumswissenschaft,
wrote summarily, " The original documents [of the Life
of Constantine] are almost all forged or highly questionable." [1]   Görres calls it inferior to the panegyrics of Eumenius and Nazarius, and Manso says it is " more shame-
less and lying " than they.   Seeck, however, completely
changed his view by 1898,[2] and in the later edition of his
Untergang der antiken Welt used all of the original documents in the Life of Constantine as genuine in accordance
with his declaration " Eusebius' reproduction of original
documents has been freed from every suspicion." [3]
Schultze in his " Quellenuntersuchungen zur Vita Constantini des Eusebius," [4] occupies commendable middle ground
in submitting each of the questioned documents to thor-
ough scrutiny with the result that some, *e. g.,* the Edict
to the Provincials of Palestine,[5] are rejected as forgeries [6]
and some are accepted as genuine.[7]   The list of questioned
documents is a long one,[8] but the case against many of
them seems weak.[9]   There are, however, statements in
others which show that they either are forgeries or con-

[1] See Article, Constantin.

[2] " Die Urkunden der Vita Constantini," in *Zeitsch. f. K. G.,* xviii, pp.
321-340.

[3] *Zeitsch. f. K. G.,* xxx (1909), p. 183.

[4] In *Zeitsch. f. K. G.,* xiv (1894), p. 503 *et seq.*

[5] *Life of Constantine* ii, 24-42.

[6] In this particular case by a later hand than that of Eusebius.

[7] *Eg.* compare *Life of Constantine* iv, 26 and *Cod. Theod.* viii, 16, 1.

[8] ii, 23-42: ii, 46: ii, 48-60: ii, 64-72: iii, 17-20: iii, 30-32: iii, 52-53:
iii, 60: iii, 61: iii, 62: iii, 64-65: iv, 9-13: iv, 20: iv, 35: iv, 36:
iv, 42: Appendix: Oration to the Saints.

[9] There is no reason, for instance, for rejecting the letter of Constantine to the churches after the Council of Nicea, iii, 17-20.

tain interpolations.[1] The work, moreover, contains rather more than Eusebius' usual proportion of minor inaccuracies.[2] His *Church History* must of course be judged independently of his eulogies. It was, for the time, a magnificent historical work. The panegyrists of the fourth century, however, and Eusebius is no exception, did not hold themselves up to even the relatively low standard of truthfulness that prevailed in their day for historical writings. They offer a curious parallel to the writers of the Italian renaissance, who were not without merit as historians but whose literary invectives against each other were pure works of art, not to be believed under oath. The *Life of Constantine* has been well called an evidence of Eusebius' "enthusiastic admiration for what he considered the good actions of the deceased emperor, and of his skill in disguising the others. No trace is found there of the murder of Crispus and that of Fausta; the author has discovered a way of telling the story of the Councils of Nicea and of Tyre, and the ecclesiastical events connected with them, without even mentioning the names of Athanasius and of Arius. It is a triumph of reticence, and of circumlocution." [3]

---

[1] *Eg.* iv, 9-13, letter to the king of Persia, under the (later) heading of Sapor, confuses Sapor II the grandson of Narses and the contemporary of Constantine with Sapor I, the predecessor of Narses. *Cf.* also ii, 51 where Constantine says he was a boy, " κομιδῇ παῖς," at the outbreak of the Diocletian persecution. *Cf.* also *supra*, pp. 53 *et seq.*

[2] *Cf.* ii, 3 with i, 50, and both with the *Church History*, x, 8 and McGiffert's note on this last passage in the N. & P. N. F. translation. iv, 53 purporting to be exact, overstates Constantine's reign by about a year. iv, 5 and 6 probably has "Scythians" for "Goths"; no such war against the Scythians is known. iv, 2 and 3 contradicts the well known financial pressure of Constantine's reign. iii, 21 and 66 entirely misstate the theological situation by representing that peace reigned after the Council of Nicea.

[3] Duchesne, *Early History of the Church* (Eng. trans.), vol. ii, p. 152.

CHAPTER II

LEGENDS OF CONSTANTINE'S ORIGIN AND RISE TO IMPERIAL POSITION, LEGENDS ABOUT HELENA

1. *Legend of Claudian Descent*

The parentage of Constantine and the beginning of his rule in Gaul and Britain are the subject of such abundant evidence that there can be little question as to the main historical facts.[1] He was born at Naissus in Dacia, about 274 A. D. (Seeck puts the date as late as 288 A. D.[2]), the son of Constantius (later Caesar in Gaul and Britain) and of his concubine, or morganatic wife, Helena, probably a chambermaid before her connection with Constantius. He spent part, at least, of his early manhood in the East at the court of Diocletian. Hence he was summoned by his father, and joined him at Bononia (Boulogne) in time to accompany him on his last expedition into northern Britain. Constantius apparently designated him as his successor, and at the death of the father, the soldiers acclaimed the son Emperor (306). Constantine contented himself for a time with the title of " Caesar ", which was recognized and confirmed by Galerius. His administration of Gaul and Britain was entirely successful, and in 308 he secured recognition as an Emperor. By his victory over Maxentius in 312 he became sole Emperor in the West.

The first legendary variation from these plain historical facts was the assertion that Constantine was descended

[1] *Cf.* article "Constantin" in Pauly-Wissowa, *Real Encyclopädie der classischen Altertumswissenschaft.*

[2] *Untergang d. antiken Welt*, vol. i, pp. 47, 435.

from the Emperor Claudius, one of the unimportant contestants of the throne who reigned in Gaul (268-270).
This assertion was first made by the rhetorician Eumenius
in a panegyric delivered in 310 in Constantine's presence.
The orator says that most men were ignorant of the fact,
but that the emperor's intimate friends knew it. He extols
Claudius as the first to restore the lost and ruined discipline of the Roman government,—praise uncalled-for by
any of the known facts of that ruler's career. Such is the
greatness of Constantine's two-fold imperial ancestry, his
eulogist maintains, that possession of imperial rank adds
nothing to his honor. He reiterates this thought: Constantine was not made ruler by any accidental, human purpose, nor by any favorable circumstances, he deserved the
empire by his birth. The imperial palace was his birth-
right.[1] This high-sounding rhetoric bears every evidence
of being inspired, not by the facts of the case, but by the
suggestion of the ruler in whose praise, and at whose in-

[1] Eumenius, *Panegyricus*, in *Pan. Vet.* no. vii, (310 A. D.) Migne; P. L.
viii, col. 624 *et seq.*, chap. ii, *et seq.* A primo igitur incipiam originis
tuae numine quod plerique adhuc fortasse nesciunt, sed qui te amant
plurimum sciunt. Ab illo enim Divo Claudio manet in te avita cognatio,
qui Romani imperii solutam et perditam disciplinam primus reformavit
. . . . Quamvis igitur ille fecissimus dies proxima religione celebratus
imperii tui natalis habeatur, quoniam te ipso habitu primus ornavit:
jam tamen ab illo generis auctore in te imperii fortuna descendit.
Quin imo patrem tuum ipsum vetus illa imperatoriae domus praeroga-
tiva provexit; ut jam summo gradu, et supra humanarum rerum fata
consisteres, post duos familiae tuae principes tertius imperator. Inter
omnes, inquam, participes majestatis tuae hoc habes, Constantine,
praecipium, quod imperator es, tantaque est nobilitas originis tuae,
ut nihil tibi addiderit honoris imperium, nec possit fortuna numini tuo
imputare quod tuum est, omissis ambitu et suffragatione.

Chap. iii. "Non fortuita hominum consensio non repentinus ali-
quis favoris eventus te principem fecit. Imperium nascendo meruisti."

Chap. iv. "Sacrum istud palatium non candidatus imperii; sed
designatus intrasti, confestimque te illi paterni lares successorem
videre legitimum. Neque enim erat dubium, quin ei comperet haer-
editas quem primum imperatori filium fata tribuissent."

H

stance it was uttered. The story of Constantine's Claudian
descent was evidently a surprise to the public, it could only
be launched as something known all the time to favored
friends. The implication must necessarily have been that
his father, Constantius, was an illegitimate son of Claudius, as there is no recognized genealogical connection.

It is significant that the panegyric in which the pronun-
ciamento was made was delivered shortly after the execution or enforced suicide of Constantine's father-in-law,
Maximian, the only emperor of the original Diocletian system from whom he could satisfactorily derive his authority. It is taken by Dessau, Seeck and others as being the
proclamation under Constantine's direction, of a new principle of legitimacy, based on a fictitious genealogy.[1]   The
substitution of hereditary right to the throne for the Diocletian system of appointment and promotion was tempor-
arily carried through successfully by Constantine's military
genius, by the continued succession of his own family to the
throne, and by the adulation of his admirers. Eusebius
went the length of writing that Constantius " bequeathed
the empire, according to the law of nature to his eldest
son," and that Constantine, by bestowing his sister, Constantia, upon Licinius in marriage, granted him the privi-
lege of family relationship and a share in his own ancient
imperial descent.[2]   The Emperor Julian, Constantine's
nephew, accepted the Claudian descent of the family.[3]
Eutropius represented Constantine as the grandson of
Claudius.[4]   Several writers described him as the nephew [5]

---

[1] *Cf.* Dessau, in *Hermes*, xxiv, p. 341 *et seq.*; Seeck, *Untergang d.
antiken Welt*, i, pp. 110-111, 451, 487-488 (with citations of sources);
Pauly-Wissowa, article " Constantin ".

[2] *Life of Constantine*, i, 21; i, 50; *cf. Church History*, x, 8, 4.

[3] *Orat.*, i, p. 6 D; ii, p. 51 C; *Caesars*, p. 313 D (ed. Hertlein).

[4] ix, 22.   [5]*Anon. Vales.*, i, 1.

or grandnephew [1] of Claudius. But in one form or another
the relationship was established, and became embodied in
the general belief.

The idea of hereditary succession to imperial power was,
of course, not original, nor in any sense unique, with Constantine. It was, however, important in this connection as
the repudiation of the Diocletian system. Under that system the imperial power was divided between emperors
with whom were associated Caesars, chosen for their merits
with a view to the transfer of the higher office to them
through the voluntary abdication of the older men. The
great scheme of Diocletian was doomed to speedy ruin
through personal ambition or necessity, and through family
pride. Imperial power continued to be the prize in whose
pursuit the declining military resources of the empire were
squandered. Hereditary succession to the throne, however,
was Constantine's theoretical substitute for the Diocletian
system, and it seems to have held a larger place in the following generation than it had in the century before Diocletian. For this, Constantine's personal success, and the
disposition of the empire at his death were chiefly respon-
sible. But the invention of a fictitious ancestry, and the
legend in which it was incorporated must also be given due
place as one of the landmarks in the development of the
idea of an hereditary kingship. While the significance of
the whole episode is largely Roman and local, it nevertheless affords an interesting instance of the way in which
some of the very foundations of society have been but-
tressed not so much by fact as by legend.[2]

[1] *Hist. Aug.*, Claudius, 13, § 2.

[2] Seeck maintains that Constantine consistently tried, even to his own
detriment, to uphold the Diocletian system (*Untergang d. antiken Welt*,
i, pp. 70-71, 112, 176, 186 *et passim*). This is one of the most curious
of the conclusions to which he is led by fixing on a motive which he

2. *Legends of Helena and the True Cross*

If legends about Constantine's paternal ancestry were artfully circulated with political motives, legends about his mother, Helena, were the spontaneous product of pious imagination. Her pronounced Christian piety not only led her to devote much of her energy and wealth to the church and to make a famous pilgrimage to the Holy Land,[1] but made her the heroine of many later traditions. Her pilgrimage especially, made her the heroine of many versions of the story of the finding of the true cross, one of the most famous of all Christian legends.[2]

The oldest document describing the finding of the cross on which Christ was crucified is generally thought to be that embodied, from an independent narrative, in the *Doctrine of Addai,* which book relates the conversion of Abgar, king of Edessa, by Addai or Thaddeus.[3]

Here Protonice, wife of Emperor Claudius, is converted by Simon (Peter) at Rome, and makes a pilgrimage to Jerusalem with her two sons and her daughter. She is received with honor by the Apostle James, and compels the Jews to turn over to him Golgotha, which they had jealously guarded. She herself entered the grave there, where

conceives to be dominant and following it to the ends of the earth. At every turn Constantine upset the Diocletian system, and instead of fitting the dynastic idea into it only by necessity, the latter was advanced from the very first. If he bore long with Licinius it may well have been that he had to do so, or deemed it advisable on other grounds than devotion to the Diocletian system. If it is agreed that there was no good material available for another joint emperor, it can hardly be proved that his sons were any better.

[1] Eusebius, *Life of Constantine*, iii, 42-43.

[2] *Cf. Acta Sanctorum*, under May 4, I, 445.

[3] Edited with Syriac text, Eng. trans. and notes by G. Phillips (1876), pp. 10-16. *Cf.* also Duchesne: *Liber Pontificalis*, i, p. cviii *et seq.*; O. Bardenhewer, *Patrologie* (Freiburg-i- B), Eng. trans., *Patrology*, (St. Louis, 1908), p. 110.

the cross of Christ was distinguished from the crosses of the two thieves by the providential, instantaneous death of her daughter, and her resurrection when the true cross was placed upon her. Protonice gave the cross to James. She then built a great and splendid building " over Golgotha on which he was crucified, and over the grave in which he was placed, so that these places might be honored." When she and her children returned to Rome, " Claudius commanded that all the Jews should go forth from the country of Italy ".[1] This legend of the finding of the true cross represents the eastern version. In the west it was overshadowed by a very different account.

Several different varieties of the western version of the story of the finding of the cross have come down to us. These ascribe the leading part in the recovery of the cross to Helena, the mother of Constantine. This group, whether derived from the legend given above, the Eastern one, or itself the original version of it, is in fact the dominant one in the Middle Ages.[2]

[1] Syriac scholars and church historians concur in dating the forged correspondence of Abgar and Christ in the late second or early third century. Eusebius refers to it as among accounts of ancient times (*Church History* I, 13) and the Abgar legend must have been widely accepted in his time. This, however, does not prove an early date for all the stories imbedded in the *Doctrine of Addai*. Though the tendency to-day is to maintain the priority of many Syrian accounts as against Latin and Greek stories about the same things, it seems to me that in some instances this is erroneous. I do not feel at all certain that the story of Protonice and the true cross may not be a later, modified version of that of Helena and the true cross. This doubt is strengthened by the fact that a church was almost certainly built over the supposed sepulchre of Christ in the time of Constantine, and there is no special reason for thinking one had been built there before that.

[2] For versions of this lengend, *cf.* A. Holder, *Inventio sanctae crucis*, Leipsic, 1889; Mombritius, *Sanctuarium sive Vitae sanctorum* (Paris, 1910 ed.), p. 376 *et seq.*; *Acta Sanctorum*, under May 1, ed. Papebroch.

In one account, probably the older variety, Helena has no particular difficulty in finding the three crosses, and the right one is ascertained by a miracle of healing in a test suggested in most versions by Macarius, Bishop of Jerusalem.[1]

In another form, after many difficulties, the crosses are brought to light by Judas Cyriac under orders and direction of Helena. Both forms exist in Syriac, Greek and Latin. The original Helena legend, as well as that of Protonice, is generally believed to have been of Syrian origin. The former, if we can judge from its literary associations, is closely connected with the legends of Sylvester both in its origin and in its later development. It is found in many manuscripts with the *Vita Sylvestri*.[2]

In one form or another the legend of the finding of the true cross by Helena became widely current throughout Christendom. Generally it displaced accounts in which the honor was assigned to other persons. Occasionally two accounts (*e. g.*, the Protonice legend and that of Helena) were combined, and harmonized by having the cross lost after its first recovery.[3] Authoritative writers in the West

[1] *Cf.* Sozomen, ii, 1; Socrates, i, 17, who tells of the recovery also of the inscription placed by command of Pilate over the head of Christ; Theodoret i, 18.

[2] *Cf. infra*, pp. 159, 164. *Cf.* E. Nestle in *Byzantinische Zeitschrift*, iv, pp. 319-345. For the whole subject of Helena and the cross, see references in Bury's ed. of Gibbon, *Decline and Fall of the Roman Empire*, ii, p. 568; Duchesne, *op. cit.*, i, p. cvii *et seq.*; Richardson, in *op. cit.*, pp. 444-445; Smith and Wace, *Dict. of Christian Biography*, art. "Helena". An old, monumental work is that of Gretser, *De cruce Christi*, 1600, vol. ii, in Opera, Ratisbone (Regensburg), 1734, which, however, is entirely uncritical. More recently Nestle, *De sancta cruce*, 1889; J. Straubinger, *Die Kreuzauffindungslegende, Untersuchungen über ihre altchristlichen Fassungen mit besonderer Berücksichtigung der syrischen Texte. (Forschungen zur christlichen Litteratur und Dogmengeschichte,* vol. xiii, part iii), Paderborn, 1913.

[3] Duchesne cites a Syriac version, MS. British Museum 12174.

and East from the end of the fourth century assume at least the recovery of the true cross to be a fact.[1]

In all the medieval texts which give in full the legend ascribing the discovery of the cross to Helena, statement is made that Constantine was instructed in Christianity by Eusebius, Bishop of Rome, and most of them add that he was also baptized by the same bishop. This statement, however, is not present in the earlier references to the finding of the true cross.[2] The legend of the finding of the cross is briefly incorporated in the *Liber Pontificalis* under the life of Pope Eusebius, though the implication that the imperial family was Christian at that time contradicts the statements given later that Constantine was baptized by Sylvester, the second bishop of Rome after Eusebius.[3]

Of the disposition made of the cross in the various legends it is enough to say that it was generally either left in Jerusalem, or taken to Rome, or divided. Part was eventually supposed to have been taken to Constantinople. One of the earliest episodes mentioned in connection with the cross was the statement that Constantine had the nails of the cross put in his diadem or helmet and in the bridle of his horse.[4] This latter was cited as fulfilling the prophecy of Zachariah xiv. 20: " On the bridles, Holiness to the Lord."

The most decisive argument against the whole story of Helena and the cross is the absence of any reference to it

---

[1] Ambrose, *Sermo in obit. Theodosii* c. 46 (Migne. *P. L.* vol. xvi, col. 1399) ; Rufinus, Church History i, 7, 8; Paulinus ep. 31 ; Cassiodorus, *Historia tripartita*, ch. ix; Socrates i, 17; Sozomen ii, 1; Theodoret i, 18.

[2] *Cf. infra*, pp. 152-153 for Ambrose and Rufinus.

[4] Ed. Duchesne, i, 167, no. xxxii. "Eusebius natione Graecus, ex medico, redit ann. vi m. i. d. iii. Fuit autem temporibus Constanti. Sub hujus temporibus inventa est crux domini nostri Jesu Christi v non. mai, et baptizatus est Judas qui et Cyriacus."

[8] Ambrose *op. cit.*, 47, Theodoret and Sozomen, *loc. cit.* Seeck gives the incident as genuine.

in Eusebius, who lived in Palestine and who describes her pilgrimage and her building of churches there at considerable length. Newman's argument to the contrary in his *Essays on Miracles* is only an illustration of Gibbon's saying that " The silence of Eusebius and the Bordeaux pilgrim, which satisfies those who think, perplexes those who believe." [1]

There are early references to the finding of the cross; *e. g.,* by Cyril of Jerusalem within twenty-five years after Helena's pilgrimage. But this, at most, shows that the empress mother may have taken back with her from Jerusalem what purported to be relics of the true cross. This much of an historical basis for the legend can not, of course, be disproved.

3. *Later Legends of Constantine's Birth and Rise to Imperial Position*

Long after the time of Constantine, romances—they can hardly be called legends—sprang up about his mother, Helena, his father, Constantius, and about his own birth. The best known of these is that told by Geoffrey of Monmouth [2] and Pierre Langloft [3] and mentioned by Henry of Huntington,[4] Richard of Cirencester, Voragine, and others. This is to the effect that Constantius was sent to Britain by the Senate, and was made king there, and married Helena, daughter of Duke Coel, and that Constantine was thus the son of a British princess.[5]

---

[1] *Decline and Fall of the Roman Empire,* ed. Bury, vol. ii, p. 456 n. The "Bordeaux pilgrim" is the anonymous itinerary of a pilgrimage to the Holy Land in 333. *Cf.* Migne, P. L. vol. viii, col. 783 *et seq.*

[2] v, 6.   [3] i, pp. 66-67.   [4] i, 37.

[5] For a short sketch of this and other stories, and for other references, see Richardson's " Prolegomena" in *Nicene and Post Nicene Fathers,* Second Series, vol. i, *Eusebius,* p. 441. A story in Hakluyt's Voyages, 2 (1810), p. 34, attributes angelic virtues and superhuman

A still wilder romance is that edited by Heydenreich in 1879 from a fourteenth-century manuscript. It makes Helena a noble pilgrim to Rome who was violated by the emperor Constantius. The son she bore was named Constantine and after remarkable adventures was recognized by Constantius and made heir to the empire.[1] This legend had been traced back to a seventh or eighth century story, which was apparently widespread in two general types, Greek and Latin. The Greek story seems to be the earlier and simpler. It is to the effect that Constantius, on his return from a victory over the Sarmatians, had intercourse at an inn with a heathen maid, Helena, with whom he left imperial insignia. Later, seeking a worthy heir to the throne, in place of his legitimate but feeble-minded son, he sent out an official who stopped at the same inn. Helena's son attracted his attention, and also his displeasure, by mounting one of the royal horses, but when Helena told that her son was the offspring of the emperor and displayed the purple robe, the boy was taken to Rome. Here he was trained in the command of troops and, as Constantine, became the emperor's heir. The Latin form varied in many places from this story and added many embellishments, such as Helena's pilgrimage to Rome as a Christian and her violation on the journey by the emperor, his rearing of her son at Rome and the son's distinguished bearing in a tourney, and his recognition thereafter as the emperor's heir. A romantic episode of a plot by certain merchants at Rome also crept into the story. Constantine is represented as having been abducted by these merchants and palmed off upon

knowledge to this British princess Helena, and tells of her pilgrimage to Jerusalem, her death at Rome, and the preservation of her body in Venice.

[1] Heydenreich (ed), *Incerti Auctoris de Constantino Magno ejusque Matre Helena*, Leipsic, 1879.

the Greek emperor as a prince, so that he married his daughter to the young man, and sent the couple back to the West, in charge of the merchants, with rich presents. The merchants deserted the couple and made off with the booty. Constantine and his bride were rescued, and eventually came to their own.[1]

But these stories and others equally fanciful take us beyond the borderline of legends into the realm of pure romance. In many of them the use of Constantine's name, rather than that of any other notable, seems merely accidental; it is only the device of the story-teller to add interest to his tale.

---

[1] For a detailed study of these legends, *cf.* E. Heydenreich, "Constantin der Grosse in den Sagen des Mittelalters," *Deutsch. Zeitsch. f. Geschichtswissenschaft* ix (1893), pp. 1-27.

CHAPTER III

THE HOSTILE, PAGAN LEGEND OF CONSTANTINE

1. *Its Meagerness*

THE hostile, pagan legend of Constantine is comparatively slight, surprisingly so in view of the significance of his reign for paganism. One finds less than one would expect of the virulence and bitterness and wild imagination that characterized, for instance, the popular Catholic stories of Luther, or the southern version of Lincoln during the Civil War. This is in part explained by the destruction of pagan society and literature which the two centuries after Constantine brought about. Possibly pagan legends afloat at the time disappeared so completely that we can find no trace of them. Yet a number of pagan writings remain. Eutropius, the Scriptores Historiae Augustae, Sextus Aurelius Victor, Praxagoras Atheniensis, Julian, Libanius, Ammianus Marcellinus, Eunapius, are represented to-day by fragments considerable enough to insure some reference to most of the pagan stories about the first Christian emperor. Furthermore, the Christian writers themselves so often quote adversaries whom they refute that we can count upon them giving a clue to most legends invented or believed in by the opponents of their faith. Yet it is after all a meagre yield that a search of this literature reveals. The explanation must, therefore, in part be sought in the fact mentioned above that contemporary paganism scarcely realized that Constantine's reign marked the beginning of the end of the older religions.[1]

---

[1] Cf. *supra*, pp. 66-67.

2. *Emperor Julian's Version of Constantine*

The emperor Julian, the failure of whose effort to restore paganism and to discredit Christianity showed how far the revolution had gone and how permanent it promised to be, gives us our first glimpse of a pagan legend hostile to the great Constantine, his own uncle. In his formal writings and orations, which he was fond of composing, Julian generally observed the utmost of imperial decorum. He gave measured and stately praise to his predecessors, even those of his own family. In one of his orations, however, that on the Cynic Heracleion,[1] the imperial orator made a veiled attack upon Constantine. He tells a long and curious fable about a man who attained great wealth, partly by inheritance and partly by acquisitions which he made, " wishing to get rich by fair means or foul, for he cared little for the gods ". His success was due to a certain knack and to luck, rather than to any real ability. At his death there came massacre and confusion, a natural result of his unscrupulousness and of the example he set his sons.[2] The rich man of the parable is none other than Constantine; the parable itself nothing but a bitterly hostile interpretation of his reign.

In " The Caesars ", however, Julian made an open attack upon the first Christian emperor. This work is an attempt at light literature, a satire written for the Saturnalia in the winter following Julian's accession to the throne. It purports to describe a Saturnalian Symposium which Romulus gives in honor of the gods, and to which the Roman emperors and Alexander of Macedon are invited. The emperors are discussed as they are introduced at the

---

[1] " Πρὸς Ἡράκλειον Κυνικον," Oratio vii in Hertlein's edition of Julian's works.

[2] *Ibid.*, vol. i, p. 295.

banquet, and as they contend for the prize of merit, and again at the end of the book, as they are asked their several ambitions and assigned to their proper divine patrons. On each occasion Julian decries Constantine's character and deeds. His admission to the contest for the highest place among the emperors is challenged by Dionysos on the ground of his imperfections and his lack of zeal for the gods, and he is finally grudgingly admitted to the contest as a man " not lacking valor, but entirely mastered by pleasure and dissipation." [1]

In pleading his cause Constantine is embarrassed by consciousness of the pettiness of his achievements " for, if the truth must be told, of the tyrants he overcame, one was unwarlike and effeminate, and the other unfortunate and incapacitated by age, and both were hated by gods and men. As to the barbarians, his efforts against them were laughable, for he gave them tribute, and spent everything on pleasure." [2] After looking lovingly at the Moon, and after a vainglorious speech, Constantine was put to shame by Silenus, the clown of the symposium, in a joking comparison of his deeds to hothouse plants that were green for a little, but soon withered.[3] Later, after an exalted discourse by Marcus Aurelius, the hero of the booklet, on his desire " to be like the gods ", Hermes asked Constantine, " And what do you consider noble? " " To get great sums," he said, " and to spend them upon your own desires, and in gratifying those of your friends." [4]

At the close of " The Caesars ", as each emperor chooses his patron, occurs the following remarkable passage:

[1] Julian, *Opera*, Ed. Hertlein, i, p. 408, l. 6-16.

[2] *Ibid.*, i, p. 422, l. 7-15.

[3] *Ibid.*, i, p. 422, l. 15—p. 423, l. 18.

[4] *Ibid.*, i, p. 430, l. 4-8.

But Constantine, not finding among the gods a pattern for his life, perceiving Wantonness near, ran to her. And she, receiving him tenderly, and embracing him, covered him with flowery feminine robes, and led him to Perdition ('Ασωτία), so that he found Jesus, who turned around and harangued them all: " Whoever is a seducer, whoever is defiled with blood, whoever is under a curse and abominable, come hither boldly, for, washing him in this water, I will make him immediately pure, and if he falls again into the same faults, I will make him pure again when he beats his breast and knocks his head." And he very gladly staid with him and led his children from the assembly of the gods. But the demons, avengers of blood, tormented him, and them no less, administering justice for the blood of kindred; until Zeus, on account of Claudius and Constantine, made them desist.[1]

This is, of course, an echo of the old accusation that the Christians welcomed the scum of the earth into their fellowship and encouraged crime by the promise of forgiveness.[2] It may have been adapted, as a parody, from the words of Eusebius in his Oration in Praise of Constantine,[3] " as a gracious Saviour and physician of the soul, calls on the Greek and the Barbarian, the wise and the unlearned, the rich and the poor, the servant and his master, the subject and his lord, the ungodly, the profane, the ignorant, the evil-doer, the blasphemer, alike to draw near, and hasten to receive his heavenly cure."

If the passage in question be a genuine part of " The

---

[1] Julian, *Opera* Ed. Hertlein, i, 431, l. 7 *et seq.* The text of this passage is uncertain. Some of the best MSS. omit the reference to Jesus and his speech, others read " the son" instead of " Jesus." I have followed the reading adopted by Hertlein in the body of his text.

[2] For a philosophical discussion of this charge and of the potency of conversion in working a moral transformation, *cf.* Origen, *Contra Celsum,* Book iii, chapters 62-69.

[3] Chapter xi, 5.

Caesars," as I think it is, it expresses Julian's scorn of the Christian idea of conversion, and especially of the idea of the magic efficacy of baptism. Its implied denunciation of Constantine, "whoever is a seducer, whoever is defiled with blood, whoever is under a curse and abominable," is one of the bitterest attacks that has survived. The punishment of Constantine which followed when " the demons, avengers of blood, tormented him and them [Constantine's sons] no less, administering justice for the blood of kindred " serves to emphasize the mockery of the parody. In the whole passage the killing of relatives is emphasized ("defiled with blood ", " under a curse ", " avengers of blood ", " justice for the blood of kindred ") as the greatest crime of Constantine. This bloodguiltiness coupled with the Christian promise of ready forgiveness and purification through baptism, are the elements which gave rise to the pagan legend of Constantine's conversion. Owing to the satirical vein in which " The Caesars " is written, it is, perhaps, not safe to infer that Julian actually attributed Constantine's adoption of Christianity to the promise which was held out to him of pardon for a profligate career and for the murder of kindred. But, that Constantine was a reprobate and that his adoption of Christianity was at once a sign and a completion of his moral turpitude, is plainly the burden of Julian's story. This, whether original with Julian or current before he wrote, is a palpable distortion of Constantine's career. The execution of his son, Crispus, his wife, Fausta, and other near relatives, is proven, but there is no historical evidence that he sought in Christianity release from remorse for these executions within his family circle. Indeed, such a view is rendered impossible, not only by Constantine's postponement of baptism and his general attitude toward the church, but by the fact that he was committed to the new religion before these executions, and by many other considerations.

3. Development of the Pagan Legend of Constantine

Certain it is, however, that the legend soon became current among pagan writers that Constantine became a
Christian because that religion alone received him after the
execution of his son and wife, and promised him forgiveness for the great crimes he had committed. Count Zosimus, one of the best-known pagan writers of the fifth century, incorporated the story in his *Historia Nova*. He is a
partisan and not a first-rate authority as to the history of
the fourth century; his work is largely a mediocre compilation from Eunapius and Olympiodorus. These very considerations, however, make his narrative invaluable as a
source for the current pagan version of Constantine's relation to Christianity. He asserted that Constantine was a
pagan until late in his reign. Then, after he had executed
his son Crispus, an able and excellent young man, and his
wife Fausta, he was stricken with remorse and asked the
philosopher Sopater how he might obtain expiation. Sopater replied that for such crimes no expiation was possible.
An Egyptian priest, however, coming from Spain (probably to be identified with Hosius) held forth the promise of
forgiveness through repentance and baptism, and gained an
ascendancy over the emperor which could be accounted for
only by magic. Constantine turned therefore to Christianity for relief and became an adherent of that religion.[1]

[1] Zosimus, *Historia Nova,* ii, 29, 3. Stated also, and refuted in Sozomen, i, 5. Seeck (*Untergang d. antiken Welt*, iii, 213, 477) assumes a
common source from which the Epitome of Victor, the account of Zosimus, and that of John the Monk in the Vita S. Artemii (*AA.SS.*,
8th October) draw, which stated that Fausta charged Crispus with
offering her violence. Crispus was therefore executed; then Helena
persuaded Constantine that Fausta was the guilty one, and induced
him to kill her by an overheated bath. Then Constantine repented, the
heathen priests declared that his deeds could not be expiated, Christianity offered forgiveness, so he became a Christian.

This account, growing, possibly, out of Julian's satire and developed by an unknown writer whose work was used by Zosimus and others, received doubtless various embellishments. We find a much later writer, Codinus (about 1450), who in part used earlier sources now lost, touching up the story of Crispus' death with the statement that Constantine afterwards erected a statue of Crispus in pure silver with the inscription " My unjustly treated son ", and did further penance.[1]

This pagan legend had a comparatively small sphere of action for it was quickly denied by Christian writers [2] and received little credence in later Christian centuries. Sozomen's refutation of Zosimus is probably the best one. It is to the effect that Crispus " did not die till the twentieth year of his father's reign, and many laws framed with his sanction are still extant" as "can be proved by referring to the dates affixed." That Sopater, or Sosipater as he calls him, " could hardly have dwelt in Gaul, in Britain, or in the neighboring countries, in which, it is universally admitted, Constantine embraced the religion of the Christians, previous to his war with Maxentius, and prior to his return to Rome and Italy; and this is evidenced by the dates of the laws which he enacted in favor of religion." And furthermore a pagan philosopher would not be ignorant that Hercules was purified at Athens by the celebration of the mysteries of Ceres, after the murder of his children and of his guest, and that the Greeks [*i. e.,* pagans] held that purification from guilt of this nature could be obtained.

Evagrius' refutation of Sozimus is far inferior to that of Sozomen. He first refutes in a most quixotic fashion

---

[1] *De signo,* ed. Bekker, Bonn, 1843, pp. 62-63.

[2] *E. g.,* Sozomen, i, 5; Evagrius, iii, 40-41; Cyril, *adv. Julian,* book vii.

[3] Book iii, chaps. 40, 41.

I

Sozimus' declaration that Constantine imposed a new tax, *chrysargyrium,* upon merchants and others including public harlots, by citing instances of Constantine's liberality in the building of Constantinople and toward the army, adding " How thou canst then maintain that the same person could be so liberal, so munificent, and at the same time so paltry and sordid, as to impose so accursed a tax, I am utterly unable to comprehend." That is, Constantine spent so much money it is impossible to think of him levying such a tax! He proceeds to prove that Constantine did not execute either Fausta or Crispus by adducing tributes to Constantine's mildness by Eusebius, his Christian panegyrist, and by the passage in Eusebius' *Church History* [1] in which Crispus is commended, and these he clinches as follows : " Eusebius, who survived Constantine, would never have praised Crispus in these terms, if he had been destroyed by his father." To modern writers, this passage is merely one of the proofs that the *Church History* was written before the execution of Crispus in 326 and was not revised at this point. The contention that Crispus was not executed at all, is one of the instances in which the defense of Constantine overshot the mark.

It was the eventual supremacy of Christianity and the disappearance of paganism as a distinct power, perhaps more than the arguments of Christian historians, that suppressed this pagan legend of Constantine's conversion.

[1] x, 9.

CHAPTER IV

EARLY LEGENDS OF DIVINE AID, CONVERSION, AND
SAINTLINESS

1. *Pagan and Christian Legends of Divine Aid*

WHILE Constantine was yet a pagan, in Gaul, pagan orators extolled the peculiar solicitude of the gods for him. Reference has already been made to Eumenius' description, in his panegyric of 310, of the close tie between Constantine and Apollo.[1] Pagan orators also attributed divine aid to Constantine in his earlier Gallic wars, and in his Italian campaign against Maxentius.[2]

The panegyric of 313, to quote one of a dozen similar passages, describes Constantine as having access in the for-

---

[1] *Cf. supra*, p. 75 *et seq.*

[2] Seeck, *op. cit.*, i, 491, Richardson, in *Nicene and Post Nicene Fathers* (second series, vol. i), *Eusebius*, p. 490, and others assert that these pagan panegyrists, and the phrase "instinctu divinitatis" on the triumphal arch refer vaguely to the vision of the monogram. They overlook the fact that Eumenius described a peculiar intimacy between Constantine and heavenly powers in the panegyric of 310, before the campaign against Maxentius (*cf. supra*, p. 75).

Nazarius, the pagan panegyrist, also predicates divine protection for Constantine on several different occasions and uses the phrase "divino instinctu" with reference to an entirely different situation from that described by Lactantius. Nazarius, Paneg. (in *Paneg. Vet.*, No. X) chaps. 14-17, 19, 26; and *Incerti Paneg.*, probably by Nazarius, in 313 (in *Paneg. Vet.*, No. ix) chaps. 2 *et seq.*; in Migne, *P. L.*, viii, cols. 592-595 and cols. 655 *et seq.*, respectively. *Cf.*, also, *infra*, p. 132, n. 2, end.

mation of his plans to the supreme divine wisdom while
other mortals are left to the care of the lesser gods.[1] The
story of heavenly warriors seen marching in behalf of
Constantine before a decisive engagement is told first in a
pagan source, the panegyric of Nazarius at Rome in 321.
He tells how all Gaul talked of the vision of celestial armies,
led, in the opinion of the orator, by Constantius, flying to
the aid of Constantine at the beginning of the war with
Maxentius.[2] He believes that this celestial army has always been fighting for Constantine but is now for the first
time revealed to other men. His deduction is not that Constantine received a revelation of the Christian god, but that
after witnessing this heavenly apparition men have no rea-

---

[1] Quisnam te Deus, quae tam praesens hortata est majestas, ut omnibus fere tuis comitibus et ducibus non solum tacite mussantibus sed
etiam aperte timentibus, contra consilia hominum contra haruspicum
monita ipse per temet liberandae urbis tempus venisse sentires? Habes
profecto aliquod cum illa mente divina, Constantine, secretum, quae
delegata nostri diis minoribus cura, uni se tibi dignatur ostendere.
Incerti Paneg., in *Paneg. Vet.*, no. ix, chap. 2, in Migne, *P. L.*, viii, col.
655.

[2] In ore denique est omnium Galliarum, exercitus visos qui se divinitus missos prae se ferebant. Et quamvis coelestia sub oculos hominum venire non soleant, quod crassam et caligantem aciem simplex et
inconcreta substantia naturae tenuis eludat; illi tamen auxiliatores tui
aspici audirique patientes, ubi meritum tuum testificati sunt, mortalis
visus contagium refugerunt. Sed quaenam illa fuisse dicitur species?
qui vigor corporum? quae amplitudo membrorum? quae alacritas vol-
untatum? Flagrabant verendum nescio quid umbone corusci, et coeles-
tium armorum lux terribilis ardebat; tales enim venerant, ut tui cre-
derentur. Haec ipsorum sermocinatio, hoc inter audientes ferebant.
Constantinum petimus, Constantino imus auxilio. Habent profecto et
divina jactantiam, et coelestia quoque tangit ambitio. Illi coelo lapsi,
illi divinitus missi gloriabantur quod tibi militabant. Ducebat hos,
credo, Constantius pater, qui terrarum triumphis altiori tibi cesserat, di-
vinas expeditiones jam divus agitabat. Magnus hic quoque pietatis
tuae fructus, quod quamvis particeps coeli ampliorem se fieri gratia
tua senserit, et cujus munera in alios influere jam possent, in eum
ipsum tua munera redundarint. Nazarius, *Paneg.*, chap. 14, in Migne,
P. L., viii, cols. 592-593. *Cf. ibid.*, chap. 16, "Quis est hominum quin
opitulari tibi deum credat?" This in reference to Constantine's early
campaigns in Gaul against Ascarius and Regaisus.

son now to doubt the story that Castor and Pollux took visible part in battles of old.[1]

A somewhat similar occurrence is described as taking place in the decisive campaign against Licinius. But this time the narration comes from a Christian writer, none other than Eusebius, the " father of Church History ", and dates from a time shortly after Constantine's death, long after the favorite of the gods had cast in his fortunes with the Christians. Eusebius tells how detachments of Constantine's army were seen marching through cities at noonday, though in reality not a single soldier was present at the time. He adds, " This appearance was seen through the agency of divine and superior power." [2] Eusebius' account was written at least fifteen years later than Nazarius'; if there is any direct connection between the two the idea of miraculous manifestations in behalf of Constantine must have been suggested to the Christian by the pagan. No connection, however, can be proved, and it is more probable that each merely gave utterance to popular tales current in his own environment.

The historical fact seems to be that direct intervention of God or gods, angels or demons, figured in most stories of great events, whether narrated by Christians or pagans. Constantine's pagan eulogists in Gaul, or from Gaul, extolled the activities of the gods in his behalf at least as late as the year three hundred and twenty-one. As Constantine's victories turned to the benefit of the Christians, they, in turn, assumed a direct interposition of their God in his affairs. As we have seen, Constantine used Christian emblems as his luck tokens as early as the year three hundred and twelve, but he took no action that precipitated an open, violent break with

[1] *Op. cit.*, chaps. 19 and 15 respectively.

[2] *Life of Constantine*, ii, 6. For another instance of divine aid cited by Eusebius, *cf. ibid.*, i, 47.

paganism. The future was with the Christians. Though Nazarius could give the pagan interpretation of Constantine's marvelous victories as late as 321, the emperor himself became more and more definitely Christian in his ideas and in his policy. It was the Christian god who fought for him and gave him the victory.

This fact, if we may believe Eusebius, found recognition in Constantine's preparations for battle, as well as in the superstitious reverence paid to the Christian labarum. In the old days the Roman armies had their praetorian altars, their questioning of the omens before important actions, and their rituals for gaining the favor of the gods. Constantine's new faith sought precisely the same objects as did the old pagan worship, but it was directed toward another deity and found somewhat different expression. He is said, in preparation for battle, to have pitched a tabernacle of the cross outside the camp and to have retired to it to pray. "And making earnest supplications to God, he was always honored after a little with a manifestation of His presence. And then, as if moved by a divine impulse, he would rush from the tabernacle, and suddenly give orders to his army to move at once, without delay, and on the instant to draw their swords." [1] This last corresponds with what we know of his military tactics; a sudden, irresistible assault won most of his battles. The tabernacle outside the camp, and the mysterious consulting of the deity suggest forms of divining common among primitive and even more advanced peoples; it may well be regarded in this case as a Christian substitute for the pagan practice of consulting the omens. Some suggestion of details came perhaps from the narratives in the Old Testament about Moses and the tabernacle.[2] The comparison of Constan-

---

[1] Eusebius, *Life of Constantine*, ii, 12-14. For the labarum, *cf. supra,* pp. 106-107.

[2] *Cf.* especially, Ex. xxxiii, 7 *et seq.*

tine to Moses was, at least, common among Christian writers; Eusebius repeatedly likened him to a new Moses, in the events of his life and in his divine mission.[1] With no other Jewish or Christian worthy was he so frequently compared.

Sozomen embellished Eusebius' account with details about the tabernacle, and adds the significant statement, " From that period the Roman legions, which now were called by their number, provided each its own tent, with attendant priests and deacons." [2] The Roman army was now definitely under the auspices of the God of the Christians. Legends of the miraculous aid of pagan gods had given place altogether to legends of the aid which the true God had vouchsafed to Constantine. It is little wonder that in the fifth century many a pagan writer found that the facts of his own time gave little ground for belief in any divine aid whatever being granted to the Roman legions and attributed the decline of the Empire to its desertion of its old religion.

2. *Early Legends of Constantine's Miraculous Conversion*

It was inevitable that Constantine's support of Christianity would be attributed sooner or later to a miraculous conversion. This is shown by the different legends upon the subject which sprang up at various times from independent origins. The earliest, and the most famous, comes direct from Eusebius and perhaps ultimately from Constantine himself. We have seen that the former's eulogistic Life of the latter is full of references to continued supernatural revelations of God vouchsafed to the emperor. Most of these references are known only to those who have read

---

[1] *Cf. Church History*, ix, 9, 5; 8; *Life of Constantine*, i, 12.

[2] *Ecclesiastical History*, i, 8.

the *Life,* but the story of the first of these revelations is
familiar to all.   Eusebius not only gave a circumstantial account of the manifestation, but in this connection ascribes
the emperor's conversion to it.   The campaign, therefore,
which furnished pagan panegyrists with their last opportunity to picture the intervention of their gods on Constantine's behalf, became to a large part of the Christian world
not only its first opportunity to portray its God as the ar-
biter of victory, but the setting of a magnificent picture of
the miraculous conversion of the great emperor to its
faith.

The importance of this legend justifies its description in
the words of its earliest narrator.   Eusebius tells how Constantine was moved at the thought of the tyrannous oppres-
sion of Rome by Maxentius to attempt the overthrow of
the tyrant.   Knowing the insufficiency of his own military
forces " on account of the wicked and magical enchant-
ments which were so diligently practiced by the tyrant, he
sought divine assistance."   Pondering over the contrast between the prosperous career of his own father, who had
" honored the one Supreme God during his whole life," and
the unhappy end of those who had put their trust in other
gods, he " felt it incumbent on him to honor his father's
God alone."

Accordingly he called on him with earnest prayer and supplications that he would reveal to him who he was, and stretch
forth his right hand to help him in his present difficulties.
And while he was thus praying with fervent entreaty, a most
marvelous sign appeared to him from heaven, the account of
which it might have been hard to believe had it been related
by any other person.   But since the victorious emperor himself
long afterwards declared it to the writer of this history, when
he was honored with his acquaintance and society, and confirmed his statement by an oath, who could hesitate to

accredit the relation, especially since the testimony of after-time has established its truth? He said that about noon, when the day was already beginning to decline, he saw with his own eyes the trophy of a cross of light in the heavens, above the sun, and bearing the inscription, " Conquer by this." At this sight he himself was struck with amazement, and his whole army also, which followed him on this expedition and witnessed the miracle.

He said, moreover, that he doubted within himself what the import of this apparition could be. And while he continued to ponder and reason on its meaning, night suddenly came on; then in his sleep the Christ of God appeared to him with the same sign which he had seen in the heavens and commanded him to make a likeness of that sign which he had seen in the heavens, and to use it as a safeguard in all engagements with his enemies.

At dawn of day he arose, and communicated the marvel to his friends: and then, calling together the workers in gold and precious stones, he sat in the midst of them and described to them the figure of the sign he had seen, bidding them represent it in gold and precious stones. And this representation I myself have had an opportunity of seeing. . . . But at the time above specified, being struck with amazement at the extraordinary vision and resolving to worship no other God save him who had appeared to him, he sent for those who were acquainted with the mysteries of His doctrine, and enquired who that God was, and what was intended by the sign of the vision he had seen.

They affirmed that He was God, the only-begotten Son of the one and only God: that the sign which had appeared was the symbol of immortality, and the trophy of that victory over death which he had gained in time past when sojourning on earth. . . .

He determined thenceforth to devote himself to the reading of the Inspired writings.

Moreover, he made the priests of God his counselors, and

deemed it incumbent on him to honor God who had appeared to him with all devotion.[1]

That the miraculous mid-day vision of the monogram of Christ in the heaven is legend and not fact, admits of little doubt. [2] Eusebius, himself, in his *Church History,* written much nearer the time of the campaign against Maxentius, makes no mention of it, or indeed of any " conversion " of Constantine to Christianity. We have considerable contemporary material upon the campaign, and this episode finds no place in it. Lactantius seems altogether our best witness. His account is simple and straightforward. He tells that Constantine was directed in a dream to cause the heavenly sign to be put on the shields of his soldiers, that he did so, and won the battle. [3] There is here no reference to a supernatural vision at mid-day, nor to Constantine's being converted to Christianity.

There is ample evidence of Constantine's use of the monogram of Christ, but aside from the passage just quoted from Eusebius there is no evidence that this originated from a miraculous vision. The repetition of the story by his continuators adds no weight to his narrative. Monumental references, sculpture and inscriptions, from the time of Constantine, have been found in many places setting forth his triumph.[4] These give no portrayal of a heavenly vision. The wellnigh universal attitude of contemporary Christians was that God had given Constantine the victory, and that

[1] Eusebius, *Life of Constantine,* i, 26-32, Eng. trans. in *N. and P. N. F., Eusebius,* pp. 488-491.

[2] *Cf. supra,* p. 77 *et seq.*

[3] *De mortibus persecutorum,* 44.

[4] For a practically complete list and short descriptions of these, *cf.* E. Becker, " Protest gegen den Kaiserkult und Verherrlichung des Sieges am Pons Milvius in der altchristlichen Kunst der konstantinischen Zeit," in *Konstantin der Grosse u. s. Zeit,* ed. Dölger.

his enemies had perished in the Tiber, precisely as God had given Moses the victory by the overthrow of Pharaoh's host in the Red Sea. All contemporary comparisons of Constantine to scriptural heroes liken him to Moses. Had there been any heavenly vision, it is inconceivable that there should be no reference to it other than Eusebius', and it is inconceivable also that no one should have thought of comparing Constantine's vision with that of the Apostle Paul. How natural this would have been is shown by the fact that Theodoret in his continuation of Eusebius summarizes in that comparison his predecessor's account, speaking of Constantine as " a prince deserving of the highest praise, who like the divine apostle, was not called by man or through man, but by God." [1]

Eusebius tells his story under circumstances which make its truthfulness highly improbable, even were it not contradicted by other evidence. He tells it as a piece of news at least twenty-four years after the event. He writes about a wonder which occurred in the other half of the Roman Empire and which left no impression in that part of the Empire. He anticipates his reader's incredulity by admitting his own, and asserting that the emperor told him the story "long afterwards" in conversation and confirmed it with an oath. He was not himself intimate with the emperor and saw him only on rare occasions; it was therefore improbable that he possessed genuine inside information of the emperor's early career. [2] He has nothing to say of the cross in the heavens in his Oration in Praise of Constantine delivered in the presence of his hero and full of allusions to the revelations with which God had favored him, but describes it only after the emperor's death. [3] It is

[1] i, 2. For comparison of Constantine to Moses, *cf.* Eusebius, *Church History*, ix, 9; *Life of Constantine*, i, 12, 20, 38.

[2] *Cf. Life of Constantine*, iv, 33, 39.

[3] The allusion in chap. 6, 21, would apply to a dream as well as, or better than, to a heavenly apparition.

possible that Constantine, never averse to enhancing the
esteem in which churchmen, and others for that matter,
held him, in conversation with Eusebius late in his life may
have embellished the facts relating to his adoption of the
heavenly sign and may even have given the bishop hints
from which his later narration developed.[1]   Indeed, Constantine's own later memories of the campaign may have
developed by some process of auto-suggestion into something like a germ of Eusebius' story.

The legend thus given birth was embodied, usually with
a few additions or modifications, in all of Eusebius' continuators.[2]   Philostorgius makes the vision a greater celestial display than did his predecessors.   " As to the cause of the
conversion of Constantine from heathen superstition to the
Christian faith, Philostorgius, in conformity with all other
writers, ascribes it to his victory over Maxentius, in a battle
in which the sign of the cross was seen in the East, vast in
extent and lit up with glorious light, and surrounded on
each side by stars like a rainbow, symbolizing the form of
letters.   The letters, too, were in the Latin tongue and
formed these words, ' In hoc signo vinces '." [3]   The soldiers
are in most accounts represented as witnessing the phenomenon, and a document is in existence purporting to give
the testimony of an eye-witness in the army, St. Artemius,
afterwards a martyr.[4]   The *Vita S. Artemii,* however, is
a crude document from a later date and entitled to no credence in this connection.

In the West, where the occurrence is represented as having taken place, it seems to have been known to few, if any,
writers.   Gibbon remarked that " the advocates for the

---

[1] *Cf. supra,* p. 106.

[2] Sozomen, i, 3-4; Socrates, i, 2; Theodoret, who begins with the
Arian controversy, refers to it in i, 2; Philostorgius, i, 6.

[3] i, 6, as preserved by Photius.

[4] October (8th) 20th in *Acta Sanctorum.*

vision are unable to produce a single testimony from the
Fathers of the fourth and fifth centuries, who, in their voluminous writings, repeatedly celebrate the triumph of the
church and of Constantine." [1] This is certainly true so far
as Western writers are concerned. Jerome makes no mention of it whatever, nor does Augustine, though both writers
had ample occasion to do so.

Another, and quite contradictory legend of Constantine's
conversion, through the agency of Bishop Sylvester (314-
336), gained credence some generations later, and this Eusebian legend remained quite in the background until its competitor was thoroughly discredited at the beginning of modern times. It then became a favorite theme of ecclesiastical
writers and in the seventeenth and eighteenth centuries
became a common subject of discussion in doctoral dissertations and elsewhere. In modern times it has unquestionably been the most popular of all Constantinian legends.

It has this in common with the hostile, pagan legend of
Constantine's career, previously described, that it assumes
a sudden and radical conversion of the emperor to Christianity. We have already seen that such a violent break
with paganism, and such an instantaneous and complete acceptance of Christianity is not indicated by the historical
evidence. Zosimus, the pagan, and Eusebius, the Christian (in his *Life of Constantine*), exaggerated and intensi-
fied the process of conversion, the former to the discredit,
the latter to the glory of the champion of the Supreme
God.

3. *Legends of Saintliness*

Irrespective of the manner of his conversion, Constantine's support, and final adoption, of Christianity became,
for all writers belonging to that faith, the central fact of

[1] *Decline and Fall of the Roman Empire,* ed. Bury, vol. ii, p. 305, n.
52.

his reign, the fact that colored all his acts and determined his personal character. Thus arose the legend which pictured him as a man of extraordinary piety, of saintly life, and of constant communion with God. Eusebius represents him as rebuking a panegyrist for prophesying that he, the emperor, was destined to share the empire of the Son of God in the world to come.[1] It was, however, only such bold flights of fancy as this, from the lips of awkward orators, that drew the imperial rebuke. Eusebius himself is not much more restrained in the praise of his ruler's character and of his favor with God. We have already seen how one-sided and fulsome with praise of the emperor's piety are both his *Oration in Praise of Constantine* and his *Life of Constantine*. In both, the emperor was described as without faults or vices, living a life wholly devoted to the service of God. His palace, in which dark intrigues took place which led, justly or unjustly, to the execution of his son and his wife, was described as modeled into a church of God.[2] Though there are strong reasons for thinking that during most of his reign he maintained irregular connection with women which, if not frowned upon by contemporary society, was contrary to all the teachings of Christianity, he was spoken of as superior to sexual desire.[3] He was, in short, one " whose character is formed after the divine original of the Supreme Sovereign, and whose mind reflects, as in a mirror, the radiance of his virtues." [4]

Constantine is said to have built a church of the apostles in Constantinople as his own sepulchre, " anticipating with extraordinary fervor of faith that his body would share

[1] *Life of Constantine*, iv, 48.
[2] *Life of Constantine*, iv, 17.
[3] *Oration in Praise of Constantine*, v, 4. *Cf. supra*, p. 90 *et seq.*
[4] *Ibid. Cf.* also, *Life of Constantine*, i, 3.

their title with the apostles themselves, and that he should
thus even after death become the subject, with them, of the
devotions which should be performed to their honor in this
place. He accordingly caused twelve coffins to be set up
in this church, like sacred pillars in honor and memory of
the apostolic number, in the center of which his own was
placed. . . ." [1] If his motive in this be correctly represented, it confirms other facts which indicate that he appre-
ciated to the full the character which others gave him for
piety, and even exerted himself to heighten his reputation
in this respect.

The legend of Constantine's extraordinary Christian virtues was accepted in full by the continuators of the *Church
History* of his first biographer; Sozomen, Socrates, Theodoret, Philostorgius, Evagrius, and, with reservations, in
the West, by Jerome. The former add very little to our
historical knowledge of Constantine, but they continued and
amplified the legend of the emperor as an ideal Christian
saint. In the East, especially, where men knew best the
last phase of his life, 323-337, when he was more closely
and publicly allied with the church than he had been before
that, and where the fierceness of the Diocletian persecution
made his reign most grateful, imagination glorified his
memory. He came finally to be regarded as a saint in the
Eastern Church with a festal day observed annually with
great ceremony, at Constantinople, the city which he had
founded. [2] He was called *Isapostolos,* " equal with the
apostles," and according to Anna Comnena was counted
among the apostles. [3] Long before this, Theodoret had

[1] *Life of Constantine,* iv, 60. Told also by subsequent writers, some
of whom were familiar with the churches of Constantinople.

[2] *Cf. Acta Sanctorum,* on May 21, pp. 13, 14. The *Chronicon Alex-
andrium* tells of the ceremony.

[3] Alexias, 14, 8.

made the comparison by describing him as " a prince deserving of the highest praise, who, like the divine apostle, was not called by man or through man, but by God." [1]

In the West Constantine did not quite attain such high rank, but he was nevertheless held in high repute as a notable Christian and classed as a saint. An equestrian statue adorning the facades of some churches in parts of France has been held by many archaeologists to represent the first Christian emperor.[2] His writings have frequently been classed with those of the Latin fathers of the church.[3]

The significance of this legendary growth is twofold. In the first place it plainly served as a sedative for uneasiness over the entrance of such a potent personage as the emperor into the affairs of the church. Over against the pagan world there could be only jubilation over the possession of such a powerful patron. Over against objectionable Christians, too, the Catholic clergy were glad to have the leverage of imperial favor, and the disposal of public funds to the exclusion of schismatics. But in the theological controversies of the early third century even the Catholic church and clergy suffered from the access to the emperors ear enjoyed by their enemies; thence the consciousness, not often expressed, that there were disadvantages attached to an imperial protector. There are two remarkable passages in Eusebius' *Life of Constantine* which seem strangely out of place in the midst of his extravagant eulogy. In the first [4] he merely says that owing to the emperor's good nature and lack of discrimination offenses went unpunished,

---

[1] *Church History,* i, 2.

[2] See Richardson's bibliography on Constantine in *Nicene and Post Nicene Fathers,* Second Series, *Eusebius,* vol. i, p. 456 ff., under Arbellot, Audiat, Berthelé and Musset.

[3] So Migne, who gives them in his *P. L.,* vol. viii.

[4] iv, 31.

and " this state of things drew with it no small blame on
the general administration of the empire; whether justly
or not, let everyone form his own judgment; for myself
I only ask permission to record the fact." In the second,
he breaks through his self-imposed reserve,[1] and writes
bitterly, " In truth I can myself bear testimony to the griev-
ous evils which prevailed during these times; I mean the
violence of rapacious and unprincipled men, who preyed on
all classes of society alike, and the scandalous hypocrisy of
those who crept into the Church, and assumed the name and
character of Christians. His own benevolence and good-
ness of heart, the genuineness of his own faith, and his
truthfulness of character, induced the emperor to credit
the profession of these reputed Christians, who craftily preserved the semblance of sincere affection for his person.
The confidence he reposed in such men sometimes forced
him into conduct unworthy of himself, of which envy took
advantage to cloud in this respect the luster of his character.
These offenders, however, were soon overtaken by divine
chastisement." [2] The only consolation for the evils of imperial control lay in the thought of the Christian disposition of the ruler, and in the hope of divine chastisement of
evil advisers. Theodoret, a staunch Athanasian, also felt
called upon to explain how Constantine had been deceived
by malicious and designing bishops and had " sent so many
great men into exile." [3] He compared him to David, received by Ziba, and ends with the sigh " However, the emperor was translated from his earthly dominion to a better
kingdom."

[1] iv, 54-55.

[2] This, it seems to me, refers to episodes in the church such as the
case of Eustathius at Antioch, or some phase of the Arian controversy,
rather than to any graft in civil affairs, with which Eusebius does not
concern himself at all in the *Life of Constantine*.

[3] i, 33.

K

In the second place the glorification of Constantine as an ideal Christian witnesses the acceptance by the church of the transformation which, beginning earlier and continuing later, proceeded most rapidly in this generation. I refer to the transformation of the church into a rigidly organized, dogmatically defined organization linked to the state. Constantine as emperor was a powerful factor in this process. He and his successors, as emperors and under the aegis of his legendary sainthood, occupied a place in the church to which as mere individuals they were not entitled. Constantine, it will be remembered, was not baptized and did not even become a catechumen, until his last illness overtook him. Yet he sat with bishops in council, and directed the church in important matters. In this the church made a sacrifice of its independence from which, in the East, especially, it never recovered. There the emperor retained a place in the church corresponding somewhat with that which he had held in paganism as *pontifex maximus*. According to the story which Theodoret relates of the discipline imposed by Ambrose upon Theodosius the Great for the massacre at Thessalonica, it had been the custom at Constantinople before that episode for the emperor to remain with the priests inside the altar-rail after presenting his gift at the communion table. It remained for Ambrose to teach him the distinction made between clergy and laity in the West: " The priests alone, O emperor, are permitted to enter within the railing of the altar, others must not approach it. Retire then, and remain with the rest of the laity. A purple robe makes emperors, but not priests." [1] It is well known that the church as a whole rose to Ambrose's position and in the Middle Ages no longer stood in awe of emperors, and that the papacy rather delighted to

[1] Theodoret, v, 18.

teach them humility, but the joy of imperial recognition
was probably too fresh and too great in the time of Constantine for church officials to fully appreciate the distinction between temporal and spiritual power.   Instead, it for-
got the darker side of the emperor's life; it extolled his
piety and his favor with God and elaborated these themes
in eulogy and in legend.

4. *Legends of Church Building*

One token of Constantine's devotion to the church was
especially magnified by tradition.   In another connection a
list has been given of the church buildings whose erection
may with some assurance be assigned to Constantine or his
family.[1]   With the facts of Constantine's munificence in
church building, and the fact of his being the first Christian
emperor, as a suggestion to the imagination of subsequent
generations, legends of buildings erected by him sprang
up on every hand.   Local pride attributed edifices by the
hundred to him, with which he had no connection whatever.[2]

When buildings actually erected by him, or those connected with him, were either destroyed or rebuilt, as all of
them sooner or later were with the exception of the Senate's
triumphal arch to him, the unmarked site or the later
structure was still permanently connected with him.

The *Liber Pontificalis* gives under the life of Sylvester
an illustration of the legendary process.   Here an enormous
list is given of Constantine's benefactions to the various
Roman churches.   But almost no benefactions by emperors, or others, of later generations are reported under the
lives of subsequent popes.   A study of the list, and comparison with other parts of the *Liber Pontificalis* shows that

[1] *Cf. supra*, pp. 57-61.

[2] *Cf.* Lethaby in *Cambridge Medieval History*, i, pp. 609-611.

the author or authors conveniently bunched documentary and other information about subsequent donations under the name of the first Christian emperor and his assumed spiritual father. These were glorified at the expense of the fame of those who came after them. Undoubtedly the same process took place with reference to many buildings.[1]

5. *Legends of the Founding of Constantinople* [2]

A most curious illustration of the work of the legend-building imagination is afforded by the fanciful way in which the story of Constantine's piety became interwoven with almost every great deed of his. Among the many successes of Constantine one of the most notable was the new city which he built on the site of the ancient Byzantium. With characteristic ambition and energy he made it a monument such as no other Roman emperor ever left. A memorial of his victory over Licinius, on the edge of the recruiting fields of the hardiest soldiers of the Roman army, Thrace, Macedonia, Illyrica and Dalmatia, the location was so admirable that this new Rome, as the Emperor named it,[3] became the greatest city of the empire and the last surviving seat of its power. It was called Constantinople within the lifetime of its founder.[4]

[1] Gregorovius, *City of Rome*, i, p. 40 n.; ii, p. 161.
Curious mistakes of identity were also made; the equestrian statue of Marcus Aurelius at Rome was called Constantine the Great throughout the Middle Ages.

[2] J. Maurice, *Les Origines de Constantinople. Memoires du centenaire des antiquaires de France* (1904), pp. 284 *et seq.*, is one of the best recent works on the historical facts involved.

[3] Augustine, *City of God*, v, 25; Sozomen, ii, 2-3; *cf.* Ducange, *Constantinopolis Christiana*, i, 6.

[4] *Panegyr. Optatianus Porphyrius*, 4, 6; 18, 33; Eusebius, *Life of Constantine*, iv, 58; Eutropius, x, 8; Julian, *Orations*, i, p. 8; *Bordeaux Pilgrim*, in Migne. *P. L.*, viii, col. 783 *et seq., cf.* Ducange, *op. cit.*, i, 5. This name was doubtless used with the emperor's approval, and perhaps by his order, *cf.* Sozomen, *loc. cit.*, Socrates, i, 16.

Aside from legends exaggerating the magnificence of the new city and the desolation of Rome, stript to people and adorn it,[1] stories of providential omens developed about it. A law of Constantine's granting special favors to Constantinople declares the divine origin of its name.[2] The site also, was later said to have been indicated to the emperor by God. Sozomen tells how Constantine, resolved upon founding a city which should be called by his own name,

repaired to a plain at the foot of Troy, near the Hellespont, above the tomb of Ajax, where, it is said, the Achaians intrenched themselves when besieging Troy; and here he laid the plan of a large and beautiful city, and built the gates on an elevated spot of ground, whence they are still visible from the sea to mariners. But when he had advanced thus far, God appeared to him by night, and commanded him to seek another site for his city. Led by the hand of God, he arrived at Byzantium in Thrace, beyond Chalcedon in Bithynia, and here he was desired to build his city, and to render it worthy of the name of Constantine. In obedience to the command of God, he therefore enlarged the city, *etc.*[3]

[1] *Cf.* Gibbon, *Decline and Fall, etc.,* ed. Bury, ii, p. 151 *et seq.,* and references given there.

[2] " Pro commoditate urbis, quam aeterno nomine jubente deo donavimus, haec vobis privilegea credidimus deferenda," *etc. Cod. Theod.,* xiii, 5, 7, Dec. 1, 334.

[3] ii, 3. Seeck accepts this as historical, and calls the night revelation a dream. He holds it to be confirmed by *Cod. Theod.,* xiii, 5, 7, " pro commoditate urbis, quam aeterno nomine jubente deo donavimus," but it will be noticed that this claims divine sanction for the name, not the site, of the city. I am inclined to look upon the whole story as an instance of the prevalent tendency to assume supernatural guidance for an accomplished fact. It is of a piece with Sozomen's explanation of the continued prosperity of the city begun; " by the assistance of God, it became the most populous and wealthy of cities. I know of no cause to account for this extraordinary aggrandizement, unless it be the piety of the builder and of the inhabitants, and their compassion and liberality toward the poor." This of Constantinople !

Burckhardt, on the other hand, cites vague reports that Constantine

The story of divine guidance extended to the details of the laying out the city. Philostorgius [1] says "that when he went to mark the circuit of the city, he walked around it with a spear in his hand; and when his attendants thought he was measuring out too large a space, one of them came up to him and asked him, ' How far, O prince?' The emperor answered, ' Until he who goes before me comes to a stop '; by this answer clearly manifesting that some heavenly power was leading him on, and teaching him what to do."

Long afterwards, in the West, the heavenly guidance was represented as coming in a very different and more romantic way. Bishop Aldhelm [2] recites that when Constantine was in Byzantium once on a time, he had the following dream. A feeble old woman appeared to him in his sleep, and, at the command of Sylvester, bishop of Rome,

---

thought of making Sardica (now Sofia, Bulgaria), Thessalonica and Chalcedon his new capital. (*Zeit Constantins,* p. 436.) He also, in his effort to show that Constantine was not a Christian, argues that he allowed the establishment of pagan cults in New Rome, and that the eternal name which he gave the city was that of Flora, Anthusa, or some other pagan deity. (*Op. cit.,* pp. 440, 441, 382 *et passim.*) This is altogether unhistorical.

[1] ii, 9.

[2] About 690 A. D., in the *Liber de Laudibus Virginitatis,* in his *Opera,* ed. Giles, pp. 27 *et seq.,* 151 *et seq.,* in Migne, *P. L.,* lxxix. Friedrich, *Constantinische Schenkung,* pp. 137-138, thinks the narrative is an invention added to the Vita Silvestri with an object, namely, to exalt Sylvester and the Roman Church of which he was bishop, by having him give directions about the founding of Constantinople. England was the great ultramontane center of that time, and Friedrich's theory is plausible. Aldhelm gives it as one of a series of stories about Sylvester, evidently taken from a copy of the Vita. It is said to be in some MS. copies of this work. Nevertheless one is not certain that it is not merely the product of a fanciful imagination inserted in the *Vita Silvestri* after it had developed in England or elsewhere. Constantine's connection with their country was not forgotten by medieval Englishmen; they made a national hero out of him, and his legendary memory blossomed more grotesquely there than elsewhere. *Cf. supra,* p. 120.

he engaged in prayer. The old woman changed into a beautiful maiden. Constantine covered her with his mantle
and put his diadem on her head. His mother Helena said
to him " She will belong to you and will never die." When
he awoke from this dream Constantine was perplexed and
sought its solution in a week's fast. Sylvester then appeared again to him in a dream and told him that the old
woman was the city of Byzantium in which he then was,
old and almost in ruins. But Constantine was to mount
the horse on which at Rome in his baptismal robes he had
ridden to the graves of the Apostles, and take the labarum
with the sign of Christ in his right hand. He was then to
let the horse take its way and to drag the shaft of the spear
along the ground so as to make a furrow. Along this the
walls of the new city were to be built, which was to bear
his name, and to be the queen of all cities. Here his de-
scendants would reign forever. As soon as Constantine
awoke he went to work as directed. This version of the
founding of Constantinople is repeated with variations by
William of Malmesbury, by Ralph de Diceto and others,
and passed into general literature.[1]

[1] *Cf.* Richardson in *Nicene and Post Nicene Fathers, Eusebius*, p.
443. Legends about Constantine and the founding of Constantinople
abound throughout the Balkan Peninsula. *Cf.* Heydenreich, " Constantin der Grosse in den Sagen des Mittelalters," *Deutsch. Zeitsch. f.
Geschichtewissenschaft*, ix (1893). *Cf.* also, art. " Roumania " (Literature) in *Encyclopedia Britannica*.

CHAPTER V

LATER LEGENDS OF CONSTANTINE'S CONVERSION AND BAPTISM

1. *Legends of Constantine's Conversion by Helena; of his Baptism by Eusebius of Rome*

THE early, Eusebian legend of Constantine's conversion through a miraculous vision, as we have seen, long had only a limited scope. Various other legends sprang up in different places. One, embodied in apocryphal letters, ascribed his conversion to the influence of his mother, Helena, thus exactly reversing the more probable account which Eusebius gives of the religious relationship of the two persons.[1] Theodoret may have ascribed to her a part in the emperor's spiritual rebirth in a reference he makes to her as "most highly blessed in her maternal capacity, having been the means of producing that great light which she still nourished by religious counsels."[2]

In the main version of the legend of the finding of the true cross in the reign of Constantine, the emperor is said to have been instructed in the Christian faith and baptized by Eusebius, bishop of Rome (309 or 310).[3] In the earlier

---

[1] *Life of Constantine*, iii, 47.

[2] i, 18. Elsewhere, however, he says Constantine "like the divine apostle, was not called by man, nor through man, but by God," i, 2. This must refer to his miraculous conversion. It is possible that the allusion in i, 18, is merely to the fact that Helena gave birth to Constantine.

[3] For this legend *cf. supra*, pp. 116-119.

152

and more fragmentary allusions to the finding of the cross, such as those of Ambrose and Rufinus, this is not included, and after the eleventh century, but apparently never before then, the name of Sylvester (314-336) is sometimes substituted for that of his predecessor [1] the change being evidently a late correction. The baptism by Eusebius of Rome may have been invented originally as an orthodox correction for the historical baptism by Eusebius of Nicomedia, the Arian, made easily and perhaps ignorantly; and furthered perhaps by the fact that Eusebius of Nicomedia, during the last four years of his life, was bishop of Constantinople, the " capital " of the East as Rome was the " capital " of the West.[2] In other writings which refer to Constantine's baptism,the name of the priest who administered it is often omitted. It will be remembered that the name is not given in the account of Eusebius of Caesarea.[3] Some subsequent writers, either through ignorance, or from theological motives, also give no name. Gelasius of Cyzicus, bishop of Caesarea in Palestine (c. 475) merely affirms that Constantine was assuredly baptized, not by a heretic, but by an orthodox priest.[4]

2. *Earliest Version of Constantine's Leprosy*

When pious story tellers of the fifth and sixth centuries, who knew none of the historical facts of Constantine's baptism, turned their attention to his conversion they produced

---

[1] J. B. Aufhauser, *Konstantins Kreuzesvision*, p. 20, in *Ausgewählte Texte*. Cf. also the *Inventio sanctae crucis*, ed. from *Cod. Paris. lat.* 2769 (6th or 7th cent.) by A. Holder (Leipsic, 1889), p. 2.

[2] Dölger develops this point at length in "Die Taufe Konstantins u. i., Problems," in *Konstantin d. G. u. s. Zeit.*, pp. 417-422.

[3] *Cf. supra*, p. 87 *et seq.*

[4] Preserved in Photius, *Bibliotheca Cod.*, lxxxix, Migne, *P. G.*, vol. 103, col. 293; given also in Dölger, *op. cit.*, p. 395, n. 2.

most extraordinary narratives. The oldest of these which has been preserved is contained in a homily upon the baptism of Constantine from James of Sarug, in Mesopotamia (452-521 A. D.), a monophysite bishop who wrote in Syriac.[1] This is his version: Constantine from birth had a leprosy upon his forehead and lips, which no physicians could heal. After his succession to the throne he sent for "Chaldeans" from Babylon. These advised him to bathe in the blood of freshly-slain infants. The infants were collected, but the chief of the slaves and the mothers tried to prevent the death of the children. The chief of the slaves urged that Constantine would be cured by baptism, and cited him an instance of its miraculous effect. Through the appearance of an angel the advice of the slave carried the day. He ran to the church and asked the bishop to prepare for the baptism of the emperor. The bishop called his priests and they met the emperor, who came from his palace with his splendid retinue. The bishop first annointed Constantine with oil, that he might be cleansed, and that the leprosy might not defile the holy water. The leprosy fell from him; he praised God, and descended with the priest into the water. He was deterred from baptism, however, by a flame which burned above the water, until his crown was removed. Then, as a simple believer, he was baptized, and afterwards he partook of the eucharist.

It is improbable that James of Sarug manufactured the whole of his interesting narrative. Judging from the use he makes of it as a homily, it must have been in more or less general circulation in his part of the world. It has been shown by Duchesne[2] that such a version of Constantine's

---

[1] A. L. Frothingham, Jr., *L'omelia di Giacomo di Sarug sul battesimo di Costantino imperator, publicata, tradotta ed annotato,* first published in *Memorie della Accademia dei Lincei,* viii, 1882 (Rome, 1883). Frothingham thinks the homily was pronounced some time after 473.

[2] *Liber Pontificalis,* vol. i, p. cxvii *et seq.*

baptism could scarcely have originated in Byzantine or Egyptian sources, and that it must probably have developed in the region of Armenia and Syria.

3. *Armenian Version*

We meet this legend, later, in the History of Armenia which bears the name of Moses of Chorene (d. 489). This work is in reality a miscellany from various sources, and while it may have as its base a genuine writing of Moses of Chorene,[1] in its present form it can not date from earlier than the seventh or eighth century.[2] Its story of Constantine's conversion runs thus: Constantine, while still only a Caesar, turned defeat into victory by putting a cross upon his banners as had been suggested to him in a dream. Later, however, induced by his wife, Maximina, daughter of Diocletian, he persecuted the Christians and was therefore smitten with leprosy. Physicians and sorcerers, even one sent by Trdat, king of Armenia, did him no good. A priest commanded a bath in infants' blood, but at the last moment Constantine shrank from the execution of the children. As a reward for his tenderheartedness, he was, in a dream, commanded by the apostle to seek healing in baptism at the hands of Sylvester, bishop of Rome, then in hiding from persecution at Mt. Soracte. He did so, and received in-

[1] So F. N. Fink, *Die Litteraturen des Ostens,* Band vii, Abt. 2, p. 92. (Leipsic, 1907.)

[2] *Cf.* A. Carrière, *Nouvelles sources de Moise de Khoren,* Vienne, 1893; *Supplement,* Vienne, 1894; A. v. Gutschmid, Moses von Chorêne, in *Kleine Schriften,* iii; Paul Vetter, in *Literarische Rundschau,* 1893, p. 264, and *Theologische Quartalschrift,* 1894, p. 49; H. Gelzer, in *Realencyclopädie für prot. Theologie;* O. Bardenhewer, *Patrologie* (1910), p. 514.

Duchesne and others, on the basis of the older studies of Armenian literature, considered the version which Moses of Chorene gave as the oldest form of the legend of Constantine's baptism by Sylvester at Rome, and dated it about the middle of the fifth century. This theory must be rejected in the light of the more recent works referred to.

struction and baptism, became sound, and continued victorious over his enemies.

This version of the legend includes various points incorporated from sources outside of Armenia and Syria, such
as the adoption of the cross for use in battle owing to a
vision in a dream, and some items which were apparently
present only in versions quite a little later than the time of
Moses of Chorene, such as the use of the name of Sylvester,
bishop of Rome. But while it shows familiarity with the
later Sylvester legend, and has other foreign additions, it
may well represent a story current in Armenia long before
the seventh century, current possibly in the days of the real
Moses of Chorene.

There were also antecedents in earlier Syrian and
Armenian stories for legends of royal leprosy and its
cure by conversion.[1] The legend of Abgar, king of
Edessa, cured and converted by Addai (Thaddeus) in
the time of the apostles, was well known throughout the
east before the fourth century. It had many points of
resemblance with the legends of Constantine's conversion as told by James and by Moses above, and as ex-
panded later,[2] such as the affliction of leprosy, conversion
accompanied with healing, conversion of nobles and peo-

---

[1] This sort of story is, of course, confined to no particular country.
Conversions through miraculous cures are found among most peoples in
all ages. One of the most remarkable legendary cases is that of the
emperor Tiberius in a Latin document, dated by its translators in the
seventh or eighth century, which combines the stories of St. Veronica
and of Nathan's embassy. Here it is said, " Tiberius was ill, and full
of ulcers and fevers, and had nine kinds of leprosy." Fortunately,
when " he adored the image of the Lord," he was healed. *Cf. Ante-
Nicene Fathers*, vol. viii (New York, 1903), pp. 472–76. Leprosy was
then, even more than now. more common in the East than in the West,
but too much stress can not be laid on this, as the Scriptures may have
suggested the type of disease by the stories of Naaman and others.

[2] *Cf. infra*, p. 161 *et seq.*.

ple following that of the king, exhibition of a picture
(in the case of Abgar, the picture of Jesus), mention of
the king's mother, hostility toward the Jews, and the
statement of the king that no one would be compelled
to become a Christian.[1]

In Armenia, the reign of Trdat (Tiridates), a contemporary of Constantine, was a time of glorious national
revival. The Roman government then, and for some
time after, supported the Armenian kingdom against the
Persians, and the country had a breathing spell before
its final political dismemberment. This was also the
time of Gregory the Illuminator, the national saint, to
whom was assigned credit for the conversion, first of the
king and ultimately of the people, to Christianity.
Trdat and Gregory probably visited Constantine and
made an alliance with him.[2] Caesarea, in Palestine, the
seat of Eusebius the historian, became later the center to
which " nascent Armenian Christianity" was bound "in
the closest ties of intimacy."[3] It was only natural that
the rich growth of legends about Trdat and Gregory
should include Constantine in its scope. From the
Armenian point of view the conversion of Constantine
would be the central fact in his career and in the history
of the Roman Empire of that time. One of the legends
about the Armenian king ran to the effect that he persecuted the Christians, was transformed into a mere dumb
animal, and was restored and converted by Gregory.

---

[1] *Cf.* Eusebius: Church History, i, 13, also Ante-Nicene Fathers, vol.
vii, p. 704. The full legend is given in " *The Doctrine of Addai*,"
Syrian text and English translation by George Phillips, 1896. Phillips
accepts the legend as having an historical basis, impossible passages
being interpolations.

[2] The copy of the treaty, however, printed in Migne, P. L., viii, 579
—582 is spurious.

[3] Baynes, in *Eng. Hist. Rev.*, xxv, p. 626 *et seq.*

Other portions of the two legends, moreover, show similarity. It is therefore plausible that Armenians or neighboring Syrians of the fifth century should have imagined Constantine to have been healed of his disease and converted by the bishop of his capital city.[1]

4. *Connection of the Legend with Rome and Sylvester*

Among the differences noted between the legend told by James of Sarug and that given in Moses of Chorene was the fact that the former left all the actors, with the sole exception of Constantine, anonymous, while the latter specifically named Sylvester, bishop of Rome, as the one who instructed and baptized the emperor. This, and some other differences, are to be accounted for, I think, by the process, common to the growth of most legends, of rounding out and completing legendary details as the story goes from mouth to mouth. The date of the final redaction of Moses of Chorene's history makes it possible that the particulars referred to may

[1] The most reliable early Armenian historian of the fourth century is now held to be Faustus of Byzantium. (French trans. in Langlois; *Coll. d. hist. Arm.*, i, 201-310. German trans. by H. Gelzer). He confirms the existence of close relationship between the Roman Empire and Armenia. For discussion of Armenian historians, see Gelzer: "Die Anfänge der Armenischen Kirche," in *Berichte ü. die Verhand. d. kön. sächsischen Gesellschaft d. Wissenschaft, Phil. hist. Klasse*, xlvii, (1895) 109-174. *Cf.* also Bury ed. Gibbon, *Decline and Fall, etc.*, ii, pp. 563-565; and Baynes, "Rome and Armenia in the Fourth Century," *Eng. Hist. Rev.*, xxv (1910), pp. 625-643.

Duchesne contended strongly for the Armenian or Syrian source of the legend, and though at points his arguments are not now conclusive, I believe that his main proposition, while by no means absolutely proven, is the best solution of the question.

Dölger, in *Constantin d. Grosse u. s. Zeit*, pp. 406-407, *et passim*, is unwilling to accept this theory as proven, and attempts to prove the Roman origin of at least many of the elements of the story. *Cf. infra*, p. 159.

have been incorporated in it from some copy of the
Vita Silvestri described below.   On the other hand, it
is entirely possible that these statements originated in
Armenia or Syria and that Moses of Chorene represents
the line by which they entered into the *Vita Silvestri*.
In either case the process was probably essentially the
same. But why was the baptism located at Rome, and
the priest who administered it identified with Sylvester?

One answer to this question attributes the development, if not the origin of the legend itself, to Rome.
Dölger thinks that Eusebius of Nicomedia, who really
baptized the emperor, becoming later bishop of Constantinople, was vaguely spoken of as performing the
rite at New Rome, or the capital city. In the West,
this phrase suggested Rome, and, as there was a Eusebius who was bishop of Rome in Constantine's time, the
Roman Eusebius was substituted for the other, and the
legend in this form proved satisfactory.[1]   Later, when it
became justly recognized that the pontificate of Eusebius came too early to admit of his having converted
Constantine, Sylvester, his second successor, was put in
his place. The legend of the finding of the true cross,
in one form of which Constantine is said to have been
instructed and baptized by Eusebius of Rome, is cited as
at once the proof of this theory and perhaps the vehicle
by which the change was made.[2]

The latter legend, however, did not contain a statement of the Roman baptism in its earliest forms,[3] probably not till after the legend of Constantine's leprosy and

---

[1] This position lends itself to the support of the theory that the legend
of the Roman baptism arose in the West, and possibly at Rome; a theory
which seems to me untenable.

[2] *Op. cit.*, 416–422.

[3] *Eg.* in Ambrose and Rufinus, *cf. supra*, p. 119.

cure had come into existence. Moreover, if as we have seen,[1] in the story of the finding of the cross, Eusebius continued to hold the place of honor until the eleventh century, this legend surely cannot be construed as explaining the belief that Sylvester converted Constantine. Nor can the fact that a baptistery connected with the Lateran church at Rome which Constantine erected was later spoken of as the place of his baptism explain the Sylvester legend, for this identification of the place of the act, also, developed too late. No direct evidence, and no important indirect evidence of this legendary identification can be adduced, earlier than the statement in the *Liber Pontificalis* of Constantine's leprosy, baptism and cure by Sylvester, which at the earliest, would not take us back beyond the year five hundred and thirty.[2] It was in any case an absurdity to represent Constantine as being baptized in a building which he had erected in gratitude for the cure effected in his baptism. Legend-makers, however, starting with the supposition that he had been baptized at Rome, might easily overlook the inconsistency of this identification of the spot, or, as they probably thought of it, of the baptismal font; but to start with the identification of the building and then develop this legend about it would have been too severe a tax upon the imagination.[3]

The locating of the baptism at Rome, therefore, and the connecting of Sylvester with it, can best be explained, if at all, on general considerations. Rome was the ancient and most famous capital of the empire, and Sylvester was bishop there during most of Constantine's reign (*i. e.*, 314–336); thus the location of the rite at Rome

[1] *Cf. supra*, p. 153.

[2] *Cf.* ed. Duchesne, vol. i, pp. 78, 172–174.

[3] *Cf. infra*, pp. 161–165 *et seq.*

and its connection with Sylvester, whether effected in the West, or as seems more probable, in the East, was inevitable.

Thus Constantine's conversion entered into the stream of one of the most extraordinary legendary developments in the church, that centering in Pope Sylvester and preserved in the *Vita Silvestri*.[1]

5. *Vita Silvestri.*

The best known version of the *Vita* (or *Gesta*) *Silvestri* is the Latin one given by Mombritius.[2] The following synopsis is based chiefly on his account:

[1] The chief apocryphal or legendary account of Sylvester is a long and fairly well defined story variously referred to as Liber Silvestri, Vita Silvestri, or Gesta Silvestri, not to be confused with the "vita" or gesta Silvestri in the *Liber Pontificalis*, though this refers to incidents in the story and evidently accepts it.

The legend has been preserved in three languages, as follows: Latin, Mombritius, *Sanctuarium, sive Vitae collectae ex codibus MSS.* (Milan, about 1479, and in a recent edition in Paris in 1910) vol. ii, folio 279 *et seq.*, and ii, 508–531, respectively. *Cf.* also *Analecta Bollandiana*, vol. i, p. 613 *et seq.*, by P. Ch de Smedt. *Cf.* also *Catalogus Cod. hagiographicorum bibl. reg. Bruxellensis*, pp. 5, 119; L. Surius, *De probatis sanctorum vitis* (Coloniae Agrippinae, 1618), in volume on December, Dec. 31, pp. 368–375, a translation from the Greek of Simeon Metaphrastes. Greek, Combefis: *Illustrium Christi martyrum triumphi* Paris, 1659), p. 254 *et seq.*, from MS. Mazarinaeus, No. 513, Bibliothèque Nationale. Another Greek text is in MS. Cod., Paris, 1448, folio 1. Syriac: Land, *Anedocta syriaca*, vol. iii, pp. 46–76, from MS. Brit. Mus. Add., 17202, of the sixth or seventh century. Another version in MS. 12174, Brit. Mus. *Cf.* Duchesne: *op. cit.*, i, cix. Later repetitions of the legend in Byzantine authors are: Ephraem (in the 14th century), ed. Bekker (Bonn, 1840), pp. 21–25; ed. Migne, *P. G.*, vol. 143, cols. 1–380. Cedrenus: *Compendium of History*, ed. Bekker (Bonn, 1838–9), vol. i, pp. 472–520; ed. Migne, *P. G.*, vols. 121–122. Zonaras: *Chronicle*, ed. Migne, *P. G.*, vol. 134, cols. 1097–1118. Glycas: *Chronicle*, ed. Bekker (Bonn, 1836), pp. 460–468, ed. Migne, *P. G.*, vol. 158, cols. 1–958. For a short summary of Glycas' version, see Richardson's "Prolegomena," in *Nicene and Post Nicene Fathers, Eusebius*, p. 442, and for comments on the other authors, pp. 453–454.

[2] See Duchesne: *Liber Pontificalis*, i, pp. cx, cxii, cxiii. Synopsis

A dedicatory letter says the accompanying life of Sylvester was taken from the Acts of the bishops of the principal sees which, together with many Acts of martyrs, were written by Eusebius of Caesarea but not included in his Church History.[1] Sylvester, a young Roman, entertained Timothy of Antioch fleeing from persecution. Timothy, however, was executed and Sylvester threatened with death, which he escaped by a miracle. Bishop Miltiades (or Melchiades) raised him to the priesthood, and at the death of that bishop, Sylvester, against his own will, was made his successor. After a long description of his administration, a visit of Euphronius from Antioch to Rome is narrated, at whose advice Sylvester changes the garb of his higher clergy, calls the days of the week by numerals instead of names, and makes Sundays and Thursdays festival days, with Wednesdays, Fridays and Saturdays fast days. Next, Sylvester frees Rome from a dragon dwelling under the Tarpeian rock. (This episode is omitted by Mombritius).

Then begins the legend of Constantine's conversion. At the instance of his wife, Maximiana, daughter of Diocletian (a gross historical error), Constantine begins a persecution from which Sylvester took refuge in Mt. Syraptim (probably an imaginary name, but afterwards identified with Soracte). The emperor is afflicted with leprosy, to cure which pagan priests order a bath in the blood of infants. Infants are collected for the purpose, but Constantine relents and sends them home. In the

given here is, in part, taken from this work, vol. i, p. cx, *et seq.* For a short summary in English, see Hodgkin: *Italy and her Invaders*, vii, p. 135 *et seq.*

[1] The version published by Surius (p. 368) does not connect Eusebius' name with the story, leaving it anonymous. *Cf.* Friedrich: *Constantinische Schenkung*, pp. 79-81.

night Saints Peter and Paul appear to him, promising in reward for this, healing from his disease if he will seek out Sylvester and do as he says.   In the presence of the emperor Sylvester shows likenesses of Peter and Paul, who are identified by Constantine as the persons who appeared to him.   Then follows Christian instruction, a solemn fast, and baptism of the emperor in the baths of the Lateran palace.   As Constantine enters the water, a bright light is seen, and he is healed.

Constantine then directs that Christ be worshipped everywhere, that blasphemy be punished, and that churches be built with public money.   There is, however, to be no new church organized without sanction from the bishop of Rome, and all other bishops are to be subject to him.   The eighth day after his baptism Constantine commenced the building of the basilica of a church of St. Peter; the next day he began to build a church in the Lateran palace, and issued edicts for the conversion of pagans.   The Senate still remaining pagan, Constantine called an assembly in the Ulpian Basilica, at which he urged conversion on the strength of his experience, but says he will not compel men to change.

Helena, then living in Bithynia with her grandchildren, writes approving Constantine's renunciation of paganism, but urging him to adopt Judaism.   The matter is decided on August 13, 315 (die iduum aug. Constantino Aug. IV et Licinio Aug. IV cons.) by a disputation before Constantine and Helena at Rome between Sylvester and twelve Jewish rabbis.   The pope successfully upholds the doctrine of the trinity and the incarnation (stating the latter so as to exclude monothelitism so thoroughly that some have detected a trace of Nestorianism).   The rabbis then show the power of their religion by whispering the name of Jehovah into the ear of a bull, killing him instantly, to the astonishment of all. Sylvester, however, raises the bull from the dead by whispering the name of Christ. Helena and great multitudes with her are thereby converted to Christianity.

The Latin versions of the legend end with two episodes, the miraculous founding of Constantinople, and the finding of the true cross, which are not found in the Greek versions.[1]

6. *Development of the Sylvester-Constantine Legend*

To understand the history of this legend it is necessary to distinguish between the legend itself (*i. e.* the bare story that Constantine was a persecutor afflicted with leprosy, and was converted, baptized and cured through the agency of Sylvester at Rome) and differences of detail or variations in the different written versions. The legend, in its bare outlines, as we have seen, probably originated, not at Rome, but on the outskirts of the Empire, among people familiar only with the great names and events of Roman history. Aside from considerations already mentioned, the scarcity and confusion of the topographical references it contains, its slow growth in popularity at Rome, and the stress it lays upon the visit and advice of Timotheus, indicate a foreign, probably an Eastern source, and possibly a source as far east as Syria and Armenia.

[1] The best discussions of this Sylvester legend are: Döllinger, *Papstfabeln des Mittelalters*, 1863, ed. by Friedrich with notes, 1890. (Döllinger's further work on the legend was left unfinished at his death). Frothingham, ed. *Homily on the Baptism of Constantine*, (L'Omelia di Giacomo di Sarug) in *Memorie della r. Accademia dei Lincei, classe di scienze morale*, vol. viii, 1883). J. Langen, *Geschichte d. röm. Kirche* (1885), ii, p. 195 *et seq.* Abbé Duchesne, ed. *Liber Pontificalis*, vol. i (1886), pp. cvii-cxx. F. J. Dölger, " Die Taufe Konstantins u. i. Probleme," in *Konstantin d. Grosse u. s. Zeit* (1913), pp. 377-381, 394-426. Friedrich, *Die Constantinische Schenkung*, Nördlingen, 1889.

At Rome itself this legend first comes to light in references to books containing it, in the time of Pope Symmachus (498–514). There is no record in writers, historians, poets, orators, official documents, liturgies or inscriptions, of any *local* Roman tradition connected with the legend until the eighth century. In fact, there is no trace of the legend in extant inscriptions or monuments in Rome before the tenth century.[1] It came into vogue very slowly and does not seem to have prevailed there until after it had been taken up in many other places. These considerations show both the lack of any historical ground whatever for the legend, and its non-Roman source.[1]

However the legend of Constantine's leprosy and cure started, it got to Rome by the end of the fifth century, possibly earlier. Duchesne thinks it may have been put into literary Latin by some eastern monk such as Dionysius Exiguus.[3] The legend and a book containing it are referred to in the forged documents brought out by ecclesiastical controversies centering about Symmachus (bishop of Rome 498–514). The pseudo [?] *Decretum Gelasii P. de recipiendis et non recipiendis libris* (c. A. D. 501, Duchesne: after 533, Friedrich)[4] says that the anonymous Acts of Sylvester are read by many of the orthodox in Rome and many churches elsewhere and does not condemn the practice.[5] The pseudo *Consti-*

---

[1] Duchesne, *op. cit.*, i, pp. cxiii, cxvi.   [2] *Ibid.*, i, cxvi.

[3] *Op. cit.*, vol. i, p. cxiii *et seq.*

[4] *Cf.* Mirbt, in Real Encyk. vi, 475, for the view that it was merely revised and interpolated under Pope Hormisdas (514–523).

[5] Actus beati Silvestri, apostolicae sedis praesulis, licet ejus qui conscripsit nomen ignoretur, a multis tamen in urbe Romana catholicis legi cognovimus, et pro antiquo usu multae hoc immitantur ecclesiae, * * * beati Pauli apostoli praecedat sententia: 'omnia probate, quod bonum est venete.'

tutum Silvestri (about 501–508, Duchesne, *op. cit.*, i, cxxxiv) mentions briefly the leprosy and cure. The pseudo *Gesta Liberii*, from the same time, refers to an old work which told of Constantine's leprosy and his cure by Silvester.[1]

These references show that there must have been in existence at Rome by the beginning of the sixth century, a book containing the legend of Constantine's leprosy and baptism by Silvester, that it was not associated with the name of any author, did not enjoy a great vogue, for its truthfulness was questioned, and it needed apology. It certainly must have contradicted not only the facts of history, but current opinion as well.[2]

It is probable that toward the end of the sixth century this anonymous *Vita Silvestri* was touched up by an enthusiast for the primacy of Rome who saw the opportunity it afforded. It was not made much of, so far as we know, in the middle of the century after the stormy days of Symmachus. But by the time of Gregory the Great[3] we find a version with added details, represented in the text published by Mombritius.[4]

[1] "Hoc cum [Liberius] legisset ex libro antiquo, edoctus a libro Silvestri episcopi Romanorum, et quod publice praedicaret, in nomine Jesu Christi a lepra mundatum fuisse per Silvestrum Constantium patrum Constantius." In emphasizing the antiquity of the *Liber* or *Vita Silvestri*, and commending it by affirming its use by Liberius, the forger probably gives himself away, as is pointed out by Duchesne, for in the *Vita Silvestri* Liberius is unhistorically represented as already dead. The forger, however, may have had another text of the *Vita Silvestri*.

[2] Friedrich thinks that this form is represented by the version published by Surius, which is also anonymous. *Cf. Constantinische Schenkung*, p. 81. For fuller discussion of the above, see Friedrich, 70–81, and Duchesne, *op. cit.*, i, pp. cxiii–cxv.

[3] Pope, 590–604.

[4] Friedrich, *op. cit.*, p. 81 *et seq.* Duchesne had, before Friedrich, given approximately the same date, but looked upon the version in Monbritius as the earliest extant form from which other versions were derived.

Here the whole legend of Sylvester purports to be taken from a collection of twenty books of Acts of martyrs and bishops of the principal sees written by Eusebius of Caesarea. The name of Sylvester's mother is given, the speech of Sylvester against the Jewish rabbis has a decided turn against the monothelites, and Constantine is made to emphasize the primacy of Rome, while Sylvester is not represented as making the trip to Constantinople, of which the version in Surius tells.

This version had apparently become known in the east before the end of the sixth century, where in fact the *Vita Silvestri* generally became popular, and seems even to have displaced the original eastern form of the legend of Constantine's conversion.[1]

Friedrich has discussed an interesting passage in the correspondence of Gregory the Great, in which Eulogius, patriarch of Constantinople, wrote to him asking for a copy of the collection of the Acts of martyrs and bishops written by Eusebius. Gregory replied[2] that he had not known whether they had been collected or not, and that he had not been able to find in his archives or in libraries at Rome any except a few scattered Acts in one manuscript volume. If he found any such collection as was asked for he would send it. Friederich's interpretation of all this is that the *Vita Silvestri*, worked over in the interest of the primacy of the bishop of Rome, and validated by a preface claiming Eusebian authorship, had

---

[1] Duchesne, *op. cit.*, i, p. cxx. One of the Greek renderings even retained the part of the preface stating that the work was translated from the Greek into Latin, thus putting his Greek into the embarrassing position of being a translation from the Greek. This process reminds one of a form of the *Autobiography of Benjamin Franklin*, which wa translated into French, then this was translated into English, and this back into French. *Cf.* Macdonald's ed., p. xv.

[2] July, 598.

fallen into the hands of Eulogius at Alexandria. He thereupon put Rome into an embarrassing situation by writing for the collection of the Acts by Eusebius from which the *Vita Silvestri* in its preface claimed to come. Gregory, in reply, could only imply that the other Acts were scattered and lost, and asks for time.[1] Though these inferences are in places overdrawn, the passage certainly looks like a reference to the preface of the *Vita Silvestri*, and the implications must, in the main, be accepted.

After Gregory, the Vita Silvestri was called to the attention of pilgrims in a Roman pilgrim book composed under Pope Honorius (625-638).[2] The *Liber Pontificalis* incorporated in its life of Silvester his flight to Syraptim, the baptism of Constantine by Silvester, and Constantine's cure from leprosy.[3]

A legend combining two such personages as Constantine and Sylvester could hardly remain entirely stereotyped. The manuscripts which have come down in different languages show considerable variation of incident. Friedrich has argued with considerable plausibility that the legend of the miraculous founding of Constantinople through a dream in which Sylvester figured, came into it not long before the end of the seventh century.[4] Not many generations after this a modified version of it appeared as the *Constitutum Constantini*, that famous document which containing the Donation of Constantine was destined to play a great part in the history of Europe.

---

[1] Friedrich, *op. cit.*, pp. 83-87.

[2] Döllinger, *Papstfabeln*, ed. Friedrich, p. 65.

[3] Ed. Duchesne, i, 170 *et seq.*, ed. Mommsen, p. 47 *et seq.* The former assigns the original compilation, including Sylvester's life, to a time not later than Boniface II (530-532). Mommsen, following Waitz, puts the work in the beginning of the seventh century.

[4] *Cf. supra*, pp. 150-151.

General Acceptance of the Sylvester-Constantine Legend

The emergence of the legend of Constantine's Roman baptism brought medieval writers face to face with a question of fact, for the knowledge of the earlier accounts of his baptism at Nicomedia had been preserved, not only in the east by Eusebius and his followers, but in the west by Ambrose, Jerome, Prosper and other authors. The former legend was also contradicted by the widely used *Historia Tripartita*, compiled from the three continuators of Eusebius' *Church History*. Confronted with this problem of historical criticism, the middle ages followed its natural bent and accepted the one which appealed most to its imagination and its orthodoxy. A few writers such as Isidore (636), Fredegar (658), Frehulf (c. 840), Hermann the Lame of Reichenau (c. 1050) and Marianus Scotus (c. 1050), held to the older version of Constantine's baptism, in some cases apparently not knowing the later legend, in some cases rejecting it. The Sylvester legend, however, won the field almost completely and in the later middle ages was seldom disputed.[1] It furnished one of the arguments at the second council of Nicea for the use of

---

[1] Döllinger in *Papstfabeln*, ed. Friedrich, pp. 65–72 *et passim*, collected a long and almost exhaustive list of references in medieval writers. Duchesne: *Liber Pontificalis*, i, p. cxv, gives a number of references in both Latin and Greek authors, concluding that after the commencement of the ninth century all the Byzantine chroniclers admit the Sylvester legend more or less completely.

In the West, at the end of the sixth century, Gregory of Tours, *Hist. Franc.*, ii, 31, described the baptism of Clovis; "procedit novus Constantinus ad lavacrum, deleturus leprae veteris morbum, sordentesque maculas gestorum antiquorum recenti latice deleturus." The Anglo-Saxon bishop Aldhelm, at the end of the seventh century, is thought to have introduced the Constantine-Sylvester legend into general literature in his "*Liber de laudibus virginitatis*," chap. 25 (*cf.* Friedrich: *Con. Schenck.*, pp. 136–137). The subsequent list includes Bede, Ado, Pope Paul I., Pope Hadrian I., Odericus Vitalis, Hugo of

images.[1] Even in modern times it was incorporated in
Baronius' *Annals*[2] and taken seriously by Severinus
Binius, whose comments are printed as notes in Migne's
Patrologia.[3]

The whole story of Constantine's leprosy, cure and
baptism gained graphical representation in a series of
ten pictures in the oratory of St. Sylvester adjoining the
church of Quattro Incoronati at Rome. These probably
date from the restoration of the oratory in the thirteenth
century, but may possibly be earlier.[4] Later tradition
located the spot where Constantine and Sylvester were
supposed to have parted.[5] It even influenced geography
by identifying the Syraptis or Syraptim of the legend
with the real Soracte and changing the latter name to
the former. Here, very fittingly, a monastery of St.
Sylvester was built in the eighth century.[6]

The reasons for the popularity and well-nigh universal
acceptance of this incredible legend are revealed by
writers who discussed it before it had entirely displaced
the historical facts. It seemed unthinkable to them that
Constantine should have presided at the Council of

Fleury, Ratramnus, Bonizo, Martinus Polonus, all the papal chroniclers
after the Liber Pontificalis, Nicholas I., Leo IX., collections of canon
law by Anselm, Deusdedit, Gratian (in the palea, or later insertions),
the Kaiserchronik, Konrad von Wurzburg, Wolfram von Eschenbach,
and others.

[1] *Cf.* the first Act of the Council.

[2] Under A. D. 324, the date to which the Roman baptism of Constantine was commonly assigned, No. 32 *et seq.*

[3] Latin series, viii, col. 795 *et seq.*

[4] *Cf.* Arch. della Societa rom. di St. patria xii (1889), p. 162. Mancini: *Vita di Lorenzo Valla*, p. 154, note.

[5] Gregorovius: *Rome in the Middle Ages*, ii, p. 361.

[6] Duchesne: *Op. cit.*, i, p. cxix. Hartmann, *Italien im Mittelalter*,
Band ii, Hälíte ii (Gotha, 1903), p. 222.

Nicea, while still unbaptized. His baptism by Eusebius
of Nicomedia, a bishop tainted with Arian heresy, seemed
either improbable, or the result of a relapse, not a natural consequence of his conversion from paganism.
Moreover, how could such a hero have postponed baptism to his death-bed? The existence in Rome of a
baptistery bearing the name of Constantine helped to
localize the place of his baptism. Moreover, the miraculous element, instead of being an obstacle to acceptance
of the legend, was fairly demanded by the great significance of Constantine's conversion. The absence of early
accounts corroborating it proved only that Constantius
had tried to suppress the story of his father's leprosy.[1]

Men of the Middle Ages were skilled harmonizers of
discrepancies. Their treatment of this legend shows
that their business was not primarily to discover facts,
but to systematize accepted teachings. They, therefore,
after accepting the legend, easily disposed of the historical Nicomedian baptism. The *Gesta Liberii* smoothed
over difficulties by postulating another emperor of the
same name. Bishop Bonizo rejected the Eusebian baptism as an error growing out of confusion of fact and
name, due to the belief that Bishop Eusebius of Rome
had instructed Constantine in Christianity. Ekkehard,
about 1100, accepted both baptisms and harmonized
them by the supposition that Constantine after his Roman
conversion had fallen into the Arian heresy which led to
his having the rite repeated by Eusebius of Nicomedia.
This happy device seems to have been generally followed. The problem was then, from all points of view,
solved to the satisfaction of the medieval mind, and the
wonderful legend of Sylvester's relations to Constantine

---

[1] So Severinus Binius. *Cf*. Migne, *op. cit.*, col. 800.

had clear sailing.   It still forms a part of the Roman
Breviary, to be read on Sylvester's Day, the last day of
the calendar year.[1]

So the piety of the early Middle Ages found one of its
most characteristic utterances.   The wonder-working
power of God was displayed in the miracles of the Sylvester legend, and the triumph of the Christian faith set
forth in glowing colors.   But the hero of these divine
manifestations was no longer Constantine, as in the
earlier legend, it was Sylvester, the priest and bishop.
The emperor took his true place as a mere creature of
this world, the object of God's wrath for his sins, and
the beneficiary of a priest's intercession when his heart
had relented.   The kingdom of heaven, the kingdom of
priests, had come into its own ; its glory and its power
made the Roman emperor himself but a miserable, help-
less mortal in comparison with the divine power dis-
pensed by the Pope, the head of the church.

[1] The revision of the *Breviary* recently completed consists merely of
a rearrangement of parts and makes little or no change in the contents.
Cf., also, under Nov. 9 and 18.

PART THREE

THE SPURIOUS CONSTANTINE: THE CONSTITUM CONSTANTINI

CHAPTER I

1. *The Constitutum Constantini and the Donation it Contains*

WE have seen that medieval legends of Constantine, especially that of his healing and baptism by Sylvester, existed in a more or less fluid state. This is true of all legends, indeed of all narratives in manuscript, and in a lesser degree even of some printed documents. Variations in printed books, however, are slight and unimportant, compared to those which develop in oral or manuscript tradition. Many medieval writers, in copying narratives of others, treated them as an author would treat his own notes, omitting, adding and changing at will. Not a little of our modern sense of accuracy and truth in historical work is due to the mechanical invention of printing.[1] When, therefore, a form of this particular legend emerged in which Constantine donated land, privileges and authority to Sylvester as bishop of Rome and pope, one scarcely knows whether to call it forgery or romance. Since the author of it, however, evidently took pains to give what he thought to be a legal form and specified grants which would really be of use and importance in his time, it is not too harsh a judgment to pronounce his words a forgery, such as even the laws of his own time severely condemned.[2]

[1] For this suggestion I am indebted to Professor J. H. Robinson.

[2] The motive of the forgery will be discussed below, p. 211 *et seq.* Cf. also *supra*, pp. 12-13.

The Donation of Constantine (or *Constitutum Constantini*, to use the original title of the entire document)[1] extended the legend of the *Vita Silvestri* by expanding and developing the emperor's expression of piety and gratitude for his miraculous cure from leprosy. It is a document of some 3,000 words, purporting to be from the hand of Constantine, running in his name, and with the imperial subscription. It contains the usual divisions of a medieval legal charter: "invocation of the Trinity," "title of the emperor," "address" to Sylvester, "greeting," then a rather long "proem" in the form of a confession of faith and a long "narration" of Constantine's leprosy and cure by baptism as contained in the *Vita Silvestri*. After this comes the "disposition" reciting that since Sylvester is the vicar of the Son of God, he and his successors shall have enlarged power and greater than imperial honor, and shall have primacy over the sees of Antioch, Alexandria, Constantinople (which even according to the legend itself had not yet been founded, much less made an episcopal see) and Jerusalem, and over the whole Church universal. Constantine proclaims that he had built the Lateran church and baptistry and makes it "head and summit of all churches." He has built and ornamented the churches of St. Peter and of St. Paul, and to supply their lamps with oil has given them endowments in Judea, Greece, Asia, Thrace, Africa, Italy and various islands. He gives to Sylvester, "chief priest and pope of the whole Roman world," the Lateran palace, his own diadem or crown, frigium, collar, purple

---

[1] Strictly speaking, the phrase "Donation of Constantine" applies only to one section of the document, that in which the grant of privileges and possessions (the *donatio*) is made, but the use of the phrase as synonomous with the whole document, the *Constitutum Constantini*, is so general that it is almost unavoidable.

robe, scarlet tunic and all imperial insignia, scepter, seals, etc. To the Roman clergy he gives the privileges of Roman nobility, the special right to use white coverings for their horses and other distinctive trappings, and, with the pope, the sole control over entrance to priestly honors. He deeds his golden diadem again to the pope, but since it would not be fitting for him to wear this over his priest's headdress which he wears to the honor of St. Peter, the emperor proposes to honor him otherwise, notably by himself acting as his squire and leading his horse. That the pope's office may not be cheapened, Constantine again gives him his own palace, also "the city of Rome and all the provinces, places and states of Italy, and the western regions," (i. e. Lombardy, Venetia, and Istria). He furthermore transfers his own empire to Byzantium, because "where the primate of priests and the head of the Christian religion is established by the heavenly emperor, it is not right than an earthly emperor should have authority there."

Then follows the "sanction" solemnly confirming this donation forever, and threatening any scoffer, oddly enough, with no physical penalty, but that he would encounter the opposition of SS. "Peter and Paul in this life and the future, and go down to be burned in the lowest hell with the devil and all the impious." The "corroboration" follows, affirming the signatures by the emperor's own hands (sic), etc.; then follow the final "protocol" with the fact of signature indicated, and the benediction, and the date (in an imaginary and impossible consulship).[1]

[1] For full text of the document, cf. Appendix ii. The text I have used is by far the best one published, from the oldest MS. and splendidly edited, namely, that of Zeumer, in the *Festgabe für Rudolf von Gneist*, Berlin, 1888. This text is also given in Haller, *Die Quellen zur Geschichte der Entstehung des Kirchenstaats* (1907,) p. 241 *et seq.* There

M

2. *Acceptance and Use of the "Donation"*

Such was the document which was incorporated in the Pseudo-Isidorean Decretals when this collection was made in the middle of the ninth century.[1] It was cited as authoritative by Ado of Vienne and Hincmar of Rheims. It was accepted in the collections of canon law by Anselm of Lucca, Cardinal Deusdedit, the so-called Ivo of Chartres, Hugo of Fleury, *de regia potestate et ecclesiastica dignitate* and, though omitted by Gratian himself, was soon put in his collection under the "palea." It was referred to as valid or used by many popes, including Leo IX, Urban II, Eugenius III, Innocent III, Gregory IX,[2] Innocent IV, Nicholas III, Boniface VIII, and John XXII. Though Gregory VII apparently did not use it, his representative, Peter Damiani, did so. It may possibly have been in the mind of other popes who exacted oaths from prospective emperors that they would preserve all the rights and possessions granted by all previous emperors to the see of St. Peter, and may also have influenced Hadrian IV.[3]

It was accepted by the great majority of the writers of the Middle Ages, lawyers, historical writers, theologians. Even those who regretted it or denied its validity, and

are also texts in Grauert, *Die Konstantinische Schenkung* and Friedrich, *ditto:* Hinschius, ed., *Decretales pseudo-Isidorianae* (1863), pp. 249–254; and elsewhere. For English translation, see E. F. Henderson, *Select Historical Documents of the Middle Ages*, pp. 319–329.

[1] Between 847 and 853, Hinschius, *op. cit.*, p. cci.

[2] For extended account of its use by Gregory IX., see Gregorovius, *Rome in the Middle Ages*, vol. v, pp. 185–186.

[3] For most of these and some other references, *cf.* Döllinger, *op. cit.*, chapter on "Constant. Schenkung." *Cf.* also *Codex diplomaticus dominii temporalis s. sedis*, I (Rome, 1861), p. 434, for Clement V in 1310. *Cf.*, also *Catholic Encyclopedia*, Art. "Donation of Constantine."

opposed extension of papal power, for the most part did not question its genuineness. Dante's feelings on the subject were very strong, but he had no thought of denying that the donation had taken place.[1] A difficulty was involved for the theologians, for they held that the Pope's power was derived from God, not from man, that he was the successor of St. Peter, and primate of the Church from the very first. Their talent for harmonizing was highly developed, however, and where they thought of the inconsistency involved they solved it by postulating that Constantine's donation was merely a restitution of what other emperors and ecclesiastics had usurped from Rome.

The Greeks took the Constitutum Constantini into their canon law in spite of its exaltation of the bishop of Rome. This was more than counter-balanced in the eyes of their clergy by the fact that the second ecumenical council granted the bishop of Constantinople privileges similar to those enjoyed by the bishop of Rome. Thus they were not averse to increasing the latter. Theodore Balsamon (about 1169) put it in his collection. Matthew Blastares (about 1335) followed his example, and it is found in many other places. It was used by Greek writers and even by the emperors.[2]

The legend was carried to the second degree in a popular story that when the donation was made an angel's voice was heard saying, "Alas, alas, this day has poison been dropt into the Church of God."[3] This saga

---

[1] Cf. *Inferno V.*, 115 *et seq.; De Monarchia*, Bcok iii., 10.

[2] Cf. Döllinger, *op. cit.*, pp. 76-78. It also entered through this channel into the Russian church. *Ibid.*, p. 120.

[3] Reginald Pecock, *Repressor of overmuch Blaming of the Clergy* (printed *Rerum britannicarum medii aevi scriptores* no. 19, London, 1860), p. 351.

evidently grew up among the Ghibellines of Germany, who saw only evil in the donation. Walther von der Vogelweide gave eloquent expression to it: " King Constantine, he gave so much—as I will tell you—to the see of Rome, spear, cross and crown. Then the angels cried, ' Alas! alas! alas! Christendom before stood crowned with righteousness. Now is poison fallen on her, and her honey turned to gall. Woe to the world henceforth!' To-day the princes all live in honor, only their highest one languishes, so works the priests' election. Be that denounced to thee, sweet God! The priests would upset laymen's rights: true is the angel's prophecy."[1]

It was maintained by some, however, that it was the devil's voice that was heard, trying to deceive the Church and lamenting his own defeat. Since the event which was lamented was entirely imaginary it will never be possible to tell which writers had the best ears for distinguishing sounds from the other world.

The part that the Donation of Constantine played in the Middle Ages has been strongly emphasized by many modern historians. The late E. M. Hodgkin[2] wrote that "the story of the Donation of Constantine fully told would almost be the history of the Middle Ages. * * * Under Innocent III, Gregory IX, Boniface III, it is constantly appealed to in support of their pretensions to rule as feudal suzerains over Italy, over the Holy Roman Empire, over the world. For three centuries after this, the canonists take the Donation as the basis of their airy edifices."

---

[1] Pfeiffer-Bartsch ed., 85, 164. Cited in Taylor, *Medieval Mind*, ii, p. 35. For reference to the saying in other writers, *cf*. Döllinger, *op. cit.*, p 113 *et seq.*

[2] Italy and her Invaders, vii, p. 135 *et seq*. Quoted in part, *supra*, p. 13.

This far overshoots the mark. The Donation undoubtedly influenced the formation of politico-ecclesiastical theories and furnished ammunition to church authorities for argument. But even in the realm of theory and argument it was not decisive. Supporters of secular authority who admitted its genuineness extracted its sting by many ingenious devices. Some maintained that it was not valid because Constantine was a heretic, baptized or rebaptizéd in the Arian heresy.[1] Some argued that it was invalid because the empire could not be alienated without the consent of the people, which was lacking.[2] Some limited the validity of the gift to Constantine's own reign. Others turned the Donation into a back-handed blow at the papacy by the fact that it represented papal primacy and honor as derived, not from God, but from the emperor.[3] On the other hand, it is significant that the first pope who gained a clear conception of the full possibilities of the papacy, the man whose genius and soaring aspirations forecast both Innocent III and the Vatican Council of 1870, Gregory VII,

---

[1] *Cf.* Geroch of Reichersperg, *Expos. in Psalm. lxiv.*

[2] Jacob Almain, of Paris, and Peter Dubois, also held it illegal. John Quidort, of Paris (1306) took a similar position. Schard, *Syntagma variorum autorum de jurisdictione imperiali, etc.* (Basle, 1566, 1609), p. 208 *et seq.*, publishes extracts from many medieval writers. *Cf.* also, Döllinger, *op. cit.*, 105.

[3] Wyclif: "Certum videtur ex chronicis quod non a Christo sed a Caesare Constantino Romanus episcopus accepit vel usurpavit potestatem." Wilkins, *Concil.* iii., 344. So also the Waldenses: "Nam error Waldensium fuit, successoribus apostolorum, scilicet papae et praelatis ecclesiasticis, dominium in temporalibus repugnare, nec eis licere habere divitias temporales. Unde ecclesiam Dei, et successores apostolorum et veros praelatos ecclesiae Dei, durasse dicunt tantum usque ad Sylvestrum papam, a quo donatione facta ecclesiae per Constantinum imperatorem, dicunt incepisse Romanam ecclesiam, quae modo secundum ipsos non est Dei ecclesia." John of Paris (c. 1322) in Schard, *op. cit.*, p. 113.

so far as we know made no use whatever of the supposed deed of Constantine.

Moreover, all these theories of canon law had less influence upon the actual course of events and growth of institutions than is often supposed. Claims might be supported by appeal to precedents and documents, but these were seldom their real source. They sprang rather out of aggressive ambition, and usually met that measure of success which their promoters had material or moral power to enforce. Claims realized embodied themselves in canon law and political theory. Here, as usual, theory generally followed after fact and practical program. The Protestant reformers and subsequent Protestant writers, holding the papacy to be a usurpation, exaggerated the importance of extreme papal claims. When they attacked it on moral grounds they greatly overstated the role of forged documents in attaining the fulfilment of these claims.

"Historical research does not support those who say that the dignity of the papacy was only acquired in the Middle Ages by violent usurpations, bold plundering and forged deeds. Such have not been wanting, indeed, but they have never been determinative nor decisive. The tree was of such sturdy and purposeful growth that we can say that even without forged deeds, bold usurpation, etc., its development would scarcely have been different. Here, as usual, the actual development of internal control and power over others came first, and then followed theories, legal maxims, occasionally also forgeries, in order to give existing power a biblical and historical foundation. These theories then, later, redounded to the advantage of the existing power, but they did not found that power."[1]

---

[1] A. Harnack, in a lecture delivered in the Aula of Berlin University

Aside from the manner of its origin and from its influence in advancing the desires of the papacy, the significance of the Donation of Constantine lies chiefly in the illustration it affords of the contrast between the church of the eighth and ninth century and that of the fourth and fifth. In the earlier days Christian imagination created an image of a pious emperor converted by miracle from paganism and doing everything for the glory of God. In the later time, this was not enough. There must be supremacy for the ecclesiastical organization, there must be lands, government, and an imperial crown to dispose of for the bishop of Rome. This had become by the eighth century one of the aspirations of medieval Christianity. "The tendency of the whole age, as expressed in the forgery, ran toward wedding the spiritual power to worldly advantages, rights, and honors."[1]

in 1911, and published in his "*Aus Wissenschaft und Leben*" (1911), vol. i, p. 214. The same view is held by Taylor, *Medieval Mind*, ii, 273-274.

[1] Hartmann, *Geschichte Italiens im Mittelalter*, Bd. ii, Hfte. ii (Gotha, 1903), p. 225.

CHAPTER II

1. *Stages of Criticism*

THE work of historical criticism in showing up the Donation of Constantine is one of the most interesting chapters in the intellectual development of Europe. In mere bulk it looms very large, larger even than the importance of the document itself would seem to warrant; many books, and short general discussions without end. The intellectual class in Europe as well as the uneducated, passed through a long stage of uncritical acceptance of it. Europe, as a whole, held to it in the face of the sharp, though limited and ineffectual, criticism it received in the twelfth century. This criticism was renewed and enlarged in the fourteenth century. But it was only the attack made upon it in the renaissance of the fifteenth century, culminating in Valla's work, that definitely exposed the forgery. The Protestant controversy concerning it, and the modern scientific, historical criticism of the last fifty years, make up the last chapters in its study.

2. *Criticism of the "Donation" previous to the Fifteenth Century*

The general acceptance of the document by the Middle Ages, in most cases without question of its genuineness, illustrates as much as any one thing could, the relative lack of the historical, scientific spirit in that stage of European thought. Consider what the Germans call the

184

shrieking inconsistencies of the whole forgery; Constantine giving the Roman see primacy over that of Constantinople, before that city was founded, even according to the account in the Sylvester Legend itself, the application of such terms as satraps to Roman officials, the purported transfer of the government of Italy to the pope in the face of the actual continuation of imperial rule without any reference to papal authority and without any records of such a change. Consider also that the Middle Ages all the time possessed, in Jerome, the *Historia Tripartita*, and elsewhere, material for refuting the forgery and the whole story of Constantine's conversion through cure of leprosy, and for getting at the approximate facts about Constantine and Sylvester. Surely we have here an illustration of the fact that truth does not always prevail. Its prevalence, even in the long run of centuries, depends on whether men really seek for it, and on what training and facilities they have in ascertaining it and its traces. In the absence of sound historical criticism, in the face of a strong tendency to harmonize inconsistencies, historical truth gives way in a single generation to wild and absurd legends.

But the so-called Middle Ages were not altogether uncritical. Our first notice of an attack comes in a document whose genuineness is open to serious doubt. If we may believe this, Otto III, at the end of the twelfth century, in a grant to Sylvester II, stigmatized the Donation of Constantine as a fiction.[1] But the twelfth

---

[1] Haec sunt enim commenta ab illi ipsis inventa, quibus Joanness diaconus, cognomento digitorum mutius (mutilus) praeceptum aureis litteris scripsit, sub titulo magni Constantini longa mendacii tempora finxit. * * * " Spretis ergo commenticiis praeceptis et imaginarii scriptis, ex nostra liberalitate sancto Petro donamus quae nostra sunt, non sibi quae sua sunt veluti nostra conferimus." (Baronius Ann. 1191, No. 57).

century brought on a fire of criticism. In the pontificate of Paschal II, in 1104 or 1105, the Donation was
used as authority by some Roman nobles for their possession, under the papacy, of a certain castle. Their
opponents, the monks of a Sabine Benedictine monastery,
Farfa, contested that at most the document could give
only spiritual power, that the pope had no earthly authority such as was claimed, and that if Constantine had
really made any such grant of land the popes would not
afterwards have sought any land for buildings, or confirmation of the emperor's name, as they did.[1]

Some fifty years later Wetzel, of the party of Arnold
of Brescia, discredited the whole legend of Sylvester and
the Donation. The Arnoldists were naturally led by
their peculiar views of the papacy to level their guns
against this buttress of its temporal power. Wetzel's
contention was that Constantine was already a Christian
before he met Sylvester. In support of this he cited the
Historia Tripartita as well as an apocryphal document,
which he found in the pseudo-Isidore and in Gratian, in
which Miltiades or Melchiades, the predecessor of Sylvester, refers to Constantine's great munificence to the
Roman Church.[2] Looking to Emperor Frederic I for
coöperation against the political power of the pope,
Wetzel wrote (1152) that the lying and heretical fable
was so thoroughly exposed that scholars could not defend it before the uneducated, and that the pope and

---

[1] *Cf.* Döllinger, *op. cit.*, p. 94; Mancini, *Lorenzo Valla*, pp. 145, 146.
For this monastery, *cf.* Kehr, *Regesta Pontificum Romanorum :* Italia
Pontificia, vol. ii, Latium, pp. 57-69. *Cf.* also *Historiae ·Farfens.* in
Pertz, *M. G. H.* xiii, 571 ; the Registrum of Farfa published by J.
Georgi and U. Balzani ; and Gregorius Catinensis in *Scriptores Rerum
Italicarum*, vol. ii, part ii, p. 637.

[2] Printed in Migne, *P. L.*, viii, col. 566 *et seq.*

cardinals hardly showed themselves for shame.[1] Unfortunately for the Arnoldists, however, the emperor had as little use for them as did the pope. Wetzel failed to produce any effect upon him, and in the overthrow of the Arnoldists, their arguments, also, for all practical purposes, fell to the ground.[2]

Echoes of this and other attacks, however, continued to reverberate through Europe. Gottfried of Bamberg in his Pantheon, dedicated to Urban III (in 1186) treats of the matter in the form of a debate between a papist who defends the Donation on the ground that God would not permit errors on such weighty points, and an imperialist who cited the continuance of imperial rule and the division of the whole empire between Constantine's sons. Leopold of Bebenburg shortly after made the same point as this hypothetical Ghibelline.[3] But neither Gottfried or Leopold gave his own conclusion.

Marsiglio of Padua, early in the fourteenth century, is also not quite clear about the matter. He speaks of the document as though he had no faith in it, but welcomes it as proving that the pope's worldly pomp and claims of universal power came not from Christ, but from the emperor. For this last proposition he cites no less authority than St. Bernard who declared that the popes in their worldly pomp were successors of Constantine, not of St. Peter.[4] Marsiglo's attitude was not an uncommon

---

[1] Martène and Durand, *Amplissima collectio veterum scriptorum*, ii (1724), 556, epist. 384.

[2] *Cf.* Döllinger, *op. cit.*, pp. 94-95. He is inclined elsewhere to place the historical criticism of the Donation in the twelfth century on a higher level than that of the fifteenth.

[3] Schard, *op. cit.*, p. 391.

[4] *Defensor pacis*, Dictio II., cap. ii. Reprinted in Schard, *op. cit.* Marsiglio's "Tractatus de translatione imperii," also touches upon Constantine's removal to the East and his supposed grant to the Pope. *Cf.* extract in Schard, *op. cit.*, pp. 154-156.

one in his time, he merely gave it the increased weight
of his authority.   Thereafter, he seems to have been a
model whom other writers copied, sometimes almost
verbally in their statement of the case. [1]

The contest in France against papal control kept the
question from entirely dying out for nearly a hundred
years longer.   It remained for the time of the Renaissance, however, to effectively establish the fact that the
Donation was a forgery unworthy of any credence.
Early writers had the acumen to arrive at or near this
conclusion, but not until the middle of the fifteenth century was the equipment of historical critics and the state
of public opinion such as to drive in and fasten down
this achievement of awakening thought.

3. *The Contest Against the Papacy in the Fifteenth Century.   Cusanus' Criticism of the " Donation "*

For more than a hundred years, that is, during the
so-called Babylonian Captivity of the papacy, and the era
of reforming councils, the papacy had been under fire.
The rising sentiment of nationality, especially in northern Europe, had been seeking intermittently to curb the
financial and the political ambitions of the Roman See.
Reformers had been seeking for some way of ending and
of preventing scandals in the church due to the confusion
into which the Roman See had fallen.   They had studied
the history of the church, they had examined, in ancient
authors, the historical grounds upon which the claims of
the papacy rested.   They had come to the council of Constance, not only with the purpose of ending the Great
Schism, but with ideas about the reorganization of
ecclesiastical government and revising the relations of

[1] *Cf.* Radulphus (Pandulfus, or Landulph) de Columna, in his " de
translatione imperii," dated by Schard, 1324 A. D., and printed by
him, *op. cit.*, p. 161.

church and state. The former purpose had been accomplished at Constance, but the realization of the latter, though to some extent accepted in principle there, had been postponed.

The Council of Basle, assembled in 1431, was the agency through which the discontented element sought to effect the desired changes and reorganization. A strong and able group there contended vigorously for a system of conciliar government for the church, instead of papal absolutism. When the pope, Eugenius IV, ordered the dissolution of the council, the latter bore itself resolutely, reasserted the principles of Constance, and continued its work.

Among the leaders in the championship of the council was Nicholas of Cues, better known as Nicholas of Cusa, or Cusanus (1401–1461), deacon of St. Florinus of Coblenz. Educated in the school of the Brethren of the Common Life at Deventer, and later at the University of Padua, he was both a pious churchman and one of the greatest, if not the greatest, ecclesiastical scholar of his generation. He wrote (1433) for the direction of the council, and in justification of its platform, a work which he called "*De concordantia catholica*," and which presented "the ideal of the reforming party, a united Church reformed in soul and body, in priesthood and laity, by the action of a Council which should represent on earth the eternal unity of Heaven." [1]

Cusanus later left the Council of Basle, as Cardinal Cesarini and others did, discouraged at the outcome of events and at the extremes to which the council went,

[1] M. Creighton, *A History of the Papacy during the Period of the Reformation*, vol. ii (1882), p. 232. For an appreciation of Nicholas of Cusa, *cf.* Janssen, *History of the German People at the Close of the Middle Ages*, Eng. trans. (London, 1908) i, 2–5.

and "labored to restore the Papal power which once he had striven to upset." [1]   He became one of the most effective representatives of Eugenius in the restoration of papal authority and influence.   At the Diet of Mainz, in 1439, he advised that only part of the Basle decrees be accepted again in 1441, and ably championed the cause of the pope against that of the council. [2]   He retained, however, at least many of his liberal ideas, and later gave expression to them in his remarkable work, "*De pace seu Concordantia Fidei* (1453), a most notable appeal for religious liberty. [3]

Among the foundations of papal power and claims which Cusanus examined in his "*De concordantia catholica*," was the Donation of Constantine.   His work was used as a sort of text-book by the council : this section of it was presented, November 7, 1433, at the fourteenth session.   It fully maintains the high standard of the rest of the work, and all things considered, is probably the most notable treatment ever given the "Donation." [4] Valla's treatise is longer, more rhetorical, and much better known ; but Valla in all probability had this work to guide him.

He called attention to the absence of any reference to the transaction or the document in early writings, which he said he had searched thoroughly with this in mind. Certain histories tell of Constantine being baptized by Sylvester, and of presents given the Church by the former, but none speak of any transfer of temporal power.

[1] M. Creighton, *op. cit*,. p. 232.

[2] For a full account of the Council of Basle and a judicious statement of Cusanus' share in it, *cf.* Creighton, *op. cit.*, vol. ii, chaps. iv-x.

[3] *Cf.* G. L. Burr: "Anent the Middle Ages," in *American Historical Review*, xviii, 710-713.

[4] For text of Cusanus' discussion, *cf. infra*, pp. 237-241.

That this last resided in the emperor was recognized by the popes after Sylvester. It was Pippin, and later Charlemagne, who conferred Italian states upon the papacy. Cusa cites passages in papal correspondence showing that imperial jurisdiction prevailed in Italy long after this grant to the pope was supposed to have been made. He makes a critical comparison of the legends of the Roman baptism with Jerome's statements and historical facts. He shows that the Donation was not in the original collection of canon laws made by Gratian, but was added later under "Palea." His conclusion is that the Donation is a more than doubtful argument for papal power, that it is really worse than nothing.

4. *Valla's Treatise*

Lorenzo Valla, however, made the most decisive onslaught upon the Donation, and the most famous.[1] Nicholas of Cusa had written about it as one of many questions, in the tone of scholarly investigation. Valla made an impassioned oratorical denunciation which singled it out as a crime against European civilization. The fame of the author, the power of his appeal, and ensuing contests against the papacy combined to connect the exposure of the forgery almost entirely with the latter name.

Valla embodied to a superlative degree most of the merits, and some of the faults, of the scholarship of the Renaissance. To find his closest analogy one must study the Italian *condottieri*, highly skilled, keen, reckless soldiers of fortune. He was an intellectual *condottiere*, well

---

[1] The best life of Valla is in Italian, G. Mancini; *Vita di Lorenzo Valla*, Firenze 1891. A good account, with many of Valla's letters, is that of Barozzi e Sabbadini, Studi sul Panormita e sul Valla, publicazioni del R. instituto di studi superiori practici e di perfezionamento in Firenze, sezione di filosofia e filologia (1891), pp. 49-265.

equipped for literary combats, now fighting as a free
lance for interests that appealed to him, now making
peace with the enemy and serving him for pay. Indeed
the real enemy was not injustice. It was not even ignorance, though he waged incessant warfaie against it. The
bitterest enemy of the Italian humanist was most likely
to be his fellow *condottiere*. Even his warmest friend
was apt to become his competitor and his rival. An attack upon the purity of one's Latinity, and Valla was
always making them,[1] was sure to provoke an invective
in which the honor of one's mother, one's character and
his private conduct were assailed with accusations as
scandalous as they were unfounded.[2] Popes at Rome
could more easily forgive attacks upon their temporal
power, than an Italian humanist a correction in his gram-
mar.

But in all these clouds of dust there was many a flash
of light. Valla, especially, had genuine critical insight
and was far from lacking scientific love of truth. Erasmus valued highly his grammatical notes on the New
Testament and his critical works on the Latin language.
"Where is the man," he wrote, "whose heart is so nar-

[1] *Cf.* Poggio's epigram:

> "Nunc postquam Manes defunctus Valla petivit,
> Non audet Pluto verba Latina loqui,
> Juppiter hunc superis dignatus honore fuisset
> Censorem linguae sed timet ipse suae."

> "Since Valla went the trembling Shades to seek
> No word of Latin Pluto dares to speak.
> Jove fears to call him to the blest abodes
> Lest carping censure vex the blameless gods."
> —Translation in Nichols, *Epistles of Erasmus*, p. 69.

[2] *Cf.* Valla's literary feuds with Fazzio, Antonio da Ro, Antonio Panormita, Poggio and Benedictus Morandus, in the works of Valla and
his opponents. For summary *cf.* Nisard: *Les Gladiateurs de la Re-
publique des Lettres*, vol. i (Paris, 1860).

rowed by jealousy, as not to have the highest praise for
Valla, a man who with so much energy, zeal and labor,
refuted the stupidities of the barbarians, saved half-buried
letters from extinction, restored Italy to her ancient
splendor of eloquence, and forced even the learned to
express themselves henceforth with more circumspec-
tion."[1] His criticism of institutions and ethics was no
less keen, even if sometimes marked by a recklessness
and lack of balance matched only by careful concealment
of his personal convictions. There are passages in his
writings which break not only with medieval but with
Christian morals as a whole. These, however, were
carefully put in the mouths of other speakers. He fore-
stalled Machiavelli's political theories in dismissing
Dante's conception of the Empire as the head of civil
power, in branding the papacy as the cause of disunion
in Italy, and in dignifying the modern state.

Such was the remarkable man who, in 1440, as royal
secretary of Alfonso at Naples, wrote the treatise *De
falso credita et ementita Constantini Donatione.*[2] He
was led to compose the treatise, not only by the echoes
of the council of Basle as they reverberated throughout
Europe, but by the local situation in Italy.

Alfonso of Aragon had claimed the Neapolitan crown

---

[1] *Cf.* Nichols, *Epistles of Erasmus*, p. 70.

[2] The theory that he wrote it at a later time and finished it in the
papal archives was a baseless invention of a later invective against him,
as was the story that he had to flee from Rome on account of it to save
his life. It apparently never caused him more than a temporary em-
barrassment later, and a feeble apology when he applied for a position
at the papal court. *Cf.* Mancini, *op. cit.* index under Valla, and Valla's
letter in Barrozi e Sabbadini, *op. cit*, pp. 94-96. The treatise is printed
in Valla's *Opera*, and in many separate editions. It is printed with a
long and uncritical, polemical introduction and French translation by
Bonneau, and with an Italian translation by G. Vincenti. *Cf. infra*,
Bibliography, under Valla.

N

upon the death of Giovanna II in 1435, on the ground of
his having been adopted heir by her, as well as of the
older Aragonese pretensions.   Pope Eugenius, however,
claimed the kingdom of Naples as a papal fief and opposed Alfonso. The latter was captured by the victorious fleet of the Genoese, who were looking after their
commercial interests, off the island of Ponza, and held
prisoner for a while by Filippo Maria Visconti, at Milan,
which then controlled Genoa, but he succeeded in form-
ing an alliance with Filippo Maria and thus finally got
control in Naples.   The pope, however, headed a league
embracing Florence, Venice and Genoa (after the revolt
from Milan) and continued the fight against Alfonso.
It was not until 1442 that the latter was able to firmly
establish himself at Naples.   The bitterness of his party
against Eugenius was naturally great, and was increased
by the pope's entrusting his interests and the conduct of
the war to the notoriously cruel Cardinal Vitteleschi.
Alfonso fought the pope, not only with an army, but
with literary forces as well.   He strongly supported the
faction hostile to the papacy at Basle, and sought in
general to undermine the moral and legal foundation of
the papal power.   For this latter purpose his secretary,
Valla, was an incomparable agent.   He contributed to
his patron's warfare a bitter arraignment of the temporal
power of the papacy, cleverly taking as his text the forgery of the Donation of Constantine.[1]

Writers who have approached this work through a
study of Valla, or from a Protestant point of view, have

---

[1] For the situation in Italian politics which called forth Valla's treatise,
cf. Creighton, *op. cit.*, ii, 170-172, 228; Barrozi, in Barozzi e. Sabbadini,
op. cit.. 222-265; Mancini, *Vita di Lorenzo Valla*, 137-145; Gregorovius, *Rome in the Middle Ages* (Eng. trans. from the fourth German
ed.), vol. vii, pp. 62-64, 84-85.

generally given it extravagant praise,[1] while many, impatient of its rhetorical form, or reading only the oratorical opening, have seen little of value in it.[2] In truth the work is not as original as has often been assumed. Valla was a friend and admirer of Nicholas of Cusa,[3] and there is reason for thinking that much of his historical criticism is based on Nicholas' earlier work. The criticism of the language and vocabulary of the Constitutum Constantini, however, which is a considerable part of the treatise, must have been largely a product of Valla's own literary studies. Errors such as the use of the apocryphal letter of Melchiades to overthrow the apocryphal Donation, the belief drawn through secondary sources from Eusebius' Church History that Constantine was always a Christian, failure to use Eusebius' Life of Constantine or even Jerome's statement of the Nicomedian baptism, were only to be expected of one writing in the fifteenth century. But Valla used old Roman coins which he had in his own possession as historical evidence, and his reasoning was usually sound and his method of approach skilfully chosen. His work is not unworthy to stand as one of the landmarks in the rise of historical criticism.

The point of Valla's treatise is that the Donation is a forgery, and that the temporal power of the pope is in any case bad and should be abolished. He makes no attempt to ascertain the date or circumstances of the

---

[1] *E. g.* Strauss, *Ulrich von Hutten*, (1877) p. 201; Gieseler, *Text-book of Church History* (New York, 1863), iii, p. 473, n. 2; Wolff, *Lorenzo Valla*, pp. 60, 79; Hodgkin, *Italy and her Invaders* (2nd ed.), vii, 154; Gregorovius, *Rome in the Middle Ages* (3rd ed.), vii, pp. 535, 571–573.

[2] *E. g.* Döllinger, ed. Friedrich, *Papstfabeln*, p. 118; Nisard, *op. cit.*, i, p. 279 *et passim*.

[3] *Cf.* letters in Barozzi e Sabbadini. *op. cit.*, pp. 115; 128.

forgery, as indeed no one does for a hundred and fifty years after him. His proof that the Donation was a forgery is varied both in form and in value. He begins with a rather clever discussion of the improbability of the whole thing, showing how Constantine could not have made the donation and how, if it had been made, Sylvester would have refused it in a speech expatiating on the incompatibility of the temporal power with the spiritual. He finds no trace of any transfer or change of officials; imperial rule continued in the west as before the supposed grant. The best historians, Eusebius and Rufinus, say that Constantine was a Christian before Sylvester's pontificate, and a letter of Melchiades [1] clearly proves it. Moreover, the Donation is not in the body of canon law, it was added under the Palea. The whole pseudo-Gelasian literature and the *Vita* (or *Gesta*) *Sylvestri* is discredited. Valla used effectively the argument from the barbarous and incorrect language of the document and inconsistencies in its account of events. Not having adequate Roman calendars or Fasti he failed to detect the error in dating. He accepted the Eusebian authorship of the *Vita Sylvestri*, but took this as discrediting it, because Greeks were proverbial liars; the *Vita* therefore is not apocryphal, but lying! As for confirmation and acceptance of the Donation as genuine by the rulers of the Holy Empire, Valla held these emperors to be creatures of the papacy. He was even less imperialist than papist. He ends as he began, with an attack upon the whole system of papal government in civil affairs.

This treatise, written before printing was developed, did not at first receive a wide circulation. Valla himself

---

[1] Which, however, is a palpable forgery.

esteemed it as one of his best and greatest works and circulated it privately among his friends.[1] Poggio, however, in his bitter invectives against Valla, did not mention this treatise, and apparently did not know of it. In a defence of himself to Eugenius IV, made in the effort to obtain a position at Rome, Valla excused himself from many damaging charges of heresy, but said nothing about the attack on the Donation, probably because it had not become well enough known to occasion controversy and call for defence.[2] He had had occasion to refer to it, though, in writing to influential friends at Rome, and to apologize for it. He protested his full devotion to the Holy See and attributed this indiscretion to bad advice as well as to his regrettable passion for controversy and fame.[3] In asking, however, in 1443, for the friendly influence of Cardinal Ludovico Scarampo in getting him back to Rome, he justified his work as solely an attempt to ascertain and establish the truth.[4]

---

[1] *E. g.* letter to Guarino, from Naples, Nov., 1443: * * * mittam ego tibi vicissim meam orationem, quae etiam ipsa prope tota in contentione versatur: "de falso credita et ementita donatione Constantini." Dices: "pacisci mecum vis." Minimi: "sed nisi orationem meam non videris, mittendam esse non puto tibi. Rescribes igitur an Pliniana Laurentianaque oratio in manus tuas venerit. Si utroque, tu Plinianam ad me mittes; si neutra, ego ad te meam Laurentianam mittam; si Laurentiana, neuter ad alterium aliquam orationem mittet." In Barozzi e Sabbadini, *op. cit*, p. 93

Valla also sent a copy to Aurispa, writing "qua nihil magis oratorium scripsi." In *"Epistolae mundi procerum"* (also referred to as *Epistolae principum*), Venice, 1574, p. 361, *cf.* also pp. 375, 346.

In 1443 he also wrote to Cardinal Ludovico Scarampo, in the letter quoted below, "Opus meum [de Constantini donatione] conditum editumque est, quod emendare aut supprimere nec possem si deberem, nec deberem si possem." Barrozzi e Sabbadini, *op. cit.*, p. 96.

[2] *Opera*, p. 795.

[3] *Cf.* letter to Landriana, c. 1445, cited by Gregorovius, *Rome in the Middle Ages*, vii, p. 574, and Nisard, *op. cit.*, i, p. 279.

[4] "At cur 'de Constantini donatione' composui? Hoc est quod pur-

His mingled protestations of innocence and veiled hints that more might be said than he had said in his treatise, produced no results during the pontificate of Eugenius IV. Nicholas V, however, finally did appoint him to an apostolic secretaryship in 1448 and gave him many marks of favor, especially in connection with his translations of Greek authors. How much the pope was influenced in this by Valla's urgency, by the policy of silencing an enemy by taking him into the papal camp, or by genuine interest in Valla's scholarly work, it is impossible to tell. I am inclined, however, to think that the last was the main reason for Nicholas' action.

Valla's treatise, however, did not remain without in-

gare habeam, ut quod nonnulli obtrectent mihi et quasi crimen intendant. Id ego tantum abest ut malivolentia fecerim, ut summopere optassem sub alio pontifice necesse mihi fuisse id facere, non sub Eugenio [the reigning pope]. Neque vero attinet hoc tempore libelli mei causam defendere nisi Gamalielis verbis, 'Si est ex hominibus consilium hoc aut opus, dissolvetur; sin autem ex deo, non poteritis dissolvere.' Opus meum conditum editumque est; quod emendare aut supprimere nec possem si deberem, nec deberem si possem. Ipsa rei veritas se tuebitur aut ipsa falsitas se coarguet. Alii de illo judices arbitrique sunt, non ego. Si male locutus sum, testimonium perhibebunt de malo; sin bene, non caedent me nervis aequi judices. Sed opus illud in sua quaeso causa quiescere sinamus. Hoc tantum consideres velim, non odio papae adductum, sed veritatis sed religionis sed cujusdam gloriae et famae gratia motum, ut quod nemo sciret id ego scisse solus viderer. Multum etiam nocere potuissem, si alieno animo fuissem in rebus quae mentem animumque magis sollicitant. Nan quod feci, hoc non modo ad pudorem praesentium, sed mortuorum etiam ac futurorum pertinet; qui enim nemini parcit, nullum laedit. Verum cum non minus prodesse in posterum possim quam uno libello offendi, per ego te superiorum temporum meam in summum pontificem benivolentiam pietatemque obsecro id, quod cum per se facile, tum vero tuae virtuti facillimum; non beneficium non munis non gratiam non veniam, sed ut similis tibi sis, ut quod semper fecisti facias, ne aliter ac sentis de animo ergo me tuo summique pontificis rescribas, etiamsi me tibi odio esse nec licere mihi in patriam redire dicas.'' Barozzi e Sabbadini, *op. cit.*, pp. 95–96.

For a letter to Cardinal Gerardo in a similar strain *cf. ibid.*, p. 104.

fluence. It probably added to Porcaro's anti-papal convictions and affected also the character of the teaching of Pomponius Laetus.[1] Valla's name more than that of any other man is associated by writers of his century, as well as by those of later times, with the refutation of the Donation. Hutten some seventy years later found it being read in Italy and got at least two copies of it there.[2] Others, however, wrote upon the subject, some probably independently of Valla.[3]

5. *Other Critics in the Time of the Renaissance*

Aeneas Sylvius Piccolomini in a treatise begun by him while on the imperialist side, some thirteen years after Valla's (*i. e.*, c. 1453) and revised, but left incomplete several months before he became Pope Pius II, describes an imaginary dialogue in which St. Bernard of Siena, Peter of Nocete and himself figure, and Valla is mentioned.[4] In this dialogue there occurs as complete a refutation of the Donation of Constantine as Valla had given, and at some points a more valid line of attack. The baptism of Constantine at Nicomedia, when an old man, is here affirmed correctly as excluding the whole story of the Roman baptism; which is quite an improvement upon Valla.

Reginald Pecock, bishop of St. Asaph, and later of

---

[1] *Cf.* Pastor, *History of the Popes*, ii, p. 221; iv, 42; Gregorovius, *op. cit.*, vii, pp. 131, 575; Creighton, *op. cit.*, ii, 308–311 *et passim*.

[2] *Cf. infra*, p. 203 *et seq.*

[3] It is interesting to note, however, that Nicholas Tudeschi, esteemed the greatest canon lawyer of Valla's time, wrote, "whoever denies the Donation of Constantine is to be suspected of heresy." Consil. 84, n. 2 cap. "per venerabilem."

[4] Pius ii, *Orationes*, i, 25; iii, 85–100; Piccolomini, *Opera Inedita*, p. 265 *et seq.;* Mansi, *Conciliorum Collectio*, xxx, 1203; *cf.* Mancini, *op. cit.*, pp. 148–149.

Chichester, discussed the "Donation" in his famous book *The Repressor of over much Blaming of the Clergy*,[1] written about nine years after Valla's treatise, but probably independently of it. Pecock's criticism shows remarkable accuracy in investigation and is based almost entirely upon genuine historical sources. He, also, accepts the baptism at Nicomedia, as did Aeneas Sylvius, as the only historical one; criticises the whole Sylvester legend; marks the absence of early references to the Donation; cites requests of early popes from the emperors, which show that the former, long after Sylvester, recognized the latter as their temporal sovereigns. He shows the actual course of events in the growth of the temporal power through the donations of Pippin, Charlemagne, Louis the Pious, and Countess Mathilda. His reasoning throughout is sound and convincing.

A scholar now little known, described as the Reverend Father in God, Hieronymus Paulus Cathalanus, Canonicus of Barcelona, LL. D., and a secretary of Alexander VI, has left a note combining the proofs of Valla and Aeneas Sylvius, and referring to other similar writings.[2] It probably represents the view of the Donation generally held among the best scholars of the papal court at the end of the century.[3]

[1] Printed in the *Rolls Series* (*Rerum britannicarum medii aevi scriptores*, no. 19), London, 1860, xix, xx, 350–366, and assigned by Wharton in Appendix, 102, to the year 1449. For a recent account of Pecock see article in *The English Historical Review*, xxvi (1911), pp. 448–468, by E. M. Blackie.

[1] Printed in the Reformation pamphlet, " De donatione Constantini quid veri habeat * * * ut in versa pagella videbis."

[3] Guicciardini (1483–1540) *Istoria d'Italia* (1775 ed.), vol. i, pp. 385–3c5, shows by his annihilation of the Donation, that it found no credence among men of letters in his circle.

Some who were acquainted with the general trend of the argument did not give it their complete assent. The celebrated theologian and casuist Antoninus, archbishop of Florence (1446–1459),[1] says that the Donation was not in the oldest manuscripts of canon law, and while accepted by theologians and canon-lawyers, is rejected by secular lawyers. For himself he holds it as at most a restitution by the emperor of power and property which belonged to the pope originally by divine right.

There was some attempt to defend the Donation as genuine. Cortesi brought forth an *Antivalla* (about 1464) which consisted chiefly of a slanderous account of Valla and of the circumstances under which he wrote, and of the condemnation he received. It still remains in manuscript.[2] There is also a report of an answer in 1458 to a trouble-making Hussite in Strassburg who insisted too vigorously that the Donation was a forgery; he was burned at the stake.[3] An equally convincing proof of the genuineness of the Donation was made later at Rome in the pontificate of Julius II, when one Bartholemeus Picernus (or Pincernus) produced a copy of it purporting to be a Latin translation of a Greek original.

The day of the Donation, however, was past. By the time of Alexander VI it had, in many quarters, become a joke. A story runs that when that pope asked for a copy of the grant on the basis of which Venice claimed control of the Adriatic, the Venetian Girolamo Donato

---

[1] In his "Chronicon partibus tribus distincta ab initio mundi ad mccclix," (Venice, 1474-9), printed, also, in "De donatione Constantini quid veri habeat," etc.

[2] *Cf.* Mancini, *op. cit.*, pp. 160-162. Another fifteenth-century refutation was by Giovanni Antonio di Sangiorgio, Cardinal Allesandrino, no longer extant.

[3] Cited by Friedrich, in his ed. of Döllinger, *Papstfabeln*, p. 118.

replied that he would find it written on the back of the Donation of Constantine.[1]   Ariosto's reference is akin to this :

> Then to a hill of vary'd flowers they went
> That sweet before, now yields a fetid scent;
> This (let me dare to speak) that present showed,
> Which on Sylvester Constantine bestowed. [2]

By the beginning of the sixteenth century the Donation was thus thoroughly discredited.   Ecclesiastical as well as secular scholarship generally recognized that it was a gross forgery.   Though we have seen that many writers contributed to this result, the refutation of the forgery seems to have been generally attributed to Valla. While not as yet printed, his treatise had become known to many in the latter half of the fifteenth century, and many manuscript copies of it seem to have been in existence.[3]   The treatise was referred to in at least one scholastic disputation in Germany, at Tübingen, as early as 1506.[4]   The literary merits of the work, the incisiveness and cleverness of its arraignment of the temporal power of the papacy, as well as the fact that it was by far the most pretentious exposé of the Donation, doubtless fostered the tendency to assign the whole merit of the critical achievement to it, a tendency which still continues among modern writers.[5]

[1] *Cf.* Mancini; *op. cit.*, p. 159.

[2] Orlando furioso, bk. xxxiv, v 80, Hoole's trans., xxxiv, l. 622 *et seq.*

> " Di vari fiore ad un grand monte passa,
> Chi ebbe gia buono odore, or puzza forte;
> Questo era il dono (se pero dir lece)
> Che Constantino al buon Silvestro fece."

[3] Hutten ran across at least two in Italy, *cf. infra*, p. 203 *et seq.*

[4] *Cf.* extract in Schard, *opus cit.*, pp. 426-434.

[5] *Cf.* G. B. Adams, *History of Civilization during the Middle Ages*, p. 378.

CHAPTER III

The "Donation" in the Protestant Revolution. Modern Scientific Historical Criticism

1. *Hutten's Publication of Valla's Treatise*

THE Protestant Revolution gave a new turn to the discussion. After being discredited by men who, however hostile they might be to the political pretensions of the papacy, had no thought of rebellion against the Church, the "Donation" was taken up by German revolutionists as proof of the fraud and deceit by which the papacy had obtained its unrighteous power. Ulrich von Hutten started the attack by the secret publication in Germany, in 1517, of Valla's treatise, which up to that time had remained in manuscript. He affixed to it, with his characteristic effrontery, a dedicatory letter to Leo X, full of pretended kindness toward that pope. Hutten had run across the book in Italy and was quick to see what an effective weapon it was.[1] After the Protest-

[1] See the following interesting letter, Hutten's *Opera*, ed. Böcking, i, p. 142.

"Joannes Cochlaeus Bilibaldo Pirckheimero Bononiae (Bologna), 5 Jul, 1517.

* * * "abiit ad vos ante octiduum noster Huttenus, homo ingenii magis acuti et acris quam placida et quieti. Dedi ei litteras, quanquam visus fuerat a nobis nonnihil abalienatus. Amo equidem hominis ingenium, ferociam ejus non ita; longe certe facilius absentem quam praesentem (ita tecum loqui libet) amicum servabo. Pridie quam recederet apud me vidit Laurentii Vallae libellum contra Constantini donationem, quem ego ad modicum tempus videndum ab alio commodatum acceperam, vult homo eum libellum in Germania rursus im-

ant movement started, his edition was frequently reprinted.[1]

2. *Luther's Attitude, Protestant Attack, Catholic Defense*

Hutten's publication fell into Luther's hands shortly
after his debate with Eck at Leipsic and added fuel to
the flame of his wrath. He wrote to Spalatin:

"I have at hand Lorenzo Valla's proof (edited by
Hutten) that the Donation of Constantine is a forgery.
Good heavens! what darkness and wickedness is at
Rome! You wonder at the judgment of God that such
unauthentic, crass, impudent lies not only lived, but prevailed for so many centuries, that they were incorporated
in the canon law, and (that no degree of horror might
be wanting) that they became as articles of faith. I am
in such a passion that I scarcely doubt that the Pope is

pressioni mandare; petit, ut libellus iste, quia correctior esset, trans-
scriberetur; non potui ei id denegare; transscriptus est a Friderico
Herbipolensi; transmittetur ei post paucos dies; sed et foris habent ex-
emplaria. Credo equidem verissima esse quae scripsit Laurentius;
vereor tamen ne tuto edi queant. at Huttenus anathema non formidat,
et indignum mihi videtur, ut veritas a veritatis gladio prohibeatur, facile
igitur illius ausu in lucem Laurentii libertas, qua haud inferiorem
Francus ille gerit, redibit. Scribunt super commenticia illa donatione
commenta multa canonistae et theologi et cucullati; sed omnium ratiun-
culas, immo captiunculas quisque cui non nihil sit cerebri, facile repelleret. At ego contra canonistas loqui non debeo, ne tibi videar rursus
ejus studii apostata; non certe id desero, quanquam magna cum displi-
centia plurima lego, praesertim ea quae sunt in Sexto et Clementinis,
ubi nulla verbositas pontificum avaritiae satisfacere potest."

It will be noticed that Cochlaeus says Hutten wanted "eum libellum
in Germania rursus impressioni mandare." This would seem to imply
that it had already been printed in Italy. I have, however, been unable
to obtain any trace of such an edition in any of the catalogues of incun-
abula or elsewhere, and infer that the above is merely a loose use of
words.

[1] 1518 (?), 1520, 1530, 1618, 1666, 1690, etc. *Cf.* Böcking, *Hutteni
Opera.* i, 18-19.

Antichrist expected by the world, so closely do their acts, lives, sayings and laws agree. But more of this when I see you. If you have not yet seen the book, I shall take care that you read it."[1]

This played no small part in the mental process by which Luther, naturally conservative and submissive to what he considered to be legitimate authority, came to look upon the papacy as a usurpation and illegitimate tyranny, and so passed on into open revolt. Thus, as the real Constantine had a large share in the development of the Catholic Church, the legendary Constantine contributed to the Protestant movement away from that church.

The Protestant attack led to a renewed defence of the Donation; indeed it probably prolonged that defence for generations after it would otherwise have been abandoned. Steuchus, librarian of the Vatican, was its ablest champion.[2] He made a general defence of the temporal power of the papacy, smoothed over some of the inconsistencies of the document in question by doctoring the text, and argued for the baptism of Constantine by Sylvester. In this last he made the mistake of assuming that Constantine would not have presided at the Council of Nicea if he had not previously been baptized, but he was entirely right and successful in overthrowing the story of Constantine and Miltiades (Melchiades) upon which Valla had relied.

---

[1] Feb. 24, 1520. I have given the translation of Preserved Smith, *Martin Luther*, p. 73. Luther wrote in a similar strain in his *Address to the Christian Nobility of the German Nation* of the same year.

[2] In his *Contra Laurentium de falsa donatione*, 1545, 1547.

3. *Baronius*

Many dissertations and compilations[1] were published in the controversy in the sixteenth century. This phase of the matter, however, ended with Baronius, the greatest Catholic church historian of these controversial generations. In his *Annales Ecclesiastici* (published 1588-1607) written in advocacy of the papacy and the Catholic Church, he took the position that the falsity of the Donation had been proven and, abandoning its defence, discussed it as a forgery.[2] Some later Catholic writers attempted a defence, and occasionally, almost down to the present, some ill-informed, ill-advised enthusiast has come forward to use it as genuine, but in educated circles this became entirely out of the question after Baronius' great work appeared. This one negative result of historical criticism was thus, in spite of the disturbing influence of the Protestant conflict, firmly established in the course of approximately one hundred and fifty years.

The way seemed clear for a dispassionate scientific study of the origin of the forgery. But Baronius, who opened the way, also carried over into the later discussion the point of view of religious controversy. He was the first to bring into prominence. after the question of genuineness was settled, the question of the source and circumstances of the forgery itself He seems to have done it, however, purely as a means of removing responsibility for the forgery from the papacy. It is inter-

---

[1] The most notable of the latter is that of Simon Schard referred to in an earlier chapter, *Syntagma variorium autorum de imperiali jurisdictione et protestate ecclesiastica*, printed also under the title, *Syntagma tractatium de imperiali jurisdictione, authoritate, et praeeminentia, ac potestale ecclesiastica*, etc. Basil, 1566. This contained reprints of most of the earlier writings attacking the Donation.

[2] Under the year 324, nos. 117-123. *Cf.* also A. D. 1191, no 51.

esting, but natural, that the very historian whose wonderful erudition and research Protestants criticized for
its lack of command of Greek, should assign the forgery
to just that field about which he knew the least, namely,
writers of the Greek Church.[1] Starting with his apologetic attitude on behalf of the papacy, and the existence
of Greek texts of the Donation, he advanced the theory
that Greeks had perpetrated the forgery and used it to
establish the antiquity of the See of Constantinople.[2]
The popes innocently accepted it as genuine and so fell
into the trap of using it.   This position is crude and untenable, for aside from other historical impossibilities involved there are numerous indications that the Greek
texts are merely translations from the Latin.[3] But it
represents one of the starting points of the modern scientific inquiry into the source of the *Donation*.   It also
forecast the survival of religious controversy in this
historical question, for down to the present there per-
sists the tendency on the part of many Catholic scholars
to find some scapegoat (nowadays the French forgers of
the ninth century usually play this rôle), and on the part
of many Protestants to attribute the Donation and its
use altogether too much to continuous, designing
knavery on the part of the papacy.

In the seventeenth and eighteenth centuries there were
occasional writings upon the Donation, but these followed the lines laid down earlier and are of no particular
interest.

[1] *Loc. cit.*

[2] He accepted the story of Sylvester and Constantine as historical (*Cf.*
A. D. 324, nos. 43–49), including the Roman baptism, most of the
material of the *Vita* or *Gesta Sylvestri*, and the actual grant of power
and possession to Sylvester, but held that the Greeks had, on the basis
of these historical facts, forged the document of the *Donation* itself.

[3] *Cf.* Döllinger, *op. cit.*, pp. 74–78.

4. *Character of Modern Scientific Criticism of the "Donation"*

The great ultramontane controversy of the nineteenth century, however, culminating at the time of the Vatican Council, brought again into prominence the medieval history of the papacy. The Donation of Constantine was made the subject of more prolonged and microscopic research than any other episode of similar importance in European history. A comparison of this series of investigation with earlier ones brings out clearly the vast improvement that had been made in the meantime in historical work. A whole library of lexicons showing the history of the use of words as well as their varying meanings, vast compilations of sources of all sorts and in all languages, accurate and detailed accounts of the course of events, careful study and comparison of manuscripts, critical editions of texts, countless organs of publication through technical reviews and learned societies, in short, all those products of what has not inaptly been termed an "industrial revolution" in learned circles, has put at the disposal of scholars an equipment with which apparent impossibilities are constantly being accomplished.

Moreover, though the old confessional and apologetic attitude has not entirely disappeared, a new spirit is clearly visible in the best modern criticism, the spirit of scientific curiosity, the effort to ascertain and understand facts, rather than to defend or to discredit existing institutions. Discussion of the *Donation of Constantine* now involves the task, beside which earlier efforts seem puerile, of discovering the process by which the story and the document came into being, and the identification of the place, the time and even the author of the forgery. The unraveling of the legendary process out of which the story of Constantine's leprosy and Roman baptism developed and the significance of the whole group of legends about the emperor has been described above.[1] The forged document has also become recognized as a composite resultant of ideas and forces lying deep in the life of the Middle Ages, with a history obscure and difficult, but intensely interesting. The materials for an understanding of this history are imbedded in scores and even hundreds of documents surviving from the eighth and ninth centuries, in peculiarities of style and vocabulary of various writers, and of various chancelleries, in political and ecclesiastical crises which might have spurred men on to the creation of false evidence. The problem has appealed strongly to scientific curiosity and has occupied the energy of many of the foremost European historians of the last two generations in Italy, France and especially Germany. It seems to have become, like the old scholastic problems, a field of exercise to sharpen the wits of scholars, deriving importance not from any practical bearing the solution may have, but from the light it throws upon the processes and possibilities of modern historical investigation.[2]

5. *Conclusions*

THIS work has not resulted in unanimity as to the place or exact time of the forgery. Differences in the

---

[1] *Cf. supra*, pp. 153–172.

[2] For list of the more important writings see Bibliography. For short summaries see the excellent articles upon Constantine, Donation of, in the last edition of the *Encyclopedia Britannica* and the *Catholic Cyclopedia*. For the most important contributions to the discussion see the works of Döllinger, Grauert, Langen, Friedrich, Brunner, Zeumer, Scheffer-Boichorst, Hartmann. The highwater mark was probably reached about the decade from 1880–1890; since then there has been a decline, at least in the volume of the discussion.

o

latter extend over a hundred years, 750–850; and both Italy and France are advanced as the source of the document.[1] Substantial arguments are not wanting for these varying conclusions; the decision, as yet must be one of probability and not of certainty. The following results, however, seem to me to best satisfy the requirements.

The legend of Constantine's leprosy and cure and of his rich gifts to the Roman church had been current at Rome long before the eighth century.[2] This legend seems to have taken on new features from time to time, chiefly by way of assigning a greater place to the bishop of Rome, and of attributing greater concessions and grants to him at the hand of the emperor.[3] Pope Hadrian I (772–795) undoubtedly was familiar with the legend in a form which represented Constantine as giving important privileges and grants to the pope and the Roman clergy, and endorsed it by his use of it.[4]

[1] The theory of a Greek origin was so completely refuted by Döllinger, *Papstfabeln*, etc., p. 74 *et seq.*, that it has been completely abandoned.

[2] The researches of Döllinger and Duchesne have thrown abundant light on this fact. *Cf. supra*, p. 165 *et seq.*

[3] Friedrich has attempted to point out definite redactions of the legend in the sixth and seventh centuries, and has also divided the document of the *Constitutum* (or *Donation*) of Constantine into two parts, the first dating from 638–641 (after 634, *cf. op. cit.*, p. 53) and the last from 752–757 (probably just before 754, *cf. op. cit.*, p. 110 *et seq.*). He is not in my judgment successful in this latter effort, but the larger fact of deviations in the legend in the direction indicated is, I think, established.

[4] In letters to the eastern rulers, Constantine and Irene, 785 A. D., given in Mansi xii, 1056–1076, and to Charlemagne in 775, 776, 778, *cf.* Cod. Car., no. lx; Jaffé, *Bibliotheca*, iv, 197; Mansi, *Concil. Coll.*, xii, 819. The resemblances between phrases of these letters and texts of the Donation of Constantine is so close at times as to suggest that Hadrian used such a text himself. This has been maintained by many scholars, *cf. e. g.* Friedrich, *op. cit.*, pp. 2–15, where some of the strik-

The earliest known manuscript of the Constitutum is the one in Codex Parisiensis Lat. 2778, found in the Collectio Sancti Dionysii of the monastery of St. Denis in France.[1] The collection contains documents dating from the last years of the eighth century (though it may have been put together later), antedating the appearance of the pseudo-Isidorean collection by a generation or more. All the other early manuscripts including those of the pseudo-Isidorean Decretals, which brought the document into general prominence, have been found in France. French writers, also, were the first to refer to the Donation. This indicates that its earliest use was there and has led to the theory that the document was forged there. The language however so clearly indicates a Roman source, and historical circumstances point so strongly in the same direction, that the Frankish origin seems untenable.

The most exhaustive and exact study of the language and use of terms in the *Constitutum Constantini* has been made by Scheffer-Boichorst.[2] He has shown a convincing resemblance in ideas, in style, and in vocabulary to the usage of the papal chancery of Stephen II (III) (752-757) and Paul I (757-767), and locates the

ing passages are put in parallel columns. However, it seems only reasonable to suppose that Hadrian would have referred to the document if he had had it before him in legal form. Other considerations also point to Hadrian's citing, not the legal document which we have in the *Constitutum Constantini*, but the legend in its literary form, probably in some text which we do not now have. Hadrian's source is therefore uncertain.

[1] For description and discussion of manuscripts, see Zeumer, in *Festgabe für Rudolf von Gneist*, pp. 39-47. For Zeumer's edition of the text of the *Constitutum Constantini*, cf. infra, pp. 228-237.

[2] "Neue Forschungen über die Konstantinische Schenkung," in *Mittheilungen d. Instituts für österr. Geschichtsforschung*, x (1889), p. 325 et seq.; xi (1890), p. 128 et seq. Also in his Gesammelte Schriften in the *Historische Studien* of E. Eberling, vol. xlii.

forgery in the time and in the chancery of the latter
pope. He attributes it not only to the effort to exalt
the authority and prerogatives of the Roman See, but
more particularly to a desire to glorify Sylvester. There
is justification for this on the further ground that Paul
I was especially interested in Sylvester, having founded
a monastery of his name in 761. The glorification of the
saint by a forgery ascribing high place to him would not
be an impossibility at that time. The argument from
the document itself is so strongly in favor of an origin
at Rome and about that time that the substance of the
Donation must be so assigned.

Reasoning from the possible motives of the forger is
uncertain, but must nevertheless be taken into account.
One motive frequently assigned seems clearly a fallacy;
namely, the supposition that the *Donation* was forged
for use as an inducement for Pippin to make grants
of Italian land to the popes. One can easily ascertain
what inducements the popes actually held out to him
to get help for the papacy. They do not use the name
of Constantine at all; that would then have had no
appeal for the Franks. They use St. Peter, however,
time and time again. [1] Stephen II even wrote a letter
in the name of St. Peter to Pippin urging and commanding the Frank to come to the help of Rome. [2] Far from
being produced by the *Constitutum Constantini*, the
donation of Pippin more likely suggested the later use
of the story of Constantine's gifts to Sylvester as a support for definite papal claims.

It is entirely probable that the forgery was not perpetrated for immediate use in support of papal preten-

[1] *Cf.* Cod. Carol., nos. 12, 42, 45, 65; see also article by Haller, *Die
Karolinger u. d. Papsttum*, in *Hist. Zeit.*, 108, 3–12, 1, pp. 39–76.

[2] Cod. Carol., 10 (A. D. 756), p. 55.

sions over against the Frankish rulers. The forger is very vague and indefinite as to donations of land, but he makes sweeping statements concerning the transfer of imperial, political power in Italy to the papacy, and very definite statements of the honor and dignity granted to the pope by the emperor. What is given most explicitly is the dignity, the aristocratic rank, what we might even call the social prerogatives, of the Roman bishop and his clergy, and Constantine's surrender to him of imperial jurisdiction in the West. These matters were not involved in the relations of the papacy and the Franks. Moreover it is doubtful whether to Pippin the old Roman emperors were more than distant names, and whether an old imperial document would have had any considerable influence upon him.

On the other hand, the latter half of the eighth century was precisely the time when the papacy finally broke the political ties which bound it to Constantinople. Such assertions as the " Donation " makes would be of great use in vindicating the independent policy of the papacy in Italy over against the lingering claims of the eastern emperor. If there was any particular occasion at Rome in the time of Stephen II and Paul I which called for magnificent assertions of that sort, it has not as yet come to light. There may well have been such an occasion, but it is not at all necessary to assume it; the general situation and aspirations of the Roman bishop and clergy in the troublous times of the eighth century were occasion enough. The forgery itself did not involve the creation of much new material, it consisted in throwing into the form of a legal document a current version of the legend of Constantine's Roman baptism with current confessions of faith inserted, and adding a grant by Constantine to Sylvester of imperial rank, of the

imperial crown, of the government of Italy, and of other
social and ecclesiastical perquisites. Indeed, it may be
said to have merely added to the Sylvester legend a
formal confession of the orthodox faith, and a pretended
official, legal grant from Constantine to Sylvester of
prerogatives and a position which the popes had already
begun to hold in central Italy.[1]

The first use made of the document to impress the
Franks and their rulers dates from after the death of
Charlemagne. It may have been cited for the purpose
for which Brunner thinks it was forged, namely, to prove
to Louis the Pious the necessity of receiving the imperial crown at the hands of the pope. There is no direct
proof of this, but the situation was appropriate, and, as
a matter of fact, Louis did repeat the coronation ceremony at Rheims in 816, and was crowned this time by
pope Stephen IV.[2] By the middle of the century the

[1] It has long been recognized that the " Donation " in granting to
the pope imperial rights over " Rome and all the provinces, places and
states of Italy, and the Western regions," dealt only with Italy, Lombardy, Venetia and Istria, and adjacent islands. In this point it was
merely in line with the requirements of the papal policy, in view of the
danger from the Lombards, etc., that the eastern empire, which could
no longer protect Italy, should not interfere so as to check or humiliate
Rome. It sanctions that policy by showing that Constantine had permanently ceded imperial authority in " Italy * * * and the Western
regions" to the popes. This is well brought out by Hartmann,
Geschichte Italiens im Mittelalter, ii, ii (1903), pp. 218-231, et passim,
the best discussion of the " Donation" in its relation to the Italian
situation. *Cf.* also, Caspar, E., *Pippin u. d. römische Kirche* (Berlin,
1914), pp. 185-189.

The rather surprising frequency of Greek MSS. of the " Donation "
and of its use at Constantinople (*cf.* Döllinger, *op. cit.*, p. 73 *et seq.*
Steuchus said he had seen four Greek MSS. of it in the Vatican Library)
may be an indication of an early attempt to cite it there. If this be so,
there is an interesting analogy between the effort of Baronius and his
successors to prove the Greek origin of the forgery, and the effort of
Grauert and others recently to prove its Frankish origin.

[2] Grauert, " Die Konstaninische Schenkung," in the *Hist. Jahrbuch*

Constitutum Constantini had gained recognition in France to such an extent as to ensure its circulation and preservation.   Its subsequent history has already been told.

des Görresgesellschaft in 1882–1884, made a strong argument for the origin of the document at a date in the eighth century (after 840). Brunner, in the *Festgabe für Rudolf von Gneist* (1888), pp. 1–35, agreed with Grauert in fixing a later date than had formerly been common, but locates the forgery at Rome (instead of in France, as Grauert had done) and between 813 and 816.   Though an earlier date than this seems called for, the document may have been touched up in one or two places for the use referred to above.

APPENDIX I

The Conversion of Constantine in the Vita Sylvestri

Vita Silvestri, from Boninus Mombritius; Sanctuarium seu Vitae sanctorum (Milan, c. 1479), Tom. II, f. 289 *et seq*. New ed. duo monachi Solesmenses (Benedictines in France), (Paris, 1910), II, p. 508 *et seq*. The text of the following is based on the 1910 edition, a careful comparison of this edition with the older one having shown that the editing was carefully done. Some of the opening sections, and the last parts, are omitted as not bearing on the subject in hand. *Cf. supra*, pp. 161-164.

PROLOGVS IN VITAM SANCTI SYLVESTRI PAPAE ET CONFESSORIS

Historiograpbus [1] noster Eusebius Caesariae Palestinae urbis episcopus cum historiam ecclesiasticam scriberet . pretermisit ea : quae in aliis opusculis sunt : uel quae se meminit retulisse : Nam uiginti libros idest duas decadas omnium pene prouinciarum passiones martyrum et episcoporum et confessorum et sacrarum uirginum ac mulierum continere fecit . Deinde secutus et ab apostolo Petro omnium episcoporum nomina et gesta conscripsit : et earum urbium : quae arcem pontificatus per apostolicas sedes tenere noscuntur : ut urbs Roma . Antiochia . hyerosolima . Ephesus et Alexandria . Harum urbium episcoporum omnium praeteritorum nomina usque ad tempus suum at gesta graeco sermone conscripsit : Ex quo numero unum episcoporum urbis Romae sanctum Syluestrum me de graeco in latinum transferre praecepisti domine sancte ac beatissime pater . Quia itaque exiguum me ad translationem hanc esse consydero : elegi hoc detergere : quod sim parui sermonis et inertis ingenii : Vnde obsecro : ut pro me tuis orationibus impetres : ne qui culpam contemptoris fugio : praesumptoris noxam incurram : sed tuis orationibus ueniam me consequi non dubito . Credo enim quod orando impleri facias : quod me arripere iubendo fecisti .

---

[1] Word misspelled in original.

Syluester urbis Romae episcopus cum infantulus esset a
uidua matre Iusta nomine et opere traditus est ut erudiretur
a Cyrino presbytero : cui quottidie sedulum exhibebat officium : Eius autem uitam imitatus et mores : ad summum api-
cem christianae religionis attigit. . . . . .[1]

In illo tempore exiit edictum : ut christiani ad sacrificandum
idolis cogerentur : unde factum est ut secedens ab urbe sanctus
Syluester Sirapti latibulo cum suis se clericis collocaret . Constantinus autem Augustus monarchiam tenens cum plurimas
strages de christianis dedisset : et innumerabilem populum per
omnes prouincias fecisset uariis poenarum generibus inter-
fici : elefantiae a deo lepra in toto corpore percussus est . Huic
cum diuersa magorum et medicorum agmina subuenire non
potuissent : pontifices capitolii hoc dederunt consilium : debere piscinam fieri in ipso capitolio : quae puerorum sanguine
repleretur : in quam calido ac fumante sanguine nudus descendens Augustus mox posset a uulnere illius leprae mundari .
Missum est igitur et de rebus fisci uel patrimonii regis ad tria
millia ; et eo amplius adducti ad urbem Romam pontificibus
traditi sunt Capitolii , Die autem constituto egrediente imperatore Constantino palatium ad hoc eunti ad capitollium : ut
sanguis innoxius funderetur : occurrit multitudo mulierum :
quae omnes resolutis crinibus nudatisque pectoribus dantes
hululatus et mugitus coram eo se in plateis fundentes lachrymas strauerunt . Percunctatus itaque Constantinus Augustus
qua de causa multitudo haec mulierum ista faceret : didicit has
matres esse filiorum eorum : quorum effundendus erat sanguis : tandiu quousque piscina repleretur : in qua medendi
causa lauandus descenderet et sanandus . Tunc imperator ex-
horruit facinus : et se tantorum criminum reum fore apud
deum existimans : quantorum esset numerus puerorum : uicit
crudelitatem pontificum pietas romani imperii : et prorum-
pens in lachrymis iussit stare carrucam : et erigens se ac conuo-
ocans uniuersos clara uoce dixit : audite me comites et com-
militones et omnes populi : qui astatis : romani imperii digni-

[1] The other opening sections are omitted as not bearing upon the
subject in hand.

tas de fonte nascitur pietatis . Cur ergo praeponam salutem
meam saluti populi innocentis ? Nunc autem ab effusione in-
noxii sanguinis sententiam crudelitatis excludam . Melius est
enim pro salute innocentum mori : quam per interitum eorum
uitam recuperare crudelem : quam tamen recuperare incertum
est : cum certum sit recuperata crudelitas . Sic semper contra
hostes nostra certamina in praeliis extitisse noscuntur : ut
reus esset legibus et capitali sententiae subderetur : quicumque aliquem occidisset infantem : Eratque hoc statutum in
bello : ut facies illa quam pubertas adhuc non nouerat gla-
dium euaderet bellatoris : et uita incolumis permaneret . Nunc
itaque quod in hostium filiis custoditum est : in filiis nostrorum ciuium exercebimus ? ut simus nostris legibus rei atque
captiuitate animae et conscientiae captiuabimur : qui pug-
nando fideliter omnium gentium meruimus esse uictores ? Quid
iuuat barbaros superasse : si a crudelitate uincamur ? Nam
uicisse extraneas nationes bello uirtus est populorum : uincere
autem uicia peccata et crimina uirtus est morum . In illis ergo
preliis extitimus fortiores illis : In his autem nobis ipsis fortiores sumus : cum uincimus nosmetipsos : dum mala uota
nostra excludimus : et quod inconsulte desyderamus : con-
sulte et utiliter exercemus . hoc autem facimus : quando uolun-
tatibus deorum uoluntates nostras postponimus : et diuinis
desyderiis obedientes nostra desyderia impugnamus : et in hoc
certamine uictos nos esse hac ratione gaudemus : ut agnos-
camus nos contra salutem nostram uoluisse pugnare . Nam
qui conatur perpetrare : quod malum est : captiuare utique
studet bonitatem . Cum ergo isto fuerit certamine superatus :
uictoriam obtinet uictus : quoniam uictor perditionem inuen-
erat : et malam captiuitatem incurrerat post triumphum : si
tamen triumphus dici potest : quando pietas ab impietate uin-
citur : et iusticia ab iniusticia superatur . Vincat ergo nos
pietas in isto congressu . Vere enim omnium aduersantium
poterimus esse uictores : si a sola pietate uincamur . Omnium
et enim uerum se esse dominum comprobat : qui uerum se
seruum ostenderit esse pietatis . Cum ad istam conctionem
omnis exercitus omnisque populus diutissime acclamasset :

Itemque conctionatus dixit : Iussit pietas romana filios suis
matribus reddi : ut dulcedo reddita filiorum amaritudinem
lachrimarum maternarum obdulcet . Et haec dicens iter quod
arripuerat eundi ad capitolium deserens : ad palatium rediit .
Non solum autem filios reddidit : uerum etiam dona simul amplissima et uehicula infinita et annonas iussit expendi : ut quae
flaentes uenerant et lugentes : ad patriam alienam : alacres
cum gaudio ad ciuitates suas reuerterentur .

Hac igiter transacta die nocturno regis facto silentio : somni
tempus aduenit : Et ecce adsunt apostoli sancti Petrus cum
Paulo dicentes : Nos sumus Petrus et Paulus : quoniam
flagitiis terminum posuisti : et sanguinis innocentis effussi-
onem horruisti : missi sumus a Christo Iesu domino nostro
dare tibi sanitatis recuperandae consilium . Audi ergo monita
nostra : et omnia fac quaecumque tibi indicamus . Syluester
episcopus ciuitatis Romae ad montem Sirapti persecutiones
tuas fugiens in cauernis petrarum cum suis clericis latebram
fouet . Hunc cum ad te adduxeris : ipse tibi piscinam pietatis
ostendet : in quam dum te tertio merserit : omnis te ista deseret leprae ualitudo : quod dum factum fuerit : hanc uicissi-
tudinem tuo saluatori compensa : ut omnes iussione tua per
totum orbem romanorum ecclesiae restaurentur . tu autem te
ipsum in hac parte purifica : ut relicta omni idolorum superstitione deum unum qui uerus et solus est deus adores et excolas : et ad eius uoluntatem attingas . Exurgens igitur a
somno Constantinus Augustus statim conuocans eos qui ob-
seruabant palatium : et secundum tenorem somni sui misit ad
montem Sirapti : ubi sanctus Syluester in cuiusdam christiani
agro persecutionis causa cum suis clericis receptus lectionibus
et orationibus insistebat : At ubi se a militibus conuentum
uidit : credidit ad martyrii coronam se uocari : et conuersus
ad clerum omnibus qui cum eo erant dixit : ecce nunc tempus
acceptabile : ecce nunc dies salutis : aduenit tempus quo nos
lectio docuit operum nostrorum assignare fructum . Ecce dominus iterum spiritaliter inter homines ambulat : si quis uult

---

[1] The paragraphing is mine. Note how closely this section is copied
in the *Constitutum Constantini, cf. infra,* pp. 230-231.

post eum uenire : abneget semetipsum sibi : et tollat crucem
suam: et sequatur eum : Ut haec dicens orationem fecit omne-
que mysterium adimpleuit commendans animam suam et dans
pacem omnibus profectus est . Secuti sunt autem eum uniuersi
clerici cum presbyteris triginta et diaconibus quinque optantes
passioni simul succumbere : melius arbitrantes cum illo pro
Christo mori quam in eius absentia epulari : erat enim tran-
quillo semper animo et sereno : ita omnes clericos diligens : et
sicut gallina pullos suos euocans : ut circa uniuersos carum
amorem ostenderet : et omni hora eos monitis caelestibus eru-
diret . Vnde factum est : ut omnes eruditionis sagena refecti
passionem magis diligerent quam timerent : et simul cum eo
alacres properarent . Profectus itaque ut dictum est : peruenit
ad regem . Tunc illico assurgens augustus prior eum salutauit
dicens : Bene uenisse te gratulamur : Cui sanctus Syluester
respondit : pax tibi et uictoria de caelo subministretur : quem
cum rex alacri animo et uultu placidissimo suscepisset : omnia
illi quae ei facta quaeque reuelata sunt secundum textum su-
perius compraehensum exposuit . Post finem uero narrationis
suae percunctabatur qui isti essent dii Petrus et Paulus : qui
illum uisitassent : et ob quam causam salutis suae latebram
detexissent . Cui sanctus Syluester respondit : deus unus
est : quem colimus : qui totum mundum fecit ex nihilo idest
caelum et terram et omnia quae in eis sunt . Petrus autem
et Paulus dii non sunt sed serui dei : qui illi per fidem pla-
centes hoc consecuti sunt : ut arcem teneant sanctitatis : et
sic in numero sanctorum omnium primi a deo apostoli facti
sunt . Ergo ipsi primi diuinitatem domini nostri Iesu christi
filii dei gentibus praedicauerunt : et omnis ecclesia ab ipsis
initium sumpsit . Hi expleto apostolatus officio ad palmam
martyrii peruenerunt : et sunt modo amici omnipotentis dei .
Cum haec et his similia gratanter augustus audisset : dixit :
peto utrum hos istos apostolos habet aliqua imago expressos :
ut in ipsis liniamentis possim agnoscere hos esse : quos me
reuelatio docuisset : qui mihi dixerunt se a deo missos esse .
Tunc sanctus Syluester iussit diacono suo ut imaginem apostolorum exhiberet : quam imperator aspiciens cum ingenti cla-

more coepit dicere : nihil inferius hac imagine in eorum ef-
figie quorum uultus in uisione conspexi . Hi ergo mihi dixerunt : mitte ad Syluestrum episcopum : et hic tibi ostendet
piscinam pietatis : in qua cum lotus fueris : omnium conse-
queris tuorum uulnerum sanitatem . Cui sanctus Syluester respondit : Audi me rex : et salutis piscinam necessariam hoc
ordine require : ut primum credas Christum filium dei ideo
de caelo uenisse : et inter homines conuersatum esse : ut istam
piscinam credentibus in se manifestaret : Cui Augustus respondit : ego nisi credidissem : ad te poenitus non misissem .
Tunc sanctus Syluester dixit : exige a te ipso una hebdomade
ieiunium : et deposita purpura intra cubiculum tuum : ibique
induere ueste humili : prosterne cylicium : et confitere modo
per ignorantiam erroris factum : ut christianis persecutionem
induceres : et ipsum esse saluatorem corporum et animarum
non solum loquendo sed et credendo pronuncia : et poenitere
multos sanctos dei occidisse : et in hac hebdomade templa iube
claudi : et cessare omnia sacrificia idolorum : debitores fisco
pauperes laxa : carceratos dimitti praecipe : in exiliis et metal-
lis aut in quibuscumque tribulationibus constitutis indulgen-
tiam dari constitue . Iube per totam hebdomada eleimosynas
fieri : beneficia etiam postulantibus exhiberi praecipe : et
idoneos qui haec exequantur constitue . Tunc Constantinus
imperator dixit : constat omnes culturas homines in superstitione diligere : nec posse ibi diuinitatis gloriam inueniri ubi
mendax assertio deum dicit hunc esse quem fecit . Nisi inuisi-
bilis iste est : qui inuocatus aquis hanc uirtutem concedit : ut
peccata animarum abluat : et corporibus conferat medicinam :
constat hunc esse uerum deum : cuius apostoli me uisitare dig-
nati sunt : et hoc monere : ut unum deum credam saluatorem
meum . Cum haec et his similia Constantinus Augustus diceret
: imposuit sanctus Syluester manus super caput eius : et bene-
dicens eum : ac faciens cathecuminum abiit . Post haec sanctus Syluester conuocatis omnibus presbyteris ac diaconibus
cum uniuerso clero indixit ieiunium biduanum omni ecclesiae
dicens : Si Nineuitae in praedicatione Ionae per triduanum
ieiunium iram dei et offensam pro meritis debitam euase-

runt : quanto magis nos in praedicatione domini nostri Iesu
christi persecutiones euadimus . lucramur animas pacem dei
ecclesiis acquirimus : et idolatriis finem imponimus : hoc autem
facimus si ieiuniis et orationibus hoc a domino impetremus .
Factum est unanimiter ieiunanitibus cum ornamento orationis
idest die sexta et sabbato in quo claudendum erat ieiunium
uespertino tempore dixit Constantino regi Syluester episcopus
: audi me rex : piscina ergo haec omnis aqua quae est sub
caelo siue maris siue fluminum siue fontium siue paludum siue
stagnorum : tanta uirtus est nominis Christi : ut ad inuoca-
tionem eius peccata uniuersa abluat : et salutem conferat :
quam fides credentis exposcit . Vocansque ipsum secum Augustum ieiunantem monitisque instruens constantia erigens :
fide certissimum reddens : Vespere itaque sabbati iubet laua-
crum caloris sui in palatio lateranensi augustum ingredi : quo
ingresso ipse ad benedictionem fontis accedit . Benedicto itaque fonte Augustus introgreditur : quem Syluester episcopus
suscipiens interrogat : si ex toto corde credit in patrem et
filium et spiritumsanctum : qui cum credere se clara uoce
diceret : et pompis se diaboli renunciare toto corde assereret :
mersit confitentis Augusti in piscina totum corpus : atque
sancto superfundens chrismate dixit : qui mundasti in Iordane
lepram Naaman Syri : et caeci nati oculos per aquam aper-
uisti : et Paulo apostolo per baptismum oculos quos amiserat
reddidisti : et fecisti nobis ex persecutore doctorem : tu
emunda hunc seruum tuum omnium terrenorum principem
Constantinum . Et sicut animam eius ab omni stercorae peccati
mundasti : ita corpus eius ab omni hac lepra elephantiae ablue :
ut ex persequente credentem et defendentem se habere uirum
hunc sancta tua ecclesia glorietur per dominum nostrum Iesum
christum filium tuum : qui tecum uiuit et regnat in unitate
spiritussancti in saecula saeculorum : Cumque omnes respon-
dissent : amen : Subito quasi fulgur lux intolerabilis per me-
diam fere horam emicuit : quae omnium et mentes exterruit :
et aspectus obtexit : et ecce sonus in aqua quasi sartaginis stri-
dentis exortus ueluti piscium ingentium Christus totam illam
piscinam fontis repletam ostendit . Ex qua mundus surgens

Constantinus imperator Christum se uidisse confessus est . Et
indutus uestibus candidis prima die baptismatis sui hanc legem
dedit : Christum deum esse uerum : qui se mundasset a leprae
periculo : et hunc debere coli ab omni orbe romano . Secunda
die dedit legem ut qui Christum blasphemasse probatus fuerit
puniretur . Tertia die promulgauit legem : ut si quis christiano
fecisset iniuriam : omnium bonorum suorum facultatem dimi-
diam amitteret . Quarta die priuilegium ecclesiae romanae
pontificique contulit : ut in toto orbe romano sacerdotes ita
hunc caput habeant : sicut omnes iudices regem . Quinta die
in quocumque loco fuerit fabricata ecclesia consecrationis suae
hanc uirtutem obtineat : ut quicunque reus ad eam confu-
gerit : a iudicis periculo qui in praesenti fuerit defensetur .
Sexta die dedit legem : nulli intra muros cuiuscumque ciuitatis dari licentiam ecclesiam construendi : nisi ex consensu
praesentis episcopi : quem sedes apostolica probasset antisti-
tem . Septima die omnium possessionum regalium decimas
manu iudiciaria exigi ad aedificationem ecclesiarum . Octaua
die processit albis depositis totus mundus et saluus : et ueniens
ad confessionem apostoli Petri ablato diademate capitis totum
se planum proiiciens in faciem tantam illic lachrymarum ef-
fudit multitudinem : ut omnia illa insignia uestimenta pur-
purea infunderentur : Dans uocem inter amaras lachrymas
quibus se errasse : se pecasse : se reum esse de presecutione
sanctorum commemorans : et ob hoc non se esse dignum eius
limina contingere : Cumque ingenti gemitu haec exclamaret :
quantus ibi ab omni populo lachrimarum fusus est numerus :
quis memorare sufficiat ? Erat autem tale gaudium flaetibus
plenum : quale solet esse in caris mortuis suscitatis aut in his :
qui euaserunt naufragia : aut in his qui uicinos dentes euadere
potuerunt.

Verum quoniam de his longum est enarrare : dicamus
quid prima die processionis suae egit : Exuens se chlamy-
dem et accipiens bidentem : terram primus aperuit ad fundamentum basilicae construendum . Dehinc in numero duodecim
apostolorum duodecim cophinos plenos suis humeris super-
positos baiulauit de eodem loco : ubi fundamentum basilicae

apostolis debuerat fundare : et ita gaudens et exultans in car-
ruca sua una cum papa residens ad palatium rediit . Altera
uero die similiter intra palatium suum lateranensem basilicae
fabricam coepit : dans talem legem : quae in his uerbis conclu-
ditur . Sit omnibus notum : ita nos Christi cultores effectos :
ut intra palatium nostrum templum eius nomini construamus :
in quo populus christianus una nobiscum conueniens deitati eius
gratias referamus . Hac itaque lege data constituit atque edicto
pendente proponi iussit : ut si quis pauper christianus fieri
uoluisset de facultatibus regiis uestimenta candida et uiginti
solidos de archa regis acciperet . Hoc autem factum est : ne
cupiditas imperaret fallaciam : et non credentibus sed temp-
tantibus istis donis proficeret . Tanta autem eo anno credidit
multitudo : ut uirorum numerus baptizatorum ad duodecim
millia tenderetur excepta mulierum populositate et infantium .
Sic quoque ex uno latere crescebat dei populus in gloria : ut
ex altero paganis confusio nasceretur . Igitur cum et senatorum
caterua huic relligioni sanctae fidem nullus adhiberet : nec ob
hoc irasci alicui . Augustum papa permitteret : praecepit Augustus sibi in basilicam excelsum tribunal statui : et senatum
ac populum romanum hac uoce affatus est : profanae dissen-
siones mentium ideo nulla ratione salubre consilium sumunt :
quia profunda ignorantiae circundantur caligine : et nullus eas
clarus ac serenus ueritatis splendor illuminat . Aperiendi sunt
ergo lumine scientiae oculi animorum et diligenti est examina-
tione cernendum : istos deos nec dici debere : nec credi : qui
ab hominibus facti noscuntur . Non enim dii sunt : sed homines magis ipsi eorum dii dici possunt : quos ipsi plasmauerunt .
Denique si quid aliquo casu in his laesum fuerit : homines qui
sua eos arte fecerunt : sua eos nihilominus arte restaurant .
Sunt ergo homines : ut dixi : dii eorum qui dum non essent
eos fecerunt : et dum fecissent : laesi ab eis restaurantur .
Vnde coniecturam summens mecum omnibus ad culturam ueri
dei exhibeo : quod in me quoque factum aspicitis ipsi et probatis : Nisi enim ipse esset deus Christus : qui me fecit : non
utique quod ab alio factum fuerat restaurare ualuisset . Pro-
batur ergo humanum genus huius dei esse figmentum : qui

P

restaurat lapsum : fractum solidat sublimat allisum . Sicut
uniuersa ista idola quae hominum figmenta sunt : ideo hominum auxilio cum laesa fuerint reparantur . Habeant itaque
habeant iam finem isti errores . abdicetur ista superstitio :
quam ignorantia concepit : stulticia nutriuit : et aluit . Adore-
tur deus solus : qui unus et uerus regnat in caelis . Desinamus
hos colere : a quibus saluari non possumus : et quos laesos ipsi
saluamus . Cessemus ab eis flagitare nostri custodiam : quos
nostri custodia tuemur ne pereant . Quid miserius quam aes
lapidesque adorare et ferrum ? Sit itaque omnibus gratum :
quod sum a Christo quem negabam pristinae redditus sanitati :
et ab isto errore ipso domino Iesu christo auxiliante cessamus .
Et quoniam sapientia romanorum non fallitur : istum deum
excolat : a quo ipsa custodiatur : non quem ipsa custodiat .
Verum ne longa oratio omnes uos intentos extendat : quid
constituendum censui breuiter pandam : Patere uolumus christianis ecclesias : ut priuilegia quae sacerdotes templorum habere noscuntur : antistites christianae legis assumant . Vt
autem notum sit uniuerso orbi romano uero deo et domino Iesu
christo nos inclinare ceruices : intra palatium meum ecclesiam
Christo arripui construendam : ut uniuersitas hominum com-
probet : nulla dubietatis in corde meo uel praeteriti erroris re-
manisse uestigia : Cumque in isto uerbo fuisset eloquium :
uox populorum per tria horarum spatia haec sunt : qui Christum negant male depereant : quia ipse est uerus deus . Dictum
est tricies . Item unus deus christianorum . Dictum est quadragies . Item templa claudantur : et ecclesiae pateant . Dictum
est decies . Item qui Christum non colunt : inimici Augustorum
sunt . Dictum est quadragies . Item qui saluauit Augustum :
Ipse est uerus deus . Dictum est tricies . Item qui Christum
non colunt : hostes romanorum sunt . Dictum est decies . Item
qui Christum colit : semper uicit : Dictum est quadragies .
Item sacerdotes templorum ab urbe pellantur . Dictum est quadragies . Item qui adhuc sacrificant diis : ab urbe pellantur .
Dictum est terdecies . Item iube : ut hodie repellantur . Dictum
est quadragies . Ad hanc uocem Imperator silentium petiit :
quo facto sic allocutus est populum : Inter diuina humanaque

seruitia hoc interest : ut humana seruitia coacta sint : diuina
autem uoluntaria comprobentur . Deus enim quia mente coli-
tur : et sincero hominis uencratur affectu : spontanea eius
debet esse cultura . In hoc enim apparet : quia uerus deus est :
quod per tanta saecula contemptoribus suis non iratus finem
imposuit : sed propitium se esse qui coli debeat demonstrauit
indulgendo crimina : et salutem animabus et corporibus con-
ferendo . Sit ergo omnibus notum : non necessitate coactos :
sed suo iudicio liberos posse fieri christianos nec humanum
metuentes imperium ad dei culturam accedere aliquos opor-
tere : sed rationabili consyderatione magis rogare : uti christianorum numero applicentur ab iis : qui huic sacratissimae
legi descruiunt . Iustum et enim uerumque conspicimus : ut
sicut petentibus culpa est : si negetur : ita non petentibus si
tradatur iniquum . Nec hoc aliqui metuant : quod a nostra
gratia diuellantur : si christiani esse noluerint . nostra enim
claementia talis est : ut opere non mutetur . Vnde hoc consy-
derandum est : quod magis nobis adhaerebunt in amiciciis ii :
qui spontanee ad christianam legem uenire uoluerint . Tunc
omnibus populis et christianis et paganis hanc legem laudan-
tibus : et uitam Augusto optantibus iteratus clamor populi
factus est diutissimus . Et cum finis huius rei factus fuisset :
reuerteni Augusto ad palatium tota ciuitas cereis lampadibus-
que repleta coronata est : erat enim omnibus gaudium : quoniam lex talis processerat : quae nullum ad culturam impell-
eret : nullum a Christi cultura repelleret . Fit uox laeticiae per
uniuersas ecclesias . honorantur uniuersa sepulchra sanctorum : omnesque confessores qui cathenati ad diuersa fuerant exilia tracti : cum gloria et honore regio ad patrias pro-
prias reuocati amici effecti sunt regis . Caetera quae facta
sunt uel dicta praetero : ne pro ipsa prolyxitate fastidium
lector incurrat : sunt enim alia plura et utiliora : quae praeterire non debeo . Exigit enim haec historia : ut ad Helenam
imperatoris matrem flectam articulum : et hoc ordine ad finem
huius operis attingam.[1]

[1] Then follows a long account of the conversion of Helena through
a disputation between Sylvester and Jewish rabbis, which forms a
regular element in the oriental form of the Sylvester legend, *cf. supra,*
pp. 163-164.

II

Earliest Text of the Constitutum Constantini, or Donation of Constatine [1]

EXEMPLAR CONSTITVTI DOMNI CONSTANTINI IMPERATORIS

[Reprinted from edition by Karl Zeumer, in *Festgabe für Rudolf von Gneist* (Julius Springer, Berlin, 1888, 8 marks), pp. 47-59, by permission of the publishers.]

1.   In nomine sanctae et individuae Trinitatis, Patris scilicet et Filii et Spiritus sancti. Imperator Caesar Flavius Constantinus in Christo Jesu, uno ex eadem sancta Trinitate salvatore domino Deo nostro, fidelis, mansuetus, maximus, beneficus, Alamannicus, Gothicus, Sarmaticus, Germanicus, Brittannicus, Hunicus, pius, felix, victor ac triumphator, semper augustus, sanctissimo ac beatissimo patri patrum Silvestrio, urbis Romae episcopo et pape, atque omnibus eius successoribus, qui in sede beati Petri usque in finem saeculi sessuri sunt, pontificibus, nec non et omnibus reverentissimis et Deo amabilibus catholicis episcopis, eidem sacrosanctae Romanae ecclesiae per hanc nostram imperialem constitutionem subiectis in universo orbe terrarum, nunc et in posteris cunctis retro temporibus constitutis, gratia, pax, caritas, gaudium, longanimitas, misericordia, a Deo patre omnipotente et Jesu Christo filio eius et Spiritu sancto cum omnibus vobis.

2.   Ea quae salvator et redemptor noster dominus Jesus Christus, altissimi Patris filius, per suos sanctos apostolos Petrum et Paulum, interveniente patre nostro Silvestrio summo pontifice et universali papa, mirabiliter operari dignatus est, liquida enarratione per huius nostrae imperialis institutionis paginam ad agnitionem omnium populorum in universo orbe terrarum nostra studuit propagare mansuetissima serenitas. Primum quidem fidem nostram, quam a prelato beatissimo patre et oratore nostro Silvestrio universali pontifice edocti

---

[1] *Cf. supra*, pp. 175-177.

sumus, intima cordis confessione ad instruendas omnium ves-
trum mentes proferentes et ita demum misericordiam Dei super
nos diffusam adnuntiantes.

3.   Nosse enim vos volumus, sicut per anteriorem nostram
sacram pragmaticam iussionem significavimus, nos a culturis
idolorum, simulacris mutis et surdis manufactis, diabolicis com-
positionibus atque ab omnibus Satanae pompis recessisse et ad
integram Christianorum fidem, quae est vera lux et vita perpetua, pervenisse, credentes, iuxta id quod nos isdem almificus
summus pater et doctor noster Silvester instruit pontifex, in
Deum patrem, omnipotentem factorem caeli et terrae, visibilium omnium et invisibilium, et in Jesum Christum, filium
eius unicum, dominum Deum nostrum, per quem creata sunt
omnia, et in Spiritum sanctum, dominum et vivificatorem uni-
versae creaturae.   Hos Patrem et Filium et Spiritum sanctum
confitemur, ita ut in Trinitate perfecta et plenitudo sit divinitatis et unitas potestatis.   Pater Deus, Filius Deus et Spiritus
sanctus Deus, et tres unum sunt in Jesu Christo.

4.   Tres itaque formae, sed una potestas.   Nam sapiens retro
semper Deus edidit ex se, per quod semper erant gignenda
secula, verbum, et quando eodem solo suae sapientiae verbo
universam ex nihilo formavit creaturam, cum eo erat, cuncta
suo arcano componens mysterio.   Igitur perfectis caelorum
virtutibus et universis terrae materiis, pio sapientiae suae nutu
ad imaginem et similitudinem suam primum de limo terrae
fingens hominem, hunc in paradyso posuit voluptatis; quem
antiquus serpens et hostis invidens, diabolus, per amarissimum
ligni vetiti gustum exulem ab eisdem efficit gaudiis, eoque
expulso, non desinit sua venenosa multis modis protelare
iacula, ut a via veritatis humanum abstrahens genus idolorum
culturae, videlicet creaturae et non creatori deservire suadeat,
quatenus per hos eos, quos suis valuerit inretire insidiis secum
aeterno efficiat concremandos supplicio.   Sed Deus noster,
misertus plasmae suae, dirigens sanctos suos prophetas, per
quos lumen futurae vitae, adventum videlicet filii sui, domini
Dei et salvatoris nostri Jesu Christi, adnuntians, misit eundem
unigenitum suum filium et sapientiae verbum.   Qui descendens

de celis propter nostram salutem natus de Spiritu sancto et Maria virgine, verbum caro factum est et habitavit in nobis. Non amisit, quod fuerat, sed coepit esse, quod non erat, Deum perfectum et hominem perfectum, ut Deus mirabilia perficiens, ut homo humanas passiones sustinens. Ita verum hominem et verum Deum, predicante patre nostro Silvestrio summo pontifice, intelligimus, ut verum Deum verum hominem fuisse nullo modo ambigamus; electisque duodecim apostolis, miraculis coram eis et inumerabilis populi multitudine choruscavit. Confitemur eundem dominum Jesum Christum adimplesse legem et prophetas, passum, crucifixum, secundum scripturas tertia die a mortuis resurrexisse, adsumptum in celis atque sedentem ad dexteram Patris, inde venturum iudicare vivos et mortuos, cuius regni non erit finis.

5. Haec est enim fides nostra orthodoxa a beatissimo patre nostro Silvestrio summo pontifice nobis prolata; exhortantes idcirco omnem populum et diversas gentium nationes hanc fidem tenere, colere ac predicare et in sanctae Trinitatis nomine baptismi gratiam consequi et dominum Jesum Christum salvatorem nostrum, qui cum Patre et Spiritu sancto per infinita vivit et regnat saecula, quem Silvester, beatissimus pater noster universalis predicat pontifex, corde devoto adorare.

6. Ipse enim dominus Deus noster, misertus mihi peccatori, misit sanctos suos apostolos ad visitandum nos, et lumen sui splendoris infulsit nobis et abstracto a tenebris ad veram lucem et agnitionem veritatis me pervenisse gratulamini. Nam dum valida squaloris lepra totam mei corporis invasisset carnem, et multorum medicorum convenientium cura adhiberetur, nec unius quidem promerui saluti, ad haec advenerunt sacerdotes Capitolii, dicentes mihi debere fieri fontem in Capitolio et complere hunc innocentium infantium sanguine et calente in eo loto me posse mundari. Et secundum eorum dicta aggregatis plurimis innocentibus infantibus, dum vellent sacrilegi paganorum sacerdotes eos mactari et ex eorum sanguine fontem repleri, cernens serenitas nostra lacrimas matrum eorum, ilico exhorrui facinus, misertusque eis, proprios illis

restitui precipimus filios suos, datisque vehiculis et donis concessis, gaudentes ad propria relaxavimus.

7. [1] Eadem igitur transacta die, nocturna nobis facta silentia, dum somni tempus advenisset, adsunt apostoli, sanctus Petrus et Paulus, dicentes mihi: ' Quoniam flagitiis posuisti terminum et effusionem sanguinis innocentis orruisti, missi sumus a Christo domino Deo nostro, dare tibi sanitatis recuperande consilium. Audi ergo monita nostra et fac quodcumque indicamus tibi. Silvester episcopus civitatis Romae ad montem Seraptem persecutiones tuas fugiens in cavernis petrarum cum suis clericis latebram fovet. Hunc cum ad te adduxeris, ipse tibi piscinam pietatis ostendet, in qua dum te tertio merserit, omnis te valitudo ista deseret leprae. Quod dum factum fuerit, hanc vicissitudinem tuo salvatori conpensa, ut omnes iussu tuo per totum orbem ecclesiae restaurentur, te autem ipsum in hac parte purifica, ut, relicta omni superstitione idolorum, Deum vivum et verum, qui solus est et verus, adores et excolas, ut ad eius voluntatem adtingas.'

8. Exsurgens igitur a somno protinus iuxta id, quod a sanctis apostolis ammonitus sum, peregi, advocatoque eodem precipuo et almifico patre et inluminatore nostro Silvestrio universali papa, omnia a sanctis apostolis mihi precepta edixi verba, percunctatique eum sumus, qui isti dii essent: Petrus et Paulus? Ille vero, non eos deos vere dici, sed apostolos salvatoris nostri domini Dei Jesu Christi. Et rursum interrogare coepimus eundem beatissimum papam, utrum istorum apostolorum imaginem expressam haberet, ut ex pictura disceremus hos esse, quos revelatio docuerat. Tunc isdem venerabilis pater imagines eorundem apostolorum per diaconem suum exhiberi precepit, quas dum aspicerem et eorum, quos in somno videram figuratos in ipsis imaginibus cognovissem vultus, ingenti clamore coram omnibus satrapibus meis confessus sum, eos esse, quos in somno videram.

9. Ad haec beatissimus isdem Silvester pater noster, urbis Romae episcopus, indixit nobis penitentiae tempus intro

[1] The almost exact copying of this paragraph from the corresponding section of the Vita Silvestri is noteworthy. *Cf. supra*, p. 220.

palatium nostrum Lateranense in uno cilicio, ut omnia, quae
a nobis impie peracta atque iniuste disposita fuerant, vigiliis,
ieiuniis atque lacrimis et orationibus apud dominum Deum
nostrum Jesum Christum salvatorem impetraremus. Deinde
per manus impositionem clericorum usque ad ipsum presulem
veni, ibique abrenuntians Satanae pompis et operibus eius vel
universis idolis manufactis, credere me in Deum patrem, omnipotentem factorem caeli et terrae, visibilium et invisibilium, et
in Jesum Christum filium eius unicum, dominum nostrum, qui
natus est de Spiritu sancto et Maria virgine, spontanea volun-
tate coram omni populo professus sum, benedictoque fonte
illic me trina mersione unda salutis purificavit. Ibi enim,
me posito fontis gremio, manu de caelo me contingente propriis
vidi oculis, de qua mundus exsurgens, ab omni me leprae
squalore mundatum agnoscite. Levatoque me de venerabili
fonte, indutus vestibus candidis, septemformis sancti Spiritus
in me consignatione adhibuit beati chrismatis unctionem et
vexillum sanctae crucis in mea fronte linivit dicens: ' Signat
te Deus sigillo fidei suae in nomine Patris et Filii et Spiritus
sancti in consignatione fidei '. Cunctus clerus respondit:
'Amen '. Adiecit presul: ' Pax tibi '.

10.   Prima itaque die post perceptum sacri baptismatis mysterium
et post curationem corporis mei a leprae squalore agnovi, non
esse alium Deum nisi Patrem et Filium et Spiritum sanctum,
quem beatissimus Silvester papa predicat, trinitatem in unitate,
unitatem in trinitate. Nam omnes dii gentium, quos usque
actenus colui, demonia, opera hominum manu facta conpro-
bantur, etenim quantam potestatem isdem Salvator noster suo
apostolo beato Petro contulerit in caelo ac terra lucidissime
nobis isdem venerabilis pater edixit, dum fidelem eum in sua
interrogatione inveniens ait: ' Tu es Petrus, et super hanc
petram aedificabo ecclesiam meam, et porte inferi non pre-
valebunt adversus eam '. Advertite potentes et aurem cordis
intendite, quid bonus magister et dominus suo discipulo
adiunxit inquiens: ' et tibi dabo claves regni caelorum; quodcumque ligaveris super terram, erit ligatum et in caelis, et
quodcumque solveris super terram, erit solutum et in caelis.'

Mirum est hoc valde et gloriosum in terra ligare et solvere, et in caelo ligatum et solutum esse.

11. Et dum hec predicante beato Silvestrio agnoscerem et beneficiis ipsius beati Petri integre me sanitati comperi restitutum, utile iudicavimus una cum omnibus nostris satrapibus et universo senatu, optimatibus etiam et cuncto populo Romano, gloriae imperii nostri subiacenti, ut, sicut in terris vicarius filii Dei esse videtur constitutus, etiam et pontifices, qui ipsius principis apostolorum gerunt vices, principatus potestatem amplius, quam terrena imperialis nostrae serenitatis mansuetudo habere videtur concessam, a nobis nostroque imperio obtineant; eligentes nobis ipsum principem apostolorum vel eius vicarios firmos apud Deum adesse patronos. Et sicut nostra est terrena imperalis potentia, eius sacrosanctam Romanam ecclesiam decrevimus veneranter honorare, et amplius quam nostrum imperium et terrenum thronum sedem sacratissimam beati Petri gloriose exaltari, tribuentes ei potestatem et gloriae dignitatem atque vigorem et honorificentiam imperialem.

12. Atque decernentes sancimus, ut principatum teneat, tam super quattuor precipuas sedes Antiochenam, Alexandrinam, Constantinopolitanam et Hierosolimitanam, quamque etiam super omnes universo orbe terrarum Dei ecclesias; et pontifex, qui pro tempore ipsius sacrosanctae Romanae ecclesiae extiterit, celsior et princeps cunctis sacerdotibus totius mundi exsistat, et eius iudicio, quaeque ad cultum Dei vel fidei Christianorum stabilitate procuranda fuerint, disponantur. Justum quippe est, ut ibi lex sancta caput teneat principatus, ubi sanctarum legum institutor, Salvator noster, beatum Petrum apostolatus obtinere precepit cathedram, ubi et crucis patibulum sustenens beate mortis sumpsit poculum suique magistri et domini imitator apparuit, et ibi gentes pro Christi nominis confessione colla flectant, ubi eorum doctor beatus Paulus apostolus pro Christo extenso collo martyrio coronatus est; illic usque in finem quaerant doctorem, ubi sanctum doctoris quiescit corpus, et ibi proni ac humiliati caelestis regis, Dei salvatoris nostri Jesus Christi, famulentur officio, ubi superbi terreni regis serviebant imperio.

13.   Interea nosse volumus omnem populum universarum gentium ac nationum per totum orbem terrarum, construxisse nos intro palatium nostrum Lateranense eidem salvatori nostro domino Deo Jesu Christo ecclesiam a fundamentis cum baptisterio, et duodecim nos sciatis de eius fundamentis secundum numerum duodecim apostolorum cofinos terra onustatos propriis asportasse humeris; quam sacrosanctam ecclesiam caput et verticem omnium ecclesiarum in universo orbe terrarum dici, coli, venerari ac predicari sancimus, sicut per alia nostra imperialia decreta statuimus. Construximus itaque et ecclesias beatorum Petri et Pauli, principum apostolorum, quas auro et argento locupletavimus, ubi et sacratissima eorum corpora cum magno honore recondentes, thecas ipsorum ex electro, cui nulla fortitudo prevalet elementorum, construximus et crucem ex auro purissimo et gemmis preciosis per singulas eorum thecas posuimus et clavis aureis confiximus, quibus pro concinnatione luminariorum possessionum predia contulimus, et rebus diversis eas ditavimus, et per nostras imperialium iussionum sacras tam in oriente quam in occidente vel etiam septentrionali et meridiana plaga, videlicet in Judea, Grecia, Asia, Thracia, Africa et Italia vel diversis insulis nostram largitatem eis concessimus, ea prorsus ratione, ut per manus beatissimi patris nostri Silvestrii pontificis successorumque eius omnia disponantur.

14.   Gaudeat enim una nobiscum omnis populus et gentium nationes in universo orbe terrarum; exortantes omnes, ut Deo nostro et salvatori Jesu Christo immensas una nobiscum referatis grates, quoniam ipse Deus in caelis desuper et in terra deorsum, qui nos per suos sanctos visitans apostolos sanctum baptismatis sacramentum percipere et corporis sanitatem dignos efficit. Pro quo concedimus ipsis sanctis apostolis, dominis meis, beatissimis Petro et Paulo et per eos etiam beato Silvestrio patri nostro, summo pontifici et universali urbis Romae papae, et omnibus eius successoribus pontificibus, qui usque in finem mundi in sede beati Petri erunt sessuri, atque de presenti contradimus palatium imperii nostri Lateranense, quod omnibus in toto orbe terrarum prefertur atque precellet

palatiis, deinde diadema videlicet coronam capitis nostri simulque frigium nec non et superhumeralem, videlicet lorum, qui
imperiale circumdare adsolet collum, verum etiam et clamidem
purpuream atque tunicam coccineam et omnia imperialia in-
dumenta seu et dignitatem imperialium presedentium equitum,
conferentes etiam et imperialia sceptra, simulque et conta atque
signa, banda etiam et diversa ornamenta imperialia et omnem
processionem imperialis culminis et gloriam potestatis nostrae.

15.   Viris enim reverentissimis, clericis diversis ordinibus eidem
sacrosanctae Romanae ecclesiae servientibus illud culmen,
singularitatem, potentiam et precellentiam habere sancimus,
cuius amplissimus noster senatus videtur gloria adornari, id
est patricios atque consules efficii, nec non et ceteris dignitati-
bus imperialibus eos promulgantes decorari; et sicut imperialis
militia, ita et clerum sacrosanctae Romanae ecclesiae ornari
decernimus; et quemadmodum imperialis potentia officiis
diversis, cubiculariorum nempe et ostiariorum atque omnium
excubiorum ornatu, ita et sanctam Romanam ecclesiam decorari volumus; et ut amplissime pontificalis decus prefulgeat,
decernimus et hoc, ut clerici eiusdem sanctae Romanae ecclesiae mappulis ex lenteaminibus, id est candidissimo colore,
eorum decorari equos et ita equitari, et sicut noster senatus
calciamenta uti cum udonibus, id est candido linteamine in-
lustrari: ut sicut celestia ita et terrena ad laudem Dei de-
corentur; pre omnibus autem licentiam tribuentes ipso sanctissimo patri nostro Silvestrio, urbis Romae episcopo et papae,
et omnibus, qui post eum in successum et perpetuis temporibus advenerint, beatissimis pontificibus, pro honore et gloria
Christi Dei nostri in eadem magna Dei catholica et apostolica ecclesia ex nostra synclitu, quem placatus proprio con-
silio clericare voluerit et in numero religiosorum clericorum
connumerare, nullum ex omnibus presumentem superbe agere.

16.   Decrevimus itaque et hoc, ut isdem venerabilis pater noster
Silvester, summus pontifex, vel omnes eius successores pontifices diadema, videlicet coronam, quam ex capiti nostro illi
concessimus, ex auro purissimo et gemmis pretiosis uti de-
beant et eorum capite ad laudem Dei pro honore beati Petri

gestare; ipse vero sanctissimus papa super coronam clericatus,
quam gerit ad gloriam beati Petri, omnino ipsa ex auro non
est passus uti corona, frygium vero candido nitore splendidam
resurrectionem dominicam designans eius sacratissimo vertici
manibus nostris posuimus, et tenentes frenum equi ipsius pro
reverentia beati Petri stratoris officium illi exhibuimus;
statuentes, eundem frygium omnes eius successores pontifices
singulariter uti in processionibus.

Ad imitationem imperii nostri, unde ut non pontificalis apex
vilescat, sed magis amplius quam terreni imperii dignitas et
gloriae potentia decoretur, ecce tam palatium nostrum, ut
prelatum est, quamque Romae urbis et omnes Italiae seu occi-
dentalium regionum provintias, loca et civitates sepefato
beatissimo pontifici, patri nostro Silvestrio, universali papae,
contradentes atque relinquentes eius vel successorum ipsius
pontificum potestati et ditioni firma imperiali censura per hanc
nostram divalem sacram et pragmaticam constitutum decernimus disponendam atque iure sanctae Romanae ecclesiae concedimus permanendam.

Unde congruum prospeximus, nostrum imperium et regni
potestatem orientalibus transferri ac transmutari regionibus
et in Byzantiae provintia in optimo loco nomini nostro civitatem aedificari et nostrum illic constitui imperium; quoniam,
ubi principatus sacerdotum et Christianae religionis caput ab
imperatore celeste constitutum est, justum non est, ut illic
imperator terrenus habeat potestatem.

Hec vero omnia, que per hanc nostram imperialem sacram
et per alia divalia decreta statuimus atque confirmavimus,
usque in finem mundi inlibata et inconcussa permanenda decernimus; unde coram Deo vivo, qui nos regnare precepit et
coram terribili eius iudicio obtestamus per hoc nostrum imperialem constitutum omnes nostros successores imperatores
vel cunctos optimates, satrapes etiam, amplissimum senatum
et universum populum in toto orbe terrarum, nunc et in posterum cunctis retro temporibus imperio nostro subiacenti, nulli
eorum quoquo modo licere, hec, que a nobis imperiali sanctione
sacrosanctae Romanae ecclesiae vel eius omnibus pontificibus

concessa sunt, refragare aut confringere vel in quoquam con-
velli. Si quis autem, quod non credimus, in hoc temerator
aut contemptor extiterit, aeternis condemnationibus subiaceat
innodatus, et sanctos Dei principes apostolorum Petrum et
Paulum sibi in presenti et futura vita sentiat contrarios, atque
in inferno inferiori concrematus, cum diabolo et omnibus
deficiat impiis.

20.   Huius vero imperialis decreti nostri paginam propriis manibus roborantes super venerandum corpus beati Petri, principis
apostolorum, posuimus, ibique eidem Dei apostolo spondentes,
nos cuncta inviolabiliter conservare et nostris successoribus
imperatoribus conservanda in mandatis relinqui, beatissimo
patri nostro Silvestrio summo pontifici et universali papae
eiusque per eum cunctis successoribus pontificibus, domino
Deo et salvatore nostro Jesu Christo annuente, tradidimus
perenniter atque feliciter possidendam.

Et subscriptio imperialis:

† Divinitas vos conservet per multos annos, sanctissimi et
beatissimi patres.

Datum Roma sub die tercio Kalendarum Apriliarum, domno
nostro Flavio Constantino augusto quater et Galligano viris
clarissimis consulibus.

III

NICHOLAS OF CUES (CUSANUS) ON THE DONATION OF
CONSTANTINE

De concordantia catholica, lib. III, cap. ii [1]

Num praeterire nequeo, quoniam pene omnium sententia
indubitata est, Constantinum Imperatorem, occidentis imperium Romano pontifici Silvestro, ac ejus in aevum successoribus perpetuo dono tradidisse; et ideo etiam si ratio de
unitate principantis, scilicet adversari bono et recto ordini,
duo capita fore non concluderet, pateret tamen in Occidente
Imperatorem nullum nisi a papa dependenter imperium cog-
nosceret, juste esse posse. Hanc radicem quoadpotui investi-
gavi, praesupponens hoc etiam indubitatum esse, Constantinum
talem donationem facere potuisse: quae tamen quaestio nec
soluta est hactenus, nec solvetur verisimiliter uncquam.

Sed in veritate supra modum admiror, si res ita est, eo quod
in autenticis libris et in historiis approbatis non invenitur.
Relegi omnia quae potui gesta imperialia ac Romanorum pontificum, historias sancti Hieronymi, qui ad cuncta colligendum
diligentissimus fuit, Augustini, Ambrosii, ac aliorum opuscula
peritissimorum, revolvi gesta sacrorum conciliorum quae post
Nicenum fuere: et nullam invenio concordantiam ad ea, quae
de illa donatione leguntur. Sanctus Damasus papa ad in-
stantiam beati Hieronymi, actus et gesta praedecessorum dicitur annotasse, in cujus opere de Sylvestro papa non ea inveniuntur quae vulgo dicuntur. Legitur in certis historiis Constantinum a Silvestro baptizatum, et ipsum imperatorem tres
illas, sancti Joannis, sanctorum Petri et Pauli ecclesias miri-
fice ornasse, ac annuos multos redditus e diversis massis terrarum in diversis provinciis et insulis pro continuando ornatu
lampadarum balsami et nardipistici, ac caeterorum, donasse,
de quibus omnibus particularem mentionem in pontificum libro

---

[1] Reprinted from the 1520 edition of the works of Nicholas Cusanus
with a few changes in the interest of modernization. *Cf. supra,*
pp. 188-191.

reperies. Sed de donatione temporalis dominii, aut imperii Occidentis, nihil ibi penitus continetur.

Verum quid postquam Astulfus rex Longobardorum exarchatum Ravennatem occupavit, cum aliis multis locis, et Stephanus secundus natione Romanus ex patre Constantino, multis legatis ad Astulfum missis rogaret imperiali ditioni loca restitui, et facere non vellet Astulfus, Stephanus Pippinum adiens, eum cum duobus filiis in reges unxit. Fuit etiam cum eodem Stephano orator missus Imperatoris, et a Pippino impetrarunt, ut Astulfum induceret, quod imperio loca restitueret. Misit Pippinus, nec profecit. Unde cum non posset sic ab Astulfo restitutionem impetrare, promisit Stephano se vi ablaturum ab eo, et sancto Petro daturum. Hoc audito revertitur imperialis missus. Pippinus, quae promiserat explevit. Forma vero hujus donationis in gestis praefati Stephani cum nominatione particulari omnium bonorum continetur. Zacharias papa monarchiam regni Franciae in Pippinum transtulit, Ludovico rege deposito, de quo legitur, XV q. VI, alius, et in gloss. venerabilem. Ex illo puto Pippinum sedi apostolicae favisse. Post hoc Desiderius rex iterum illas civitates aut earum aliquas, tempore Adriani sexti coepit. Adrianus papa multis missis ad eum legatis, repetiit jus sancti Petri, impetrare non potuit. Tunc Carolus magnus invocatus per Adrianum, recuperavit, et iterum donavit sancto Petro solenni donatione, quae in gestis ejusdem Adriani papae continentur. Ex istis constat Constantinum imperium per exarchatum Ravennatem, urbem Romam, et Occidentem minime papae dedisse.

Unde continue legitur, Imperatores usque ad tempora praefata sicut prius pleno jure Romam, Ravennam, et Marchiam cum aliis locis possedisse. Et probat textus XCVI, distin. "bene quidam," ubi dicit de Patricio praefecto nomine Adoacris regis; et LXIII, distin. "Agatho"; XCVI, distin. "cum ad verum," cum similibus. Et Romanos pontifices legimus Imperatores sateri dominos. Scribit enim Agatho papa ad Imperatorem Constantinum, qui sextam Synodum congregavit, et multis annis secutus est primum, quomodo urbs Roma

sit ipsius Imperatoris servilis urbs. Et Bonifacius papa ad
Honorium, qui dicit, quod ecclesiae Romanae ipse habet
regere sacerdotium, sed Imperator humanas res, et in fine
dicit Romam esse urbem suae mansuetudinis; hic textus habetur XCI distin. " ecclesiae." Et ut breviter dicam, nullibi con-
trarium legi quin usque ad illa praefata Pippini tempora Imperator remanserit in possessione locorum praetactorum. Nec
unquam legi aliquem Romanorum pontificum usque ad tempora
Stephani secundi, in illis locis nomine sancti Petri aliquid
juris praesumpsisse habere.

Haec credo vera esse, non obstante famigera opinione de
contrario, quae in palea habetur Constantinus, XCVI distin.
quoniam absque dubio, si non fuisset illud dictamen apro-
cryphum, Gratianus in veteribus codicibus, et canonum collec-
tionibus invenisset, et quia non invenit, non posuit. Unde
quae postea addidit, pro palea ita illam confictam scripturam
posuit, sicut multa alia inveniuntur ex apocryphis libris nostris inscripta. Ego etiam ad longum hanc scripturam in
quodam libro inveni, quae multo plus continet, quam ea quae
in decreto ponitur loco praeallegato, et diligenter eam exami-
nans reperi ex ipsamet scriptura, argumenta manifesta con-
fictionis et falsitatis, quae pro nunc longum et inutile foret his
inserere. Etiam est advertendum, quod textus Constantinus,
XCVI distin. est ex legenda sancti Silvestri extractus, et fundat
ille qui imposuit decreto, autoritatem ipsius textus in appro-
batione Gelasii in Synodo. Rogo videatur XV disin. " sancta
Romana " illa approbatio, et inveniet pauci roboris, quia dicit
auctorem ignorari, et tamen per catholicos legi, et ea propter
legi posse, qualis sit approbatio, quisque considerare potest.
Multae enim sunt historiae sancti Silvestri; una in quo hoc
non invenitur, quam sanctus Damasus ponit, alia cujus auctor
ignoratur, quam textus non dicit veram sed legi posse, neque
dicit in illa hoc contineri. Etiam antiqua decreta non habent
textum, nisi usque ad ver. " Item decreta Romanorum pontificum " inclusive, et sic non invenitur in illis libris iste ver. de
historia Silvestri. Quinta etiam universalis Synodus, quae de
approbatis doctorum omnium, et scripturarum approbatarum

libris mentionem facit, ac etiam ipsa synodus Martini papae,
quae fuit contra afferentes unam voluntatem in Christo, scilicet contra Petrum et Sergium, renovans approbatas scripturas, ut egomet vidi, nullam de istis historiis faciunt mentionem, nec quisquam approbatus aut nominatus inter veri-
dicos, quem unquam vidi.

Ego legi in Vicentio historiarum, XXIIII libro, in fine,
secundum sanctum Hieronymum, Constantinum uxorem Faus-
tam, et filium Crispum crudeliter occidisse, et in extremo
vitae ab Eusebio Nicomediae episcopo baptizatum, in Arianam
haeresim declinasse.   A quo tempore, inquit Hieronymus,
ecclesiarum rapinae, et totius orbis discordia secuta est usque
in praesens tempus.   Ista libro de actibus Silvestri, quem Vin-
centius dicit a quondam cujus nomen ignorat e Graeco trans-
latum, ut eodem libro cap. IX habetur, manifeste contradi-
cunt.   Quis non crederet potius Hieronymo approbato, quam
ignoti auctoris scripturis, quae apocryphae dicuntur, quando
auctor ignoratur?

Textus etiam qui asscribitur Melchiadi papae, qui habetur
XII q. i. futuram, qui videtur huic dicto aliquantulum obstare,
non est Melchiadis papae secundum glossam quandam, et etiam
rei veritatem, quia Melchiades praecessit Silvestrum, ut patet
in catalogo Romanorum pontificum.   Et si Constantinus fuit
baptizatus a Silvestro secundum commune dictum, tunc patet
titulum illius textus falsum, quia loquitur de baptismo Constantini.   Et etiam si Melchiadis foret ille textus, adhuc non
haberetur argumentum ex eo contra praemissa, quia non dicit
aliud quam Constantinum sedem Romanam imperialem reli-
quisse, et Petro et successoribus consessisse.   Hoc est, quod
ubi fuit sedes imperialis, quod ibi sit modo papalis, quod non
negatur.   Et verum est Constantinum imperatorem tempore
Melchiadis papae fuisse, et tunc Christianum, ut per Augus-
tinum in multis locis hoc habetur, et maxime in epistola ad
Glorium et Elusium, et quibus hoc gratum est, quae incipit,
" Dixit quidem apostolos," et hoc concordat cum Hieronymo.

Vidi etiam decretum Leonis papae in synodo Romana cum
subscriptione episcoporum et clericorum et civium Roman-

Q

orum, ubi Leo papa Othoni primo restituit omnia loca per
Pippinum et Carolum et Robertum reges sancto Petro data.
Et nominantur in eodem decreto omnia loca, et nullam facit
de donatione Constantini mentionem. . . . . . [1]

Sunt meo judicio illa de Constantino apocrypha, sicut for-
tassis etiam quaedam alia longa et magna scripta sanctis
Clementi et Anacleto papae attributa, in quibus volentes Romanam sede omni laude dignam, plus quam ecclesiae sanctae
expedit et exaltare, se penitus aut quasi fundant. . . . . .

Sicut nec de Constantini donatione se majorem arguere
deberet, quae si etiam indubia foret, quid in spirituali cathedra
potestatis ecclesiasticae augere possit, quisque intelligit. Non
adhuc dubitaretur de ejus validitate solum quae diligenti in-
quisitione, quam pro veritate scienda reperire potui scribo,
salvo in omnibus judicio sacrae Synodi. Et si omnia illa quae
praenarrata sunt, ex acceptatione ecclesiae firma censeri de-
bent, placet et mihi, quia etiam illis omnibus scripturis e medio
sublatis, sanctam Romanam ecclesiam primam, summae potestatis, excellentiae. inter cunctas sedes quisque catholicus
fateretur.

[1] The two following paragraphs on this page I have taken from
the reprint in Schard, *op. cit.*

BIBLIOGRAPHY

Constantine and Early Legends

For Bibliography of material published before 1890, see *Nicene and Post Nicene Fathers*, ed. Philip Schaff (New York, 1890), series II, vol. I, *Eusebius*, pp. 411-467, list compiled by E. C. Richardson. For shorter but later list see Gibbon, *Decline and Fall of the Roman Empire*, ed. Bury (1895), vol. II, pp. 530-540. This gives a good discussion of most of the sources about Constantine. For a recent, long, unannotated bibliography see, *Cambridge Medieval History*, vol. I (1911), and vol. II (1913), appendices.

I. SOURCES

a. *General Collections*

Acta Sanctorum, ed. by the Bollandists, vols. 1-54 in 2nd. ed. (1863-1869), in process of publication.

Ante-Nicene Fathers, 10 vols. (New York, 1886-1905).

Corpus Inscriptionum Latinarum (C. I. L.), ed. Mommsen and others (Berlin, 1862, in progress), new ed. (1893, in progress).

Corpus Scriptorum Ecclesiasticorum Latinorum (Vienna, 1866, in progress).

Corpus Scriptorum Historiae Byzantinae (Bonn, 1828-97).

Collection des historiens anciens et modernes de l'Arménie, by Victor Langlois. Containing Moses of Chorene. (1868.)

Fragmenta Historicum Graecorum, ed. C. Mueller, 5 vols., (Paris, 1841-83).

Monumenta Germaniae Historica (M. G. H.), ed. Pertz, Mommsen and others (Berlin, 1826, in progress).

Nicene and Post Nicene Fathers, ed. Philip Schaff (New York, 1890-1907).

Panegyrici Latini, ed. Bährens (Leipsic, 1874).

Patrologiae Cursus Completus, ed. Migne, J. P.

—— *Ser. Graeca* (P. G.), 166 vols. (Paris, 1857-1866).

—— *Ser. Latina* (P. L.), 225 vols. (Paris, 1844-1855).

Sacrorum Conciliorum Collectio, ed. J. D. Mansi (Florence and Venice, 1759-1798). Reprint (Paris, 1901, in progress).

Patrum Nicaenorum nomina Latine, Graece, Coptice, Arabice, Armeniace, sociata opera, ed. H. Gelzer, H. Hilgenfeld, O. Cuntz (Leipsic. 1898).

b. *Individual Works*

Addai, Doctrine of. Syriac Text and English translation, ed. George Phillips (London, 1876).

Ambrose, *Opera*, in Migne, *P. L.*, vols. XIV-XVII; *in Corpus Scriptorum Ecclesiasticorum Latinorum*, vol. 32; Eng. translation, by Romestin, in *Nicene and Post Nicene Fathers*, series 2, vol. 10.

Ammianus Marcellinus, *Rerum Gestarum Libri (qui supersunt)*, ed. in Teubner Texts, by V. Gardthausen, 2 vols. (Leipzig, 1874-1875), Eng. trans. by N. H. Baynes (London, 1912).

Anonymi Itinerarium [Anno Domini 333] a Burdigala Hierusalem usque, et ab Heraclea per Aulonam et per urbem Romam Mediolanum usque, etc., (the *Bordeaux Pilgrim*), *P. L.*, VIII, col. 783 et seq.

Anonymus Valesii, printed with Ammianus Marcellinus: ed. Mommsen in *Chronica Minora* (M. G. H., 1892). Part about Constantine is in vol. I under *Origo Constantini imperatoris. Cf.* also Ohnesorge, W., *Der Anon. Valesii de Constantino*. Kiel, 1885.

Augustine, *Opera*, in Migne, *P. L.*, XXXII-XLVII; Eng. translation in *Nicene and Post-Nicene Fathers*, series I, vols. 1-8 (New York, 1903-1907).

Chronica Minora, ed. by T. Mommsen (M. G. H.), auct, antiq., vols. 9-12 (Berlin, 1892-98).

Codex Justinianus, ed. by P. Krüger (Berlin, 1877-99), 2 vols.

Codex Theodosianus, or *Theodosiani libri XVI cum constitutionibus Sirmondianis*, ed. by T. Mommsen and P. M. Meyer, 3 vols. (Berlin, 1905); also by Haenel (Berlin, 1842); also by J. Gothofredus, 6 vols. (Leipsic, 1736-45).

Codinus, *De originibus Constantinopolitanis*, in *Corpus Scriptorum Historiae Byzantinae;* also in *Scriptores originum Constantinopolitanarum*, ed. T. H. Preger (Leipsic, 1901-7).

Constantine, *Opera*, in Migne, *P. L.*, vol. VIII.

—— *Oration to the Assembly of the Saints* (the Easter Sermon). Published as an appendix to *Eusebius' Life of Constantine, q. v.*

Eumenius, *Panegyricus Constantino Augusto.* In Migne, *P. L.*, viii, cols. 619-640. Also in *Panegyrici Latini.*

Eunapius, *Opera*, ed. by C. Müller, in *Fragmenta Historicorum Graecorum*, vol. IV (1868); also by L. Dindorf, in *Historici Graeci Minores*, 2 vols. (Leipsic, 1870-71); and by F. Boissonnade, 2 vols. (Amsterdam, 1822).

Eusebius, *Historia Ecclesiastica*, ed. by Schwartz and Mommsen, 2 vols. (Berlin, 1903), Kleine Ausgabe (1908); also by W. Bright (Oxford, 1872). *Vita Constantini*, and other writings in Migne, *P. G.*, vol. II; also, ed. by Heinichen (1830, 1869); ed. Heikel in

G. C. S., (Berlin, Leipsic, 1902), Eng. translation of these and of
his Oration in Praise of Constantine in *Nicene and Post-Nicene
Fathers,* series 2, vol. I. *Cf.* Heikel; Kritische Beiträge zu dem
Constantin-Schriften des Eusebius, in Texte u. Untersuchungen,
ed. Harnack u. Schmidt XXXVI, 4, (Leipsic, 1911).

Eutropius, *Breviarium ab urba condita.* Ed. Ruehl (1887) ; ed., H.
Droysen in *M. G. H.,* II (1878-1879). Trans. in Bohn series by
Watson, *Abridgement of Roman History* (1853).

Faustus, *History of Armenia,* German translation by H. Gelzer.
French translation in Langlois, *Coll. d. hist. Armenie,* vol. I.

Hydatius, *Consular Fasti,* in Mommsen, *Chron. Minora,* I.

James of Sarug, *L'omilia di Giacomo di Sarug sul Battesimo di Constantino imperatore, trad. ed. annot.* da Arthur L. Frothingham,
Jr., in *Memorie della Reale Accad. dei Lincei,* (Rome, 1883).

Jerome, *Opera,* Migne, *P. L.,* 22-33. Eng. translation by Lewis and
Martley in *Nicene and Post-Nicene Fathers,* series 2, vols. 6.

Julian, *Opera,* ed. Hertlein (Leipsic, 1875) ; the *Caesares,* ed. also by
Ezekiel Spanheim (Gotha, 1736).

Lactantius (L. Caecilius Firmianus Lactantius), *De Mortibus Persecutorum* (authorship questioned), *Divinarum Institutionum,* libri vii,
Migne, *P. L.,* vol. 7; also ed. Brandt and Laubmann, in *Corpus
Scriptorum Ecclesiasticorum Latinorum,* vol. xxvii, ii, 2 (Vienna,
1897). Eng. trans. of Lactantius' works in *Ante-Nicene Fathers,*
vol. 7.

Libanius, *cf.* Sievers, *Das Leben des Libanius* (1868), *Orations and
Declamations,* 4 vols., ed. Reiske (1784-1797) ; *Speeches and Letters,*
ed. by Wolf (1738).

Moses of Chorene, ed. Le Vaillant de Florival. *Cf. supra, Collection
des historiens . . . de l'Armenie.*

Nazarius, *Panegyricus,* 321, in Migne, *P. L.,* viii, cols. 583-608; also in
Paneg. Lat.

Philostorgius, *Kirchengeschichte,* ed. J. Bidez, in *Die griechischen
christlichen Schriftsteller der ersten drei Jahrhunderte* (Leipsic,
1913. *Ecclesiasticae Historiae Libri Septem,* ed. by H. Valesius,
in Migne, *P. L.,* vol. 65. Eng. trans. in Bohn's *Ecclesiastical
Library* (London, 1855).

Prudentius, *Carmina,* ed. by A. Dressel (Leipzig, 1860), in Migne,
P. L., vols. 59-60. Eng. trans. by Thackery (London, 1890).

Socrates, *Historia Ecclesiastica,* ed. by R. Hussey, 3 vols. (Oxford,
1853) ; also ed. by W. Bright (Oxford, 1878) ; also Migne, *P. G.,*
vol. 67. Eng. trans. in *Nicene and Post-Nicene Fathers,* series 2,
vol. 2 (New York, 1890), and in Bohn's *Eccles. Library* (London,
1874).

Sozomen, *Historia Ecclesiastica,* ed. by R. Hussey, 2 vols. (Oxford,
1858-60; also in Migne, *P. G.,* vol. 67. Eng. trans. in *Nicene and*

Post-Nicene Fathers, series 2, vol. 2 (New York, 1890), and in Bohn's *Eccles. Lib.* (London, 1855).

Theodoret, *Historia Ecclesiastica,* ed. by L. Parmentier (Leipsic, 1911); also in Migne, *P. L.,* vol. 82. Eng. trans. in *Nicene and Post-Nicene Fathers,* series 2, vol. 3 (New York, 1892), and in Bohn's *Eccles. Lib.* (London, 1854).

Victor, Sextus Aurelius, *Opera,* ed. F. Pichlmayr (Munich, 1892).

Vita Artemii, in *Acta Sanctorum* (October 20).

Zosimus, *Historia Nova,* ed. by L. Mendelssohn (Leipzig, 1887). Eng. trans. (London, 1814). German trans. by Seybold and Heyle (Frankfurt-a-M., 1802).

II. LITERATURE

Ayer, J. C., Jr., *A Source Book for Ancient Church History* (New York, 1913).

Bardenhewer, Otto. *Patrologie;* Eng. trans., *Patrology.* (Freiburg i.B. and St. Louis, 1908.)

Baynes, N. H. *Rome and Armenia in the Fourth Century.* Eng. Hist. Rev., xxv (1910), pp. 625-643.

Boissier, Gaston. *La Fin du Paganisme: étude sur les dernières luttes religieuses en occident au quatrième siècle,* 2 vols. (Paris, 1891.) 5th ed. (Paris, 1907).

—— *Essais d'histoire religieuse; II, la conversion de Constantin,* in *Rev. de deux mondes,* July, 1886, pp. 51-72.

Boyd, W. K. *The Ecclesiastical Edicts of the Theodosian Code,* Columbia University Studies in History, Economics and Public Law, vol. XXIV (New York, 1905).

Brieger, Theod. *Constantin der Grosse als Religionspolitiker,* in *Zeitsch. f. Kirchengeschichte* (1880).

Burckhardt, Jakob. *Die Zeit Constantins des Grossen* (Basle, 1853). 2nd ed. (Leipsic, 1880). 3rd ed., reprint (Leipsic, 1898).

Bury, J. B. *Cf.* Gibbon.

Cambridge Medieval History, planned by J. B. Bury, vol. 1 (London and New York, 1911), vol. 2 (London and New York, 1913).

Carter, J. B. *The Religious Life of Ancient Rome* (Boston, 1911).

Ciampini, Joan. *De sacris aedificiis a Constantino magno constructis synopsis historica* (Rome, 1693).

Clinton, H. F. *Fasti Romani,* 2 vols. (Oxford, 1845-50.)

Cohen, H. (continued by Feuardent). *Descriptions des monnaies frappées sous l'Empire romain communément appelées medailles impériales,* 8 vols., 2nd ed. (Paris, 1880-1892.)

Crivellucci, A. *Storia delle relazioni tra lo stato e la chiesa.* (Livorno, 1888.)

Cumont, Franz. *Textes et monuments figurés relatifs aux mystères de Mithra.* (Brussels, 1899.)

—— *The Mysteries of Mithra*, trans. by J. T. McCormick. (London, 1903.)

—— *Les Religions orientales dans le paganisme romain.* (Paris, 1907.) Trans., *Oriental Religions in Roman Paganism,* by Grant Showerman. (Chicago, 1911.)

Cutts, E. L. *Constantine the Great; the Union of Church and State.* (New York, 1881.)

Delahaye, H. *Legends of the Saints.* (London, 1907.)

Dill, Samuel. *Roman Society in the Last Century of the Western Empire.* (London, 1898.)

Dölger, ed. *Konstantin der Grosse und seine Zeit.* XIX Supplementheft der *Römischen Quartalschrift* (Freiburg i.Br., 1913).

Ducange. *Constantinopolis Christiana.*

Duchesne, L. *Histoire ancienne de l'Eglise,* 3 vols. (Paris, 1906-10.) Eng. trans. from 4th ed. *Early History of the Christian Church,* 2 vols. published. (London, 1909-12.)

Duruy, Victor. *Histoire des Romains depuis les temps les plus reculés jusqu'a l'invasion des barbares.* (Paris, 1870, and later editions.) Eng. trans., J. P. Mahaffy ed., *History of Rome and of the Roman People.* (London, 1883, and later.)

—— *La politique religieuse de Constantin, A. D. 312-337,* in *Compte rendu acad. scien. mor. polit.,* XVII (1882), pp. 185-227.

Finlay, G. *History of Greece, B. C. 146-A. D. 1864.* 7 vols., ed. Tozer, H. F. (Oxford, 1877.)

Firth, J. B. *Constantine the Great.* (New York, 1905.)

Frothingham, A. L. *Cf. supra,* James of Sarug.

Geffcken, Johs., *Aus der Werdezeit des Christentums* (Leipsic, 1904).

Gelzer, H. *Die Anfänge der Armenischen Kirche,* in *Berichte über die Verhandlungen der kön. sächs. Gesellschaft der Wissenschaft zu Leipzig.* XLVII (1895), pp. 109-174.

Gibbon, E. *The History of the Decline and Fall of the Roman Empire.* Ed. by J. B. Bury, 7 vols. (London, 1900-1902.)

Gieseler, J. C. L. *Lehrbuch der Kirchengeschichte,* 3 vols.(Bonn, 1824) ; 5th ed. 6 vols. (1828-37). Eng. trans. from 2nd ed. *Textbook of Ecclesiastical History,* by Hull, revised and ed. by H. B. Smith, 5 vols. (New York, 1863), also Davidson, 5 vols. (Edinburg, 1854).

Glover, T. R. *The Conflict of Religions in the Early Roman Empire.* (London, 1909.)

Görres, Franz. "Die Verwandtenmorde Constantins des Grossen," *Zeitsch. für wiss. Theol.* XXX (1887), pp. 343-377.

—— "Die Religionspolitik des Kaisers Constantins." *Ibid.,* XXXI (1888), vol. I, pp. 72-93.

—— "Das Edikt von Mailand." *Ibid.* (1892), p. 282 et seq.

Grauert, Hermann, *Konstantin der Grosse und das Toleranz-Edikt von Mailand, Festrede* (Munich, 1913).

Gretser, J. *De cruce Christi*, in *Opera*, vol. 2. (Ratisbonae, 1743.)

Grisar, Hartmann. *History of Rome and the Popes in the Middle Ages*. Ed. Luigi Cappadelta, translation from the German. (1912.)

—— "Die vorgeblichen Beweise gegen die Christlichkeit Constantins des Grossen," *Zeitsch. für kathol. Theolog*. VI (1882), pp. 585-607.

Gwatkin, H. M. "Constantine and his City." Chap. I of *Cambridge Medieval History*, vol. I, pp. 1-23.

Hamilton, Mary. *Incubation, or the Cure of Disease in Pagan Temples and Christian Churches*. (London, 1906.)

Healy, Patrick J. "Constantine's Edict of Toleration," in *Catholic University Bulletin*. XIX (1913), No. 1, pp. 3-22.

Hülle, Hermann. *Die Toleranzerlasse römischer Kaiser für das Christentum*. (Berlin, 1895.)

Jeep, L. *Quellenuntersuchungen zu den Griechischen Kirchenhistorikern*. (Leipzig, 1884.)

—— "Zur Geschichte Constantins," in *Festschrift für E. Curtius*. (Berlin, 1884.)

—— *Zur Ueberlieferung des Philostorgios*, in *Texte und Untersuchungen*, Neue Folge. (Leipzig, 1899.)

Keim, Theodore. *Der Uebertritt Constantins des Grossen zum Christenthum, Academ. Vortrag*. (Zurich, 1862.)

Langen, Jos. *Geschichte der römischen Kirche*, 4 vols. (Bonn, 1881.)

Lipsius, R. A. *Die edessenische Abgarsage*. (Brunswick, 1880.)

Madden, W. "Christian Emblems on the Coins of Constantine the Great," etc. *Numismatic Chronicle*. New Series, vols. XVII, XVIII. (London, 1877-78.)

Manso, J. C. F. *Leben Constantins des Grossen*. (Breslau, 1817; Vienna, 1819.)

Maurice, Jules. *Numismatique Constantinienne*. Vol. I. (Paris, 1908.) In process of publication.

—— *Les Origènes de Constantinople*, in *Memoires du centenaire des antiquaires de France*. (Paris, 1904.)

Monod, Paul. *La politique religieuse de Constantin*. (Montauban, 1886.)

Müller, I. E. P. von. *Handbuch der klassischen Alterthumswissenschaft*. New ed. (Berlin, 1892.) In progress of publication.

Newman, J. H. *Essays on Miracles*. (London, 1875.)

Pauly-Wissowa. *Real-Encyclopädie der klassischen Alterthumswissenschaft u. s. w.* New ed. (Stuttgart, 1901-, in process of publication).

Peter, Hermann. *Die geschichtliche Litteratur über die römische Kaiserzeit bis Theodosius I und ihre Quellen*. 2 vols. (Leipsic, 1897.)

—— *Wahrheit und Kunst; Geschichtschreibung und Plagiat im klassischen Altertum*. (Leipsic, 1911.)

Pfättisch, J. M. *Die Rede Konstantins des Grossen an die Versammlung der Heiligen, u. s. w.* (Freiburg i.B.; also St. Louis, 1908.)

Preger. "Konstaninos-Helios," in *Hermes.* XXXVI (1901), p. 457 *et seq.*

Rapp. *Das Labarum u. der Sonnenkultus,* in *Jahrb. des Vereins von Altertumsfreunden im Rheinlände.* (1866.)

Reitsenstein, R. *Hellenistische Wundererzählungen.* (Leipsic, 1906.)

Richardson, E. C. Ed. *Eusebius' Life of Constantine,* etc., in *Nicene and Post-Nicene Fathers,* Series 2, vol. I.

Savio, F. "La Conversione di Costantino Magno e la Chiese all' Inizio del Secolo IV", in *La Civiltà Cattolica.* February 15, 1913.

Schaff, P. "Constantine the Great and the Downfall of Paganism in the Roman Empire," in *Bibliotheca Sacra.* XX (1863), p. 778 *et seq.*

Schanz, M. *Römische Litteraturgeschichte,* in Müller, *Handbuch,* etc.

Schiller, Hermann. *Geschichte des römischen Kaiserzeit.* 2 vols. (Gotha, 1883-87.)

Schultze, Victor. *Geschichte des Untergangs des griechisch-römischen Heidentums.* 2 vols. (Jena, 1887-92.)

—— "Untersuchungen zur Geschichte Konstantins des Grossen," in *Zeitsch. für Kirchengeschichte.* VII (1885), VIII (1886.)

—— "Quellenuntersuchungen zur Vita Constantini des Eusebius." *Ibid.,* XIV (1894).

Schwartz, Ed. *Kaiser Constantin und die christliche Kirche, fünf Vorträge.* (Leipsic, Berlin, 1913.)

Seeck, Otto. *Geschichte des Untergangs der antiken We:t.* 5 vols. Berlin, 1895-1913.) 2nd. ed. 1897 *et seq.*; 3rd. ed. 1910 *et seq.* Volumes used in this work: I (1897), II (1901), III (1909), IV (1911).

—— "Die Verwandtenmorde Constantins des Grossen," in *Zeitsch. für wiss. Theol.* XXXIII (1890), pp. 63-77.

—— "Das sogenannte Edikt von Mailand," in *Zeitsch. für Kirchengeschichte.* Vol. XII (1892), p. 381 *et seq.*

—— "Die Bekehrung Konstantins des Grossen," in *Deutsche Rundschau.* VII (1891), pp. 73-84.

—— "Zur Geschichte des Nicänischen Konsils," in *Zeitsch. für Kirchengeschichte.* XVII (1897),

—— "Die Urkunden des Vita Constantini," in *Zeitsch. für Kirchengeschichte.* XVIII (1898).

—— "Urkundensfalschung des 4n Jahrhunderts." *Ibid.,* XXX (June, 1909).

Sesan, Valerian, *Kirche und Staat im römisch-byzantinischen Reiche seit Konstantin dem Grossen und bis zum Falle Konstantinopels.* Vol. I (Czernowitz, 1911).

Ulhorn, Gerhard. *Der Kampf des Christentums mit dem Heidenthum.* (Stuttgart, 1875.) Eng. trans. by Smyth and Ropes, from 3rd German ed., revised. (New York, 1891.)

Zahn, Theodor. *Constantin der Grosse und die Kirche.* (Hanover, 1876.)

—— *Geschichte des Sonntags.*

Venuti, Tomaso de Bacci. *Dalla grande Persecuzione alla Vittoria del Cristianesimo.* (Milan, 1913.)

Wissowa, Georg. *Religion und Kultus der Römer.* (Munich, 1902.)

Workman, H. B., "Constantine," in *Encyclopaedia of Religion and Ethics,* vol. iv (New York and Edinburg, 1912).

LATER LEGENDS AND HISTORICAL CRITICISM

(Works not included *supra*)

I. COLLECTIONS AND SOURCE BOOKS

De donatione Constantini quid ueri habeat eruditorum quorumdam judicium, ut in uersa pagella uidebis. (Mainz, 1518, reprinted later.)

Godfray, Thomas. *A treatyse of the donation or gyfte and endowment of possessyons gyven and graunted unto Sylvester, pope of Rhome, by Constantyne, emperour of Rome,* etc. (London, 1525.) Apparently a translation of the preceding item.

Fabricius, J. A. *Bibliotheca Graeca.* (Leipsic, 1705-1728.)

Goldast, Melchior. *Monarchia s. Romani imperii, sive Tractatus de jurisdictione imperiali, etc.,* vol. I (Hanover, 1611), vol. II (Frankfort, 1614), vol. III (Frankfort, 1613).

Kehr, Paul Fridolin. *Regesta Pontificum Romanorum.* Vol. I. Italia, 1906. Vol. II. Latium, 1907. Rome and Berlin. 6 vols. published.

Martène et Durand. *Amplissima Collectio veterum scriptorum* (1724).

Mirbt, Karl. *Quellen zur Geschichte des Papsttums und des Römischen Katholizismus.* 3rd ed. (Tubingen, 1911.)

Schard, Simon. *Syntagma variorum autorum de imperiali jurisdictione et potestate ecclesiastica,* or *syntagma tractatuum de jurisdictione, autoritate, et praeminentis imperiale, ac potestate ecclesiastica.* (Basil, 1566. Under slightly different title, 1609.)

II. WRITINGS BEFORE THE 16TH CENTURY

Aldhelm, *Opera,* ed. Giles (1844).

Codex Carolinus, in *Mon. Ger. Hist., Epistolae,* III.

Corpus juris canonici, ed. Friedberg. (Leipsic, 1879-81.)

Cusanus, Nicholas. *De Concordantia Catholica.* (Basle, 1568.) Also printed in *Opera.* (Basle, 1520, 1565.)

Decretales Pseudo-Isidorianae et Capitula Angilramni, ed. Hinschius. (Leipsic, 1863.)

Gratian, *Decretum*, in *Corpus juris canonici, q. v.*
Liber Pontificalis, ed. Duchesne, with introduction and commentary.
   2 vols. (Paris, 1886, 1892.)
———ed. Mommsen, in *M. G. H.* (Berlin, 1898.)
Marsiglio of Padua, *Defensor pacis.* (Frankfort, 1592.)
Mombritius (Mombrizio). *Sanctuarium, sive vitae sanctorum co lectae
   ex codibus.* (Milan, c. 1479.)   New edition. (Paris, 1910.)
Moses Chorensis, ed. Whiston. French translation in Langlois, *Col-
   lection des historiens anciens et modern de l'Armenie.*
Pecock, Reginald. *The Repressor of Overmuch Blaming of the Clergy.*
   In Rolls Series, in *Rerum Britannicarum medii aevi scriptores.*
   (London, 1860.)   Ed. Wharton and Babington.
*Regesta pontificum Romanorum ab condita ecclesia ad annum post
   Christum natum* 1198, ed. Jaffé. 2nd ed. 2 vols. (Leipsic, 1885,
   1888.)
——— ed. Kéhr, P. F. (Berlin, 1906-1913.)   In progress, six vols. already published.
Valla, Lorenzo. *Opera.* (Basel, 1543; Venice, 1592.)
——— *de falso credita et ementita Donatione Constantini,* manuscript
   copies, *Cod. Vat. Urbinates Latini,* No. 337 (all except a few paragraphs destroyed), also *Cod. Vat.,* No. 5314, dated December 7,
   1451, in splendid condition.
——— *Ibid.* Printed by Ulrich von Hutten in 1517, frequent reprints,
   also in *Opera.*
——— *Ibid.* Translations: English, Thomas Godfray (London, 1525?);
   French, Anonymous (c. 1522), Alcide Bonneau, with Latin text
   and historical study (Paris, 1879); Italian, without typographical
   indication (1546); ed. also by G. Vincenti under title, "La dis-
   sertazione di Lorenzo Valla su la falsa e menzognera donazione di
   Costantino tradotta in italiano da G. Vincenti." Latin and Italian
   (Naples, 1895, out of print).
Voragine. *Golden Legend,* ed. Graesse. (Breslau, 1890.)   Trans. by
   Wm. Caxton, revised by Ellis. (London, 1900.)

III. WRITINGS AFTER 1500

Baronius, Caesar. *Annales Ecclesiastici una cum critica historica
   chronologica,* ed. Pagii (1588 *et seq.*) ; ed. Mansi, 34 vols. (Lucca,
   1738 to 1746.)
Banck, V. *De tyrannide Papae in Reges et Principes Christianos.*
   (Franequerae, 1649.)
Barozzi, L. and Sabbadini, R. *Studi sul Panormita e sul Valla. Reale
   institutio di studi superiori practici e di perfczionemento.* (Florence, 1891.)
Bayet. *La fausse donation de Constantin,* in the *Annuaire de la*

Faculté des Lettres de Lyon. (Lyons, 1884), also separately (Paris, 1884).

Binius, Severinus. *Collection des Conciles.* 4 vols. (Cologne, 1606.)

Böhmer, H. "Konstantinische Schenkung," in *Real-Encyklopädie für protestantische Theologie.* Vol. XI (1902).

Brunner, Heinrich. *Das Constitutum Constantini,* in *Festgabe für Rudolf von Gneist,* pp. 1-36, and separately. (Berlin, 1888.)

Cambridge Medieval History. Vol. II. (New York and London, 1913.) Especially chapter XVIII, by G. L. Burr.

Caspar, Erich. *Pippin und die römische Kirche.* (Berlin, 1914.)

Catholic Encyclopedia, especially art. "Donation of Constantine," J. P. Kirsch. Vol. V. (New York, 1909.)

Colombier. "'La Donation de Constantin," in *Études Religieuses.* Vol. XI (1877).

Combéfis. *Illustrium Christi Martyrum Triumphi.* (Paris, 1659.)

Döllinger. *Papstfabeln des Mittelalters.* (Munich, 1863.) Also ed. J. Friedrich. (Stuttgart, 1890.)

Duchesne, ed. *Liber pontificalis,* q. v.

Fournier, P. *Études sur les fausses Décrétales.* (Louvain, 1907.)

Friedrich, J. *Die Constantinische Schenkung.* (Nördlingen, 1889.)

Frothingham, A. L., Jr. *L'omelia di Giacomo di Sarûg sul battesimo di Costantino imperatore,* in *Atti della R. Accademia dei Lincei* (Rome, 1883).

Gmelin. *Das Schenkungsversprecken und die Schenkung Pippins.* (Leipsic, Vienna, 1880.)

Grauert, H. "Die Constantinische Schenkung," in *Hist. Jahrbuch der Görresgesellschaft,* III (1882); IV (1883); V (1884).

Gregorovius, F. *Geschichte der Stadt Rom im Mittelalter.* 8 vols. Stuttgart, 1859-1872); 5th. ed. (1903 *et seq.*) Eng. trans., A. Hamilton, 8 vols., *Rome in the Middle Ages.* (London, 1894-1902.)

Guicciardini. *Istoria d'Italia.* (Freiburg, 1775-1776; Pisa, 1819.)

Haller. *Die Quellen zur Geschichte der Entstehung des Kirchenstaats.* (Leipsic and Berlin, 1907.)

—— "Die Karolinger und das Papsttum," in *Hist. Zeit.,* 108, 3-12, I, pp. 39-76.

Hartmann, Ludo Moritz, *Geschichte Italiens im Mittelalter.* In *Allgemeine Staatengeschichte,* hrsg, v. K. Lamprecht, Abt. I, Werk 32. Vols. I-III (Leipsic, 1897-1911).

Hauck, A. "Zur donatio Constantins," in *Zeitsch. f. kirchl. Wissenschaft u. kirchl. Leben* (1888).

Henderson, Ernest F. *Select Historical Documents of the Middle Ages.* (London, 1892.) Trans. of *Donation of Constantine,* pp. 319-329.

Heydenreich, E. Ed. *Incerti Auctoris de Constantino Magno ejusque matre Helena libellus* (Leipsic, 1879).

—— *Ueber einen neugefundenen Roman von der Jugendgeschichte Constantins des Grossen*, in *Verhandel. d. Philologenversammlung in Trier;* also in *Berliner Zeitschrift f. d. Gymnasialwesen* (1880).

—— "Constantin der Grosse in den Sagen des Mittelalters," in *Deutsch Zeitsch. f. Geschichtswissenschaft*, IX (1893), pp. 1-27.

—— "Griechische Berichte über die Jugend Constantins des Grossen," in *Griech. Stud. H. Lipsius zum Geburtstag dargebracht* (1894).

Hodgkin, Thomas. *Italy and her Invaders.* 8 Vols. (Oxford, 1880-1899.) Second edition (1892-1896, Vols. I-IV, in V).

Hutten, Ulrich von. *Opera*, ed. Münch. 5 Vols. (Berlin, 1821-1825.) Ed. E. Böcking. 7 Vols. (1859-62).

Janssen, Johannes. *History of the German People at the Close of the Middle Ages.* Trans. from the German (15th ed.) by M. A. Mitchell and A. M. Christie. 16 Vols. (London, 1905.)

Kaufmann, George. "Eine neue Theorie über die Entstehung und Tendenz der angeblichen Schenkung Constantins," in *Allgem. Zeitung* (1884).

Kirsch, J. P. "Die Heimat der Konstantinischen Schenkung," in *Römische Quartalschrift für christliche Altertumskunde und Kirchengeschichte*, Bd. xxiii, 110-114. (Rome, 1909.)

Krüger, G. "Die Frage nach der Entstehungszeit der Konstantinische Schenkung," in *Theologische Literaturzeitung*, XIV (1889), cols. 429-435, 455-460.

Lamprecht, C. *Die römische Frage von König Pippin bis auf Kaiser Ludwig den Frommen.* (Leipsic, 1889.)

Langen, J. "Entstehung und Tendenz der Konstantinischen Schenkungsurkunde," in *Historische Zeitschrift* L. (1883).

Langen, J. *Geschichte der römischen Kirche.* 4 vols. (Bonn, 1885.)

Lea, Henry C. *Studies in Church History* (1883).

Löning, E. "Die Entstehung der Konstantinischen Schenkungsurkunde," in *Hist. Zeitschrift*, LXV (1890).

Martens, W. *Die römische Frage unter Pippin und Karl den Grossen.* (Stuttgart, 1881.)

—— *Die falsche Generalkonzession Konstantins des Grossen.* (Munich, 1889.)

—— *Beleuchtung der neuesten Kontroversen über die römische Frage unter Pippin und Karl dem Grossen.* (Munich, 1898.)

Mayer, E. "Die Schenkungen Konstantins und Pippins," in *Deutsche Zeitschrift für Kirchenrecht*, XXXVI, p. 1 *et seq.* (Tübingen, 1904.)

Mancini, Girolamo. *Vita di Lorenzo Valla.* (Florence, 1891.)

Nisard, Charles. *Les Gladiateurs de la république des lettres aux XVe, XVIe et XVIIe siècles.* 2 Vols. (Paris, 1860.)

Pastor, Ludwig. *The History of the Popes from the Close of the Middle Ages.* Trans. and ed. by F. I. Antrobus. Second ed. 10 Vols. (London, 1898.)

Scheffer-Boichorst, Paul. *Neue Forschungen über die Konstantinische Schenkung,* in *Mitteilungen des Instituts für österr. Geschichtsforshung,* X (1889), XI 1890). Also printed in *Historische Studien,* pub. by Eberling, Vol. 42.

Schwahn, Walther. *Lorenzo Valla; ein Beitrag zur Geschichte des Humanismus.* (Rostock, 1896.)

Steuchus. *Contra Laurentium Vallam de Donatione Constantini* (Lyons, 1547.)

Strauss, D. F. *Ulrich von Hutten* (1857), 4th ed. (1878). Eng. trans. by G. Sturge, from second ed. (1874).

Taylor, Henry O. *The Medieval Mind.* 2 Vols. (New York, 1911.)

Tiraboschi, Girolamo. *Storia della letteratura Italiana.* (Rome, 1783, 1806.)

Voigt, G. *Die Wiederbelebung des classischen Alterthums* (1880-1881).

Weiland, L. " Die Konstantinische Schenkung," in *Zeitschrift f. Kirchenrecht,* XXII, 1 (1887), XXII, 2 (1888).

Wolff, Max von. *Lorenzo Valla, sein Leben und seine Werke.* (Leipsic, 1893.)

Zeumer, Karl. " Die älteste Text von der Donation von Constantin. (Die Konstantinische Schenkungsurkunde,") in *Festgabe für Rudolf von Gneist.* (Berlin, 1888.)

Zinkeisen. " The Donation of Constantine as Applied by the Roman Church," in *Eng. Hist. Rev.,* IX (1894).

INDEX

Names of modern writers are indicated by SMALL CAPS, titles of writings by *italics*.

F